Blue Remembered Years

For S, V and L
who put up with it all

Willie,
with very best wishes,

Ian

July 2002

BLUE
REMEMBERED
YEARS

A Politcal Memoir

IAN
LANG

Politico's
PUBLISHING

First published in Great Britain 2002
by Politico's Publishing
8 Artillery Row
Westminster
London SW1P 1RZ

www.politicos.co.uk/publishing

Copyright © Ian Lang 2002

The right of Ian Lang to be identified as the author of this work has been asserted by
him in accordance with the Copyright, Designs & Patents Act, 1988.

A catalogue record for this book is available from the British Library.

ISBN 1 84275 009 7

Printed and bound by Creative Print and Design, Wales

CONTENTS

ACKNOWLEDGEMENTS

I suppose I should start with thanks to my wife for suggesting the title of this book and with apologies to the late A. E. Housman for using it. When Politico's asked me to write the book, they insisted on knowing at once what it would be called. My own preoccupation was with whether or not I should write it. I used to subscribe to the Alec Home school of politics: 'Better keep your mouth shut and be thought a fool, than open it and remove all doubt.'

On looking back through the detritus of my years in active politics, however, I was surprised to find how much had accumulated – layer upon indiscriminate layer of mementoes and reminders, like an archaeological dig. Even so, I wondered how on earth I would disentangle the themes and events I wanted to cover from that random mass of paper and the foggy recesses of memory.

Politics in those years was lived at such a pace and under such pressure that there was never time to digest and reflect. The shooting stars and comets of this crisis and that drama recede into a blurred constellation of fading light. One's memory plays tricks; and for every tale satisfyingly pinned down on the page there are many more that escape and drift off into space, unrecorded.

John Peyton, Lord Peyton of Yeovil, set out in his eloquent autobiography *Without Benefit of Laundry* to 'gather up the fragments'. 'Memory', he wrote, 'has no rules or regular habits; it loses much that was important and yet clings on to and preserves quite small things which, like stray, unconnected footprints, have escaped erosion by the winds and tides of time. Recalling people, times, places and events is, to an extent, an affair of chance. Many are lost beyond recovery. The remainder some glimpsed for a moment like a fish in clear, still water, vanish as you move towards them; the outstretched hand comes back empty save for some bits of unmemorable debris from the bed of the stream.'

In gathering up my fragments, I started with those episodes in my political career that I particularly wanted to address: Scottish devolution; John Major's leadership campaigns; the Scott Report. On all of these I did have notes, press releases, speeches, published reports, even occasional fragments of diary to fall back on. Then I started to fill in the gaps and what started as an episodic record began to take on a fuller narrative form. At any rate, that is what I hope has happened.

I am grateful to a number of people for encouraging and trying to help me, not least to Iain Dale and Sean Magee of Politico's, who patiently moved back several deadlines. Special thanks are due to my long-suffering secretary Dounie Stanley-Clarke, who never complained as she typed and retyped the ever-changing text. Lord Waldegrave of North Hill and Sir Nicholas Lyell QC gave me helpful guidance on aspects of the Scott Report; so did Lord Howe of Aberavon. John Major offered invaluable insights on one or two chapters. I also sought advice, generously given, from Eileen Mackay, Kirsty Wark and Drusilla Fraser, and from my three former special advisers: Alan Young, Gregor Mackay and Dr Greg Clark. Lord Peyton of Yeovil kindly consented to my use of the above quotation and Bernard Levin to the quotations in Chapter Two.

To all these – and to others unnamed – I am most grateful. However, the opinions expressed and any errors are mine alone.

ONE

First Beginning

I was born in the Park Nursing Home in Glasgow on 27 June 1940, though we lived in Greenock, lower down the Clyde. My first weeks of life were spent in Turnberry, in Ayrshire, in a white house that still stands alone on the golf course side of the road, not far from the sea. For as far back as I can trace, the Lang family have lived close to the sea. For several generations they earned their living from it.

In the eighteenth century they lived in and around Dumbarton, on the north bank of the Clyde, trading mainly as maltsters, but also engaging in farming, shopkeeping and shipowning. One ancestor, known as James 'A'thing' Lang because he would tackle anything, built in 1811 a dry-dock in the town and a shipyard next to it. In 1821 he built there the *Comet II* for Henry Bell, as a replacement for the historic *Comet*, which had foundered. In other steamships which he and his relation William Denny built, he used engines designed by the celebrated Napier cousins. By 1832 he had built fifteen of the fifty-nine paddle-steamers then in service on the Clyde. At the same time one of his brothers, John, opened a successful distillery and another, Alexander, a brewery.

Another relation of his, also named James Lang, started his career articled to a Dumbarton lawyer, but was soon lured to sea in 1823 as a steward on the paddle-steamer *Dumbarton* built by 'A'thing' and owned by his Dumbarton Steamboat Company. It plied the Clyde between Dumbarton and Glasgow and by 1826, at the age of twenty-one, young James had become its master. As Captain James Lang, he continued in this role on a succession of steamers for several years, taking on also the role of 'ship's husband' to the elegant little steamer *The Lady of the Lake* on Loch Lomond.

In 1835 he took command of the *Vale of Leven*, only the second iron steamer to trade on the Clyde, and, three years later, of the new steamer, the *Loch Lomond*. He is immortalised in oils by the great Clyde marine painter of the time, William Clark, standing on the bridge of his new command in top hat and frock coat, with Dumbarton Rock behind. The painting remained in the family's possession for 130 years but we have now lost track of it – sadly, because Captain James Lang was my great-great-grandfather. Whilst commanding the *Loch Lomond* he invented a new mechanical indicator whereby the captain and pilot could communicate with the engine room, which was speedily adopted by other shipowners at home and abroad. Previously instructions had been passed down simply by kicking the engine casing, or by shouting.

In 1835 Captain Lang had crossed the river to marry Agnes MacCallum, the daughter of Peter MacCallum, a successful iron merchant and shipowner in the rapidly growing port of Greenock, which lies on the south bank just where the river broadens before turning south into the Firth of Clyde. Thus were formed through matrimony the twin tracks of the family's fortunes for the next hundred years: ships and steel. The couple settled in Renfrewshire, buying Horsewood House in the little village of Kilbarchan, from where James commuted by ferry daily to run the Dumbarton Steamboat Company. In 1836 their son John was born.

Captain James Lang died in 1850; and in due course John joined his grandfather's firm of Peter MacCallum & Sons. The firm, which had begun supplying nails to wooden ship builders around 1780, was by now trading in iron in growing quantities. Such future giants as Scotts, Dennys and Russells (later to become Lithgows) were among the early major customers. John Lang became a partner in 1869 and by 1874 was running the company, steering it safely through major recessions and the collapse of many debtors as well as the failure of the City of Glasgow Bank. By the 1880s open hearth steel was taking over from iron and John had soon established good links with all the major Scottish steel-making concerns such as Clydesdale, Colvilles and Beardmores, as well as Consett in Northumberland and Carnegie in America. There were boom years and bust years, the beginning and ending of the Boer War accounting for both, but the firm steadily grew and prospered.

In the 1870s they diversified into shipping. There had been earlier *ad hoc* forays, but John Lang formed the separate partnership of Lang & Fulton with his head clerk James Fulton, to acquire the 1331-ton *Lady Clarendon* as their first ship. Over the next three decades they owned a total of thirteen ships and managed eight more: these were mainly three or four-masted barques, iron-hulled at first and then steel, some with 'double four top gallant and royals', as the ship lists record, and nearly all capable of sailing the world's oceans. The ship lists also record, though, the hazardous nature of such voyages at that time. For example, the *Ormsary*, the last sailing ship to be built by Russells in Port Glasgow, was lost with all hands off Cape Horn in 1906; and in 1908 the *Australian* was also lost with all hands on passage to Sydney. Sadly, these were not the only such losses, nor was Lang & Fulton's experience uncommon.

John Lang died in 1903 after a career that had spread from shipping and steel into marine insurance, underwriting through the Glasgow Underwriters Protection Committee, to whom he must have been familiar as a client. He had also become a town councillor in Greenock in 1875 and Provost in 1898 and 1899, and had served as President of the

Chamber of Commerce and Chairman of the Greenock Provident Bank, as well as on several local charitable bodies, such as the Greenock Working Boys and Girls Society and the Sunday Morning Free Breakfast movement. A keen member of the United Evangelists and an elder of St Paul's Presbyterian Church, he was also president of the Greenock Total Abstinence Society and in 1896 celebrated his jubilee as an abstainer, with what I know not.

I don't know what John's politics were – he may have been a Liberal, in the days when Liberals stood for Liberal ideals, as Greenock was a Liberal stronghold – but his local council career, which was of course non-political, was the nearest any of my ancestors seems to have got to a political life.

His son Peter, my grandfather, inherited his entrepreneurial flair and, again in volatile economic conditions, continued to build up the steel stock-holding and shipping interests. By 1914 steel purchases totalled 226,000 tons, 17 per cent of the total Scottish ingot make. On the shipping side sail had given way to steam and between 1906 and 1922 Lang & Fulton's steamship fleet had numbered almost thirty vessels, mainly of around 8,000 tons each. Close links had developed with various shipyards, especially Lithgows. They wanted the orders to build and, to help secure them, would buy much of the steel from MacCallums and take a share of the ship, with other interested parties also taking shares. Lang & Fulton would manage these ships, as well as owning usually the largest share in the single-ship company they formed to own each vessel.

As a young man, Peter Lang had served as a captain in the Renfrewshire battalion of the Argyll & Sutherland Highlanders' Volunteer Brigade, the equivalent of the territorial army, but when war came in 1914 his knowledge of the steel industry was needed for what his later obituary in the *Greenock Telegraph* was to describe as 'special service for the Government in the control of steel in the west of Scotland'.

So far as I know, the only perk that went with this position was the issue of a gold disc that secured for him free travel on the London Midland Scottish Railway. On one occasion in 1917 he travelled to Liverpool, for a breakfast meeting in the Adelphi Hotel with Stanley Baldwin of Baldwins Ltd, then Financial Secretary to the Treasury, and Winston Churchill, Minister of Munitions. This encounter with two future Prime Ministers was said to have been dominated by Churchill, who had stepped off the night train in a black mood that could only be dispelled by a large glass of brandy.

Peace brought a bumpy return to free markets both for steel and shipping after the controls of wartime. Steel production had been under government control since 1915 and many ships had been requisitioned, or sunk by U-boats. Values had risen and continued to do so for the first year or two after the war, but so had replacement costs as the large shipping companies jostled to rebuild their fleets.

To add to the problems, America and Japan had displaced the depleted British fleet in many parts of the world and Peter Lang decided that a small family shipping firm could no longer compete. Lang & Fulton had owned over forty ships in the previous half-century and managed half a dozen more. By 1922 the last of the Ard Fleet of steamers (as it was known, because most of the ships had such names as *Ardgryffe*, *Ardgrange*, *Ardgowan* – though local wags preferred *Ardtimes* or *Ardgoing*) had been sold and the remaining fleet of seven Ard coasters was transferred to MacCallums, the family's steel stockholding firm, to own and manage, with a core cargo base of steel.

The Lang and Fulton families had cemented their business links with marriage when Peter Lang had married Margaret Fulton in 1903. My grandmother was a competent oil-painter and a friend of William McTaggart, the great Scottish impressionist. She probably met him at Machrihanish, on the Mull of Kintyre, whose green and rocky coastline and broad, sandy beach is immortalised in many of McTaggart's Atlantic seascapes.

Machrihanish was a favourite holiday destination of the family, with its wonderful links golf course, but home was in Greenock, where they lived at Lindores, an imposing Victorian house, built for one of the Lyle sugar barons in the lea of the Lyle hill, which rises behind the town. Later they also owned Ardmillan, a country house near Girvan, on the Ayrshire coast, and it was in these agreeable settings that their family grew up, comprising two sons, Ian and James (my father), and a daughter, Dorothy, who was to die tragically in a train crash at the age of eighteen.

'West End Gentleman's Sudden Death', proclaimed the *Greenock Telegraph* when their father Peter died unexpectedly in 1930, adding that 'he was an able businessman' but, by way of mitigation, that he had 'likeable qualities, quiet and modest in his bearing' and that he had been President of Greenock Cricket Club for a number of years. He was only fifty-three. His elder son, Ian had joined him in the family business and James, then twenty, had followed his uncle Charles Fulton into the marine insurance world, an interest originally developed to handle the insurance of the family's shipping interests. Both sons succeeded their father as underwriting members of Lloyd's, but James was also to run a successful underwriting syndicate in Glasgow which, by the time he came to wind it up in the late 1950s, was the last remaining such syndicate outside Lloyd's itself. In 1963 he and his partners were to sell the business, with its offices in Glasgow, London and at Lloyd's, to a thrusting young businessman and rising politician by the name of Peter Walker.

The fortunes of MacCallums, still the core of the family's business activities, which also included by now interests in ship-building, marine engine building and steering gear manufacture, moved with the fortunes of the great Scottish industries it served. As shipping, ship-building and steel-making were to wane on the Clyde, so did MacCallums. Nationalisation of both industries took ownership and control away from the entrepreneurs and families who had built them up and understood them, to civil servants in Whitehall. A whole class of owner–managers disappeared, and so did the investment and the drive with which they had built up several important pillars of the Scottish economy. It was a tragedy that was to dog Scotland for decades.

My own family's business story is not exceptional. There was no particular distinction that singles it out for praise. My forebears simply did what countless other family businesses did all over Britain, during and after the industrial revolution. They applied the Victorian virtues of enterprise, integrity, hard work and civic obligation to the creation of small firms that struggled with the countless commercial hazards of that age to survive and prosper. I know of and admire many of their achievements. I wish I could know more about them as people.*

My mother's family also lived in Renfrewshire, though some time before they had farmed in Arran and before that, she claims, they had hailed from Appin in Argyll. They, too, had developed loyalties to the Argyll & Sutherland Highlanders. Her grandfather, Major James Stewart, commanded A company 1st (Renfrew) Volunteer Brigade, when not preoccupied with his grain shipping business. His young cousin Arthur Stewart fought in the Boer War with the same territorial battalion before making a career in the Indian Army, finishing as Colonel of the 3-10 Baluchi Regiment. In 1928 Arthur published a book on tiger shooting, in which he volunteered the view that: 'Every officer in the Regiment should be able to say that he has shot a tiger, panther and a bear'. His book told them how to go about it.†

Her father Charles Stewart was quite small and, though a good horseman, was found to be too light to bear arms, so he took on the family grain business in Glasgow. For many years it prospered, but even-

---

* A bicentennial history of P. MacCallum & Sons Ltd. entitled *A Bed of Nails* was written in 1981 by John Hume and Michael Moss

† *Tiger and Other Game* by Col. Arthur E Stewart, Longmans, Green & Co., 1928

tually, after the combined effect in the 1920s of depression, the return to the gold standard of an overvalued currency and the General Strike of 1926, he decided to sell up and take his wife and three daughters to America to make a fresh start. They settled in Wisconsin, where he carved a new career in fruit farming and real estate.

A decade or so later his wife Maude (née Bruce) – who was an enthusiastic poet and composer, a talented pianist and the sixth child of an explorer, James Bruce – returned to Scotland to visit old friends, bringing my nineteen-year-old mother, Maudie, with her. One of the old friends was Margaret Lang and within three weeks Maudie and James Lang were engaged. In due course they married and settled in Greenock in a house with a fine view across the river to the hills of Argyll. In 1937 my elder brother Ronald was born, followed by me in 1940 and later by my two sisters, Patricia and Judith.

I was to have been christened Charles after my maternal grandfather, but my birth coincided with the fall of France to Hitler and, in gratitude for my Uncle Ian's safe evacuation as one of the last off the beaches of Dunkirk, I was named after him. Three months later his own son Peter was born and we became not just cousins but friends for life.

I could not have had a better example to follow than my namesake, Uncle Ian. He had a quiet courtesy and charm throughout his life and an impish sense of humour that made him greatly liked and respected. His main joys were fishing and shooting, which were only slightly impaired by the serious wounds he received in Tunisia, serving as a major with the Highland Division. He was more fortunate than his two Fulton cousins: Robert was killed in Tunisia on the same day as Uncle Ian was wounded, and James perished when *HMS Goodall*, the frigate he commanded, was torpedoed on a Murmansk convoy one week before the war ended. James's son Robin Fulton is managing director of MacCallums today – a company diminished but still in business. So conscious, however, was Uncle Ian of the loss of his Fulton cousins and fellow directors of the firm during the war that, from the day he returned to work after recovering from his own wounds to the day he retired thirty years later, he declined to take any increase in salary out of the firm.

My father Jim Lang loved speed. Although he was a keen shot and a competent golfer, his main passions in life were driving fast cars, sailing and flying. The love of sailing ran in the family. His first yacht, *Gometra*, which he owned for a few seasons in the mid-1930s, was to make her final journey on a cradle on the deck of a Norwegian freighter, crossing the Atlantic at the beginning of the Second World War, carrying some of Norway's gold reserves to the safety of Canada. The theory was that if the freighter were torpedoed the yacht would float off as it sank.*

By then he owned his second yacht, *Noreine*, a 25-ton Bermudan sloop in which after the war he won many races, before converting her to a ketch for family cruising. We had many wonderful holidays aboard her as children, cruising the magical waters of the west of Scotland. Later, Ronald, Peter and I took her over and ran her for several seasons before costs and the responsibilities of married life overwhelmed us.

My father also owned speedboats from time to time, so when war came and his ambition to fly – he already had a pilot's licence – was thwarted by RAF regulations and his need of spectacles, he switched happily to air-sea rescue. After a spell at Dover, including backing up the Dieppe raid in 1942, he spent the rest of the war in his high-speed launch patrolling the Mediterranean. Like so many of that generation, he never talked about the war in later years, but I do know, because it is recorded on a wooden shield presented to him by his crew at the end of hostilities, that he saved the lives of fifty-four Allied airmen in thirteen different rescues. It was many years later that I discovered he had been awarded the Distinguished Service Cross for one of his exploits.

---

* A fuller account of this story, by Charles Rawlings, appeared in the American magazine *Yachting* in February 1941.

In 1944 the southern invasion of France made the Mediterranean a less dangerous place and his role largely redundant. He spent the last part of the war in charge of the shore-station at a little French coastal village called St Tropez. The living was not hard. Stores of precious wines re-emerged from their wartime hiding places. A bar opened, named Jimmy's Bar after him. Two more which he recorded carefully in his logbook were Le Pingouin and L'Escale. When the time came to take up civilian life again in post-war Britain some of his French friends tried to lure him, with the offer of one hundred metres of sea-front, to bring his wife and young family out to St Tropez. I occasionally ponder how different my life might have been, had he weakened.

In the meantime my mother, like thousands of other wartime mothers, was struggling to bring up the said young family, without their father on hand to assist. True, there was a nanny, a maid and a cook at Glenelg, Octavia Terrace, but there were also several army officers billeted on us and in due course, the house requisitioned, my mother decided to move from the bomb-prone Clyde and we settled for the duration in The Pines, a sturdy, semi-detached house in quiet Church Road, Pitlochry, in the heart of rural Perthshire.

So it is of there that I have my first memories, a little blurred now, but still capable of being conjured back to life. There were my escapades in the garden, taking a knife to a tree trunk because I wanted a rubber for my drawing, helping the Almighty to open the flowers by forcing my fingers into the first buds of spring. There were the walks in my pram and later alongside my sister Patricia's pram, past the solid stone houses with their distinctive Perthshire gables, past the Town Hall where the iron railings were being taken down to turn into guns, off to collect our weekly ration of concentrated orange juice, out along the roads from the town with their drystone walls and high trees. There were the hills around Pitlochry where I used to watch for invading Germans, the mixed feelings I had about my brother Ronald's German mouth organ, the occasional parade through the town of troops or tanks, the visits to the faded elegance of Fisher's Hotel where my grandmother had taken up residence with her companion Miss Martin (formerly governess to her children), over whose head I once smashed a china dog.

I can remember, towards the end of the war, crowding round the big, black Bakelite wireless at The Pines to listen to an important broadcast by Mr Churchill. I was not so precocious as to understand what he said, but I did register the magnetism of his voice. Most memorably of all, there was my first remembered sighting of my father, home on leave, whose sun-tanned balding pate I spied over the garden gate, before I ran off to hide, overwhelmed by shyness.

It must have been far more difficult for him to adjust, after five years of war to the ready-made and self-contained family that awaited his return, than it was for us. But after the initial excitement of seeing the myth made flesh, I don't think I ever quite closed the gap created by those first missing years. He was always kind and thoughtful, but I wish there could have been a greater sense of intimacy between us. I remember one very wet afternoon a year or so after his return from the war when, golf cancelled, he sat down and, at my insistence, drew for me on one sheet of paper every instrument and artefact of warfare that I could think of. On another occasion – the only time I can recall it – he suddenly sat down at the piano and revealed an unknown expertise, but such occasions were rare.

Although to me at the time my childhood was a great and important adventure full of incident and drama, it can really be briefly recorded in tidy, conventional terms. I went at seven to prep school, at Lathallan in Fife; and when the school burned down one holidays, destroying my treasure-filled tuck box, we moved to the coldest spot in Britain at Johnshaven on the east coast of Kincardineshire. I shone at nothing, but was blessed with a beautiful treble voice, for which I won the only silver cups I have ever won in my life. As the soloist in the choir I used to have to sing the opening verse of 'Once in Royal David's City' at the annual carol concert, my throat constricted with terror. I was never really to shake off my childhood diffidence at any kind of public performance yet constantly felt impelled to perform, in music, in theatre and later in politics. There was always some gnawing challenge that had to be met, some yearning to achieve that had to be assuaged, however inconvenient.

I read a lot – all the Biggles books, starting with *Biggles in the Baltic* when I was seven and recovering from having my tonsils removed, followed by Billy Bunter, Sherlock Holmes, *The Scarlet Pimpernel*, a little Dickens and any book I could find about the war. Photography followed stamp-collecting as an early hobby, developing and printing my own films in the basement of our home in Greenock by the time I was eleven. I was very fond of my Lang grandmother, who now lived, with Miss Martin, in a suite of rooms at Greenock's Tontine Hotel. On my regular bicycling visits there she plied me with peppermints and taught me to play pelmanism, canasta and bezique. My cousin Peter and I, when not sitting up a tree smoking cigarettes or refighting the Battle of the Atlantic, would go for long bicycle rides up into the hills and moors behind Greenock or, if wet, to one of the seven cinemas in the town. We were once arrested for riding our bikes along the pavement of the Esplanade. We were sent home chastened, but not charged.

From Lathallan I went to Rugby, attempting but failing to win a scholarship. The voice slowly subsided and eventually broke. I played most games without distinction, finding them increasingly boring. My work was usually above average, but never outstanding. 'Competent and conscientious' was the damning verdict of one form master in my end-of-term Report but whilst, coming from Scotland, I initially felt like an immigrant amongst my new English colleagues, I gradually got the hang of them and of England. It was no better than Scotland (though it clearly thought it was) and anyway we were all British (though they clearly thought that was another word for English).

I performed in house plays and school plays and to my piano lessons

I added the flute – not a sensible instrument for those of a retiring nature, since its mistakes are not drowned out by the rest of the orchestra. I had never made a public speech, and decided that before I left school this rite of passage had to be endured. The school magazine, *The Meteor*, reported in its November 1958 edition that in the second debate of the Advent term, on the motion that 'Great Britain should acknowledge that she is no longer a world power', Mr I. B. Lang had 'said that the motion was a socialist doctrine, and Britain's relegation to the second rank would be the inescapable consequence of socialist policy.' This report hardly did justice to the subtlety of my arguments but it generously glossed over the inarticulate speed and panic of my delivery.

After the conventional five years I left, in December 1958, with the requisite A-levels for Cambridge. Like Neil Kinnock's family, none of mine had been to university and I was desperately keen to break with this tradition. It all hinged on a few essays and interviews and, on a leaden, dank day in early January with snow on the ground, I presented myself at Sidney Sussex College (chosen because John Chase, my revered Rugby housemaster, had been there). It was the first time in my life that nothing seemed automatic, even pre-ordained. I had finished at one institution but not yet secured a safe haven at the next. Despite my unsettled mood, all seemed to go well. A couple of weeks later the fateful letter arrived. I took it out into the garden of the house in Troon, in Ayrshire, where we now lived.

I don't know if, like my father, I had always been diffident and shy of displaying emotion, or whether the rigours of two boarding schools had branded me, as perhaps they had him. But of all the passing ambitions of youth, often hidden but carefully nurtured, going up to Cambridge was the greatest – being Foreign Secretary could wait. So when I opened that letter joy really was unconfined, not least because the impossible decisions about what to do with one's life could be put off for another three years. Childhood was over and whatever came next – not quite adulthood – beckoned

A Gale of Ridicule

I suppose it's not unusual for young people to go through a phase of wanting to perform or show off in front of their peers. Most outgrow it. In some, often the shy and diffident, it persists beyond childhood. Looking back, I can see that my affliction took several forms. There were parodies of poetry – Victorian and mock-modern – cartoons and satirical articles, all published in school magazines, at my prep school and at Rugby. I agonised as I wrote them, panicked when I saw them in print and cringe now to look back on them – always hiding behind the façade of mockery and pastiche, never daring to create something that might stand up for itself, to be judged on its own merit.

At home, there were plays and revues put on with friends for our baffled parents. Usually I wrote them myself but once, at a precocious fourteen, I remember producing a one-act Chekhov play in a friend's garden. At Rugby there were school plays and house plays and end-of-term concerts. So my father should not have been altogether surprised when, in answer to his enquiry about my future career plans, I told him

I wanted to be an actor. 'Very overcrowded', he replied, 'and not at all secure. What about accountancy?'

The matter remained unresolved as I went up to Cambridge in 1959 to read history. Sidney Sussex was a small college, founded in 1596 by the Countess of Sussex. Former alumni included Oliver Cromwell, whose head, recently returned from a Norfolk vicarage, was reburied in the college ante-chapel just before I arrived.

In the days before the gap year became such a well-defined part of growing up, I had taken a job for six months at Prestwick Airport, working for Scandinavian Airlines, whose flights had to stop there *en route* to New York. I drove a truck, washed dishes, set trays of hot meals and carried them up the steps to every flight that stopped there between Sweden and America, working day shift, back shift and night shift. It was brainless work, but there was some compensation in the chance to read the American newspapers that came off the eastbound flights. To this broadening experience I was to add after my first year at Cambridge a voyage to Canada as supernumerary crew on an iron-ore carrier – my family's links with the Denholm shipping line came in useful here – followed by a night shift job in a paper mill near Ottawa. I was taught there how to mix pulp to make paper, but when one night I added too much water to one large load I had to ask the sleepy supervisor during his rounds what to do. 'Let it go,' was his reply, laconic – and ambiguous, as I soon realised. Should I let it go out into the mighty machine, hungry to spin it out into (very thin) paper, or should I let it go down the drain and wait for the machine to grind to a halt? I chose the former and went unrebuked, but the next night I was on log-washing. At least I earned enough to hitch-hike to my cousins in Wisconsin.

By 1959 the war seemed a lifetime away to my generation, but it had only been over for fourteen years and its disciplines and attitudes still dominated the outlook of many. We lived in a reticent and deferential society. This was still the Cambridge of sports jackets and flannels; of women outnumbered eight to one by men; of gowns worn to lectures and after dark; of college gates closing at ten o'clock; of the proctor and his bulldogs (two burly bowler-hatted runners) who patrolled the town at night looking for miscreant undergraduates. As it happened, I had the key to one of the garden gates into Sidney Sussex, sold to me by a graduating friend, so I never had to risk the spikes on the perimeter walls. In due course I sold it on at a profit. National Service had just ended, so there was a wide range of ages and degrees of maturity among the undergraduate population. I suppose class distinctions did still exist at Cambridge, as in the country at large, but I was never conscious of them. Indeed, meeting contemporaries from other kinds of schools and from abroad was one of the enlivening features that university life offered. I think most of us were more concerned to seize the day and plunge into all the stimuli of life at Cambridge, than to succumb to the inhibitions of the world outside.

But at first, although getting to Cambridge had fulfilled my greatest ambition thus far, I felt curiously directionless. I didn't quite know how I wanted to shape my life or what interests I wanted to pursue. The *Varsity Handbook* offered a bewildering range of choices and, liberated from the disciplines and ritual of school life, I took some time to get used to the freedom of making my own decisions.

During Freshers' Week, I wandered round the Societies Fair.

Page 70 of the *Handbook* listed, amongst the Dramatic Societies, the Footlights Dramatic Club. 'Membership is strictly male and is by election only. Those interested should see the President: Peter Cook (Pembroke)'. Peter Cook was already becoming famous, with a revue named *Pieces of Eight* playing in the West End. A large crowd of confident-looking people – they had probably done National Service – milled around the Footlights stall. I felt sure I would not be able to compete, so I passed on. I auditioned for the Mummers, one of the main theatre groups, and was given a part in their forthcoming production of Arnold Wesker's *The Kitchen*.

But the part really needed a guitarist, and when before the first rehearsal they found one, I was told politely to wait for the next production.

I also joined the Union, where during my first year I was to admire the eloquence of such luminaries as Leon Brittan and Christopher Tugendhat. We freshmen had been told that the Union was the centre of university life, but I soon found that I could live without it, and by my third year I looked with satirical disdain at the self-important posturing of those embryonic politicians, alongside whom I was later to sit in Cabinet.

I joined CUCA, the Cambridge University Conservative Association, handing over my life subscription of 17/6d to a charming girl at one of their wine parties. I had little political curiosity: I had been through the rebellion bit and then formed my views on the inadequacies of socialist theory and the irrelevance of the Liberals. From the age of ten I had grown up under Conservative governments and, though I thought some of them needed a boot up the backside, I felt comfortable with them. They were my kind of people. Unfortunately, my kind of people did not send me my promised membership card and, when I tried to attend my first function, I was refused entry. They could find no record of my membership and the charming girl was known to none. My political development stalled.

For a year or two I did all the normal things. I drank beer, joined dining clubs, rowed in my college second boat (Sidney was not one of the great rowing colleges), went a great deal to the cinema, where the audience repartee was usually more fun than the film, and turned in one history essay a week. I soon found that I could manage without attending lectures – though some, such as Geoffrey Elton on the Tudors, Denis Brogan on America and F. R. Leavis on the English tripos – were worth a visit. On one occasion, having neglected to tackle the long reading list I had been given for that week's essay, I wrote it entirely by reference to the relevant (short) chapter in Winston Churchill's *History of the English*

17

Speaking Peoples. My supervisor had not deigned to read Churchill and gave me an alpha, complimenting me on some original ideas.

One afternoon in April 1961 I went with two friends, Bill Stansfield and Tim Denison, to the matinée at the Cambridge Arts Theatre of a new revue in which Peter Cook was performing, called *Beyond the Fringe*. Its effect on me was electrifying. It was the funniest thing I had ever experienced. I ached with laughter as Peter and his three colleagues, Jonathan Miller, Alan Bennett and Dudley Moore, deftly slew a herd of sacred cows and uncovered a whole new world of comedy.

It was the kind of comedy that already peppered the conversation of some of us undergraduates at the time: ironic, absurdist, anti-establishment. But where our caustic chit-chat merely mocked authority and tweaked at convention, they were completely uninhibited in their comic assault on all the humbug and affectation that so stifled our lives in those days. *Beyond the Fringe*, though it triggered the new satire era, was not simply, or even mainly, satirical. It owed more to *The Goon Show*, to which I had been an avid listener at school, than it did to the pre-war cabarets of Berlin. But its voice was distinctively its own. Its targets were not politics or religion, but politicians and prelates. There was no serious message, just the wish to share a laugh at life's absurdities and pretensions in buttoned-down Britain. It relied less on tightly scripted punchlines than on free-ranging fantasies, full of wit and parody. Above all, it was liberating: it released me, like many others, into the world of humour and seemed to change the whole landscape of comedy.

Distracted only briefly by the summer exams for Part I of the History tripos, I started to write material in the Cook and Bennett mould. In the autumn, I confronted the Secretary of the Footlights, Humphrey Barclay, who was standing alone behind a little stall like a Punch and Judy tent at the Societies Fair. Humphrey arranged an audition for me. Then early one afternoon at the Footlights Clubroom, before a selection committee that included Graham Chapman, Tim Brooke-Taylor and John Cleese, I performed a couple of my sketches, with John Shrapnel, another applicant, playing a part in one of them. There was more kindness than amusement in their laughter, but I got in and I was off.

I now belonged to the club that Peter Cook and David Frost were making famous. I was among kindred spirits, off whom humour would spark as we fed each other ideas and punchlines and we shared that heady brew: the excitement of making people laugh. There were two 'Smokers' each term. These were traditional cabaret concerts at which we all performed our latest pieces. Tim Brooke-Taylor, a natural comic actor, formed a dry, hilarious double-act with Chris Stuart-Clark, who was later to become a master at Eton. Richard Stilgoe wrote and performed scintillating patter songs. Bill Oddie's greatest success was impersonating the pop star Adam Faith. Graham Chapman did Jacques Tati-style mimes, always with a pipe clamped in his teeth. He and John Cleese formed a cabaret act, the highlights of which were two Nazi officers strutting around saying 'Velkom to mein kampf. Ve haf vays of making you valk' (fore-runner of the Ministry of Silly Walks?) and a wrestling match between two karate wrestlers, who told each other hysterical jokes in mock-Japanese, peppered tastelessly with references to Pearl Harbor and Nagasaki. For us the war was over and, though we all revered the courage of our parents' generation, we no longer felt the need to talk about the war as though we were in church. Copies of a new, seditious magazine called *Private Eye* began to do the rounds, confirming to us that there were others out there with the same mildly anarchic tendencies. But its distribution arrangements were erratic and we all agreed it wouldn't last.

In my first two Smokers, I performed a sketch I had written as a television commercial, that sold religion as though it were a detergent, followed by a sardonic piece on nuclear war and a Flanders and Swann-type song, in which I was accompanied at the piano by Tony Branch. Tony and I later teamed up to do cabarets at May Balls and dances around East Anglia. At one Hunt Ball near Norwich we started with a song he had written that poked fun at hunting. The audience fell strangely silent. When we followed it with my sparkling sketches that poked fun at such establishment heroes as Montgomery of Alamein and Harold Macmillan the silence took on a kind of menace. After we'd finished we were escorted to the kitchen where, instead of the promised lavish helpings of food and drink, we were given a plate of ham sandwiches and orange squash and told to see ourselves out. I suppose we were lucky to leave in one piece.

We had a better experience in February 1962, when a team of us went by bus to Bristol to put on a show for Bristol University. I was our stage manager and also performed a couple of pieces. We were complete amateurs and the stage facilities in our Falcon Yard clubroom in Cambridge were basic. So when the technician at Bristol's Victoria Rooms asked me at our afternoon rehearsal what I wanted him to do about gells, I was at a complete loss. 'You do want them, don't you?' 'Oh yes, of course we do'. I think he was offering us a particular kind of stage lighting, but I'm still not sure. Somehow we got through the show and the audience were wonderful. Our kind of humour was spreading. Our host at Bristol, who I think was President of their Union, was an articulate and courteous young man by the name of David Hunt. I would meet him again many years later at Westminster.

Bristol was where I first performed a sketch I had written as a take-off of a Richard Dimbleby outside broadcast. Originally entitled 'Uncle Richard', because its target was the urbane, rather pompous smoothness in all circumstances of this most famous of BBC commentators, it was later to earn some notoriety: the event described was the departure of the Queen from the Pool of London for an overseas visit on the royal yacht *Britannia*. Everything went wrong and the royal barge sank *en route* to *Britannia*, leaving the Queen swimming across the Pool of London, smiling radiantly, whilst the Band of the Royal Marines struck up 'God Save the Queen' and Dimbleby calmly described the silk ensemble Her Majesty was wearing.

Some construed this as an outrageous attack on the monarchy. Nothing could have been further from my mind. I revered the monarchy. I knew the Coronation order of service by heart; and my admiration and respect for the Queen knew no bounds – then as now. I also rather admired Dimbleby, then the supreme master of his craft, but I did think there was a kind of suffocating dullness in the BBC's numbingly deferential approach at the time that did neither the Crown nor the Corporation any good. Now, of course, it has moved tastelessly to the other extreme.

I hadn't intended to perform the sketch at Bristol – indeed, I had only begun to memorise the lines – but we hadn't finished rehearsing the show during the afternoon and the grand finale was to be a particularly ambitious piece. The Footlights resident singer, Leonard Pearcey, later to find fame as music director of the Guildhall School of Music and Drama, was to belt out in his rich baritone voice a romantic ballad of that era written by Tony Branch, whilst *le tout ensemble*, dressed as angels, were to provide a heavenly chorus. The highlight was when John Cleese set aside his harp and processed up to an unsuspecting Pearcey, bearing a very large custard pie that he had secreted on to our bus in Cambridge that morning. As the song reached its final climax, the custard pie and Leonard Pearcey met their ineluctable fate in a messy fusion and the curtain descended. I suppose the old ones are the best ones.

However, before this towering monument to the sophistication of the humour of the Cambridge Footlights could be unveiled, there was an agonising pause after the previous sketch. Behind the stage curtain, the scenery was shifted and the angels struggled into their surplices and wings, but out in the auditorium the audience began to fidget. Old trouper that I was, I seized the initiative. I called up to the lighting man to give me a spotlight, front left, and 'gells' if he had any left. Then I stepped out in front of the curtain to save the day in the best theatrical tradition. As I said, they were a good audience, quick on the uptake and it went well. I experienced for the first time the heady drug of thunderous applause, to be enjoyed again only fleetingly years later, in the party conference halls of Blackpool, Brighton and Bournemouth.

That Dimbleby sketch was pretty tame stuff by today's standards and I doubt if it would stand the test of time in the world of contemporary comedy, but in its day it was thought rather forward. It was to have quite a history, but for the moment it simply entrenched me among my Footlights colleagues; and I performed it again to similar success at a Smoker in Cambridge the following week, which was good for my self-confidence. In the same Smoker I also did a satirical sketch on a British Foreign Secretary being interviewed by an *Observer* journalist and another one in which I impersonated the Prime Minister Harold Macmillan, speaking at a French State Banquet, in French. I revived the latter sketch forty years later for a charity show at Westminster, to find that it did still contain a grain of humour and its theme, Britain's membership of the Common Market, still had some resonance. A few years before that, one newspaper marked my Harold Macmillan the best impersonation of the Bournemouth Conference and my Michael Heseltine the worst.

The Footlights became an all-consuming interest in my undergraduate career and the club emerged to increasing prominence in university life. Smokers were packed. Agents came up from London. Peter Cook came back, to a hero's reception. More serious cabaret bookings began to arrive. Tony Branch and I performed on Anglia Television, for the princely fee of four guineas. The eerie silence in the studio for sketches that relied on the response of a live audience was a little disconcerting.

Somehow, Tony got us a professional booking at the Royal Court Theatre Club, a nightclub run by the gourmet (and later MP) Clement Freud, at the top of the Royal Court Theatre in Sloane Square. *Varsity*, the university newspaper, proclaimed the fact and described our act as 'satire and songs'. There, 'nightly at midnight', we performed our newly fashionable 'satire and songs' for three weeks in April. Introducing us on our first night, Clement Freud demonstrated his own entertainment skills as, in lugubrious tones, he warmed up our audience. He had warned us that we might have to deal with drunk hecklers. He had two stock lines, as I recall: 'You should get together with the ceiling. That's plastered too', or alternatively 'You and I should get together in a double-act. I will play the front legs of a pantomime horse; and you can be yourself.'

The audiences varied in their ability to grasp our genius, but their numbers grew over the weeks. I remember gratefully the loud laughter of the actor Terry Thomas on one evening. After our first performance Clement Freud had taken to his bed with a temperature, but at the end of our three weeks he asked us to come back. Max Setty at the Blue Angel, off Berkeley Square, where David Frost had been performing, said that he too would book us, but our Cambridge finals were looming.

In the May Smoker of 1962, which I co-produced with Anthony Buffery, I am listed in the programme as having written or performed in nine sketches, most of which I can barely remember. One, billed as 'Allegro con multo panache', which John Cleese and I wrote and performed together, I remember not at all. John, who sported a bushy, black beard at that time, and answered to the nickname 'Otto', was a tall, lanky, rather diffident individual, keen on cricket and constantly making imaginary batting strokes. Off stage he was funny in a deadpan way, but on stage he was volubly hilarious. His party pieces included a very fast football commentary, a gawkish astronomer explaining what light years were and a civil servant espousing birth control. Perhaps his best piece was a BBC news item on a dog stuck down a mineshaft and the death and disaster that befell all who tried to rescue it before it escaped, unharmed, of its own accord. Then there were his various catch-phrases that had us all in hysterics. For some reason, 'Here come Cardinal Richelieu's men' was one. It loses something on the written page. Even the lunch menu in the Footlights clubroom bore his influence, with 'Roll with cleese ... 9d'. *Fawlty Towers* it was not.

John seemed to inhabit a detached world of his own such that, much though we all liked him, we feared for his ability to survive in the outside world when the time came. If we had had a shred of perception, we should have known that he would prosper. He had all the necessary qualities: he was highly articulate and had a strong stage presence, perfect timing, subtle writing skills and a well-developed sense of the absurd. His talents blended satire, fantasy and farce and his later achievements, especially in *Fawlty Towers* and *A Fish Called Wanda*, must put him in the ranks of the all-time greats of British comedy.

Graham Chapman, by contrast, with whom Cleese would later share fame in the television series *Monty Python's Flying Circus*, was stolid, down-to-earth and pipe-smoking and when not performing would go off and climb something. On-stage, however, he was rather different. He once persuaded Tony Branch to go on a round of cabaret engagements as his pianist. Tony's sole contribution to the performance was to touch one note on the piano when Graham asked him for 'carrot' music. Where Cleese was voluble and often manic, Chapman was more measured, often understated, but like Cleese showed a real gift for comic timing.

Beyond the Fringe was to open in New York in the autumn of that year, and in the spring I was asked to audition as a possible replacement for one of the cast in the continuing London run. I rather fancied myself in the Peter Cook role. Rigid with nerves, I stepped through the stage door of the little Fortune Theatre, near Drury Lane, and found myself in pitch darkness. I was amazed at how cramped it was backstage and eventually stumbled through acres of black cloth, which formed the set of the revue, on to the dimly lit stage. Of the four stars, only Jonathan Miller was present that day. He and the other examiners, lost somewhere in the auditorium, were friendly enough and I heard his guffaws as I performed some of my material. But it was not to be. Whether I might have made it, I don't know; perhaps all of us who auditioned were hopeless. Anyway, they decided in the end to take on professional actors – Andrew Ray played the part I had auditioned for – and that was that.

Back in Cambridge the annual Footlights Revue was in preparation. I was to be on the script committee rather than on-stage, and later was to go with the team to the Edinburgh Festival, to perform on the Fringe. *Double Take*, which Trevor Nunn was brought in from the ADC to produce, was a success both in Cambridge and in Edinburgh, where it became 'The Après-Show'. Also co-opted was Miriam Margolyes, whose acting skills and beautiful speaking voice were later to carry her to great success, though the *Spectator* review complained that she was starved of good material.

My role in Edinburgh, however, was to produce and perform in a twice-nightly cabaret in a nightclub we were establishing in what was said once to have been a famous brothel, high in a centuries-old tenement in the Lawnmarket, not far from the Castle. The Sphinx, as it was called, was at 15 James Court, and late into the night at the start of the Festival we were hammering and sawing and nailing and painting as we prepared our little auditorium for the public. Humphrey Barclay, later to be Head of Light Entertainment at London Weekend Television, designed our sphinx logo, which hung from a sign at the entrance to the dark close. He also produced caricatures of the performers, which were stuck on the tiled wall of the dingy staircase outside our door.

'Could you hammer more quietly?' asked a passing policemen, drawn in from the street by the noise. Lord Kilbrandon, the well-known judge, later to chair the Royal Commission set up by Harold Wilson to consider plans for Scottish devolution, was more helpful. He kept a grand piano on the floor above, as his own flat next door was too small, and when he put his head round our door and discovered our plans, he invited us all back for scrambled eggs and agreed to be our patron.

Tony Branch and I were to do the Sphinx's first show, whilst the others performed in the revue in the Central Hall, Tollcross; then Graham Chapman, John Cleese and Tim Brooke-Taylor would take over for the midnight show. We had no licence to serve alcohol, although we managed coffee and tea, and like most Fringe shows, not much advance publicity either. Not for us the prestigious Official Festival Programme, with its distinctive Jean Cocteau motif. On the first night, two bemused customers climbed the stone stairs to our little club, as much to get out of the rain as anything else. The next night saw our searing wit fly above the heads of an audience of eight. But gradually word got around and the numbers grew. The *Scotsman*'s review helped. We were 'entertaining a growing number of visitors with sophisticated humour, which pokes fun at the Establishment . . . One can see the chair where Lawrence Durrell sat and the cup from which Henry Miller sipped coffee.'

They had indeed come: two short, grizzled men in damp and crumpled raincoats. I remember discussing jazz with them – they wanted us to play Thelonius Monk, but all we had was Chris Barber. Then other stars of the Festival came, in increasing numbers. We became the 'in' place. Our wall gathered the signatures of a long list of distinguished visitors, from Dušan Popovic, the Prince Igor of the Belgrade Opera Company, to Lord David Cecil. I may be wrong, but I think that glamorous couple Ludovic Kennedy and Moira Shearer came one night. Willie Merrilees, the Chief Constable of Lothian, was cheerfully present with over ninety others on another evening, in a room licensed for a maximum of forty.

It was a great Festival year, with a strong Russian musical theme. Shostakovich was the featured composer and I remember sitting in the gods at the Usher Hall to hear David Oistrakh play Beethoven's 'Kreutzer' sonata, and in a back pew at St Cuthbert's Church for the magical experience of Rostropovich playing Bach's six suites for unaccompanied cello. Then there was the Royal Shakespeare Company with *Troilus and Cressida*, *The Devils* and *Curtmantle*, and the English Opera Group's production of Britten's *The Turn of the Screw*, from which John Cleese returned in ecstasy: 'Such precision, such accuracy, such timing!'

I had a little car and one day Cleese, Chapman, Branch and I all squeezed into it to drive up to Stirling, where we toured the castle. The pre-Pythonesque clowning that took place on the battlements there caused a mild stir among the other visitors and nearly an arrest. Sadly, none of us had a camera to record the scene. On another occasion Tim

Brooke-Taylor, Jamie Dugdale (who was the drummer in the Footlights band), and I played golf at Muirfield on the introduction of Jamie's uncle, the film director Anthony Asquith. Our golf, I recall, was of a standard that might well have been described as satirical.

It was at North Berwick, where Jamie's family had a house, that I first met his aunt, the legendary Kay Elliot, who was one of the famous Tennant sisters, painted in childhood by John Singer Sargent and brought up in 10 Downing Street as Herbert Asquith's step-daughter. I remember her playing Brahms duets at North Berwick on two grand pianos, with her half-brother Anthony. In later years at Westminster, where she was a life peer, I asked her whether it was true, she being then in her nineties and having been born when her father was over seventy, that her grandfather had been a friend of Robespierre. She thought for a moment before replying, 'No, I don't think that's right. But it is the case that my father, at the age of eight, walked with his father in a procession through London in support of the 1832 Reform Bill.' How one wishes that she had written her memoirs.

The days in Arcadia were over now. I had already graduated, with a modest second-class degree, and was living on borrowed time. Those three weeks in Edinburgh had provided a fitting coda to my undergraduate career. It was forty years ago, but the memory of them lives in my mind like sun on a distant landscape. I took down my Barclay caricature from the dirty white tiles outside the door. We said our farewells and drifted away, the spell broken. However, our Festival performances ended on a high note, because such had been our success that various local entrepreneurs decided to take over the nightclub as a going concern, and convert it to a small experimental theatre. To this day I don't know who really deserved the credit for that, but the Sphinx survived, with Lord Kilbrandon remaining as its patron, under its new name: the Traverse. In new premises behind the Usher Hall, the Traverse exists to this day and is an established part of the Edinburgh theatrical scene.

My not-quite show business career continued, but fitfully and at one remove, for I now started to earn my living. Whilst Cleese, Chapman and the rest returned to Cambridge for another glorious year I, unsure how to maintain the momentum, succumbed to the delights of the Glasgow office of my father's insurance-broking business. It was not a setting conducive to creative writing. Nevertheless, I persevered. I helped with the script of a short comedy film called *The Six-Sided Triangle*, which a film director friend Christopher Miles was making, starring his sister Sarah Miles and Nicol Williamson. In it he cleverly satirised the film-making styles of six different fashionable directors, from Kurosawa to Bergman, via Visconti and Truffaut. It was later nominated for an Oscar.

The name of Ned Sherrin had been cropping up increasingly in Footlights circles, as the proposed producer of a television satire show to be broadcast by the BBC in the autumn. It was to be topical, late-night instant humour, all of which seemed highly improbable in the BBC of those days. But Ned got hold of my name as a possible candidate to contribute to the show and I responded to his summons to meet for a drink in the Café Royal. The show in question was to become the satirical phenomenon of the early 1960s, *That Was The Week That Was*, which burst on our screens with the impact of a comet in November 1962, only to burn out a few months later.

I couldn't get to London regularly to be one of the script-writing team who wrote up the week's topical stories for every show, but I fed in my few contributions from Scotland and enjoyed the thrill of hearing the studio audience respond as my material went out live across the airwaves. The image of *TW3* was very much ad lib, informal, anything-may-happen, and the bare sets, minimal props and obvious under-rehearsal all added to the sense of danger that gave it such an edge. The star of the show, and of its successor *Not So Much a Programme, More a Way of Life* (to which I was also to contribute) was David Frost. He and Peter Cook were between them to dominate what came to be called the satire boom.

But really satire was only part of the story. As is well known, the 1960s was a time of liberation. The war and post-war austerity had receded. Life was less serious, in the sense that growing prosperity was helping people to relax again, emotionally as well as physically. True, there was still the overhang of a potential nuclear holocaust, but that engendered light-headedness rather than despondency.

People began to break ranks, and the stultifying humour that had been handed down from the music-halls gave way to something fresher and more free-ranging. *The Goon Show* had led the way with its mixture of surrealism and anarchy. All my generation at school had tuned in, quietly in our studies, with the volume low, like wartime resistance fighters. But our laughter must have given the game away. The acid songs of Tom Lehrer, the Harvard don, added spice. Then came *Beyond the Fringe*, which was like the first splitting of the atom. For me, Peter Cook was comedy's Rutherford. A convivial man of gentle courtesy yet fearless invective, he was an original, a clear spring from which poured forth humour so sparkling and inventive as to defy definition. A little of its magic faded in the cooled-down mechanics of the film or television studio, but he remained a comic genius, with all the burdens that brought.

Satirist is just one of the labels that could be tied to him. He was fantasist, mimic and verbal wizard, whose stream of consciousness found humour of all kinds in unexpected places. But if satire is scorn wrapped in humour, or parody with an agenda, then Peter was more interested in the humour than the scorn and his agenda was simply to amuse, which he did as none before or since. He cracked the code for many who came later.

David Frost, the other figure to dominate this period, was quite different. His humour was journalistic. Where Peter built a confection from a torrent of words, David went for the honed one-liner. Quick-witted and astute, he quickly sensed the new trends and rode them with a drive and efficiency none could match. He certainly had an agenda, and humour, old and new, was more a vehicle to him than an end in itself, as his highly successful subsequent career demonstrates. But his was the right image for *TW3* – though, it has to be added, he was no actor – and he gave it the cutting edge that made it such a seminal programme, even if at times its skits were characterised more by abuse than by humour. Had Peter Cook hosted *TW3*, as by rights perhaps he should have done, it would have been funnier, but probably less successful. As it was, Peter found other outlets for his talents, through his ownership of *Private Eye* and his satirical nightclub, The Establishment.

Frost relied on others for much of his material, whilst Cook almost always wrote his own, though much of it never reached the written page. With their quite different talents, there should have been room for both of them in the world of satire and literate comedy that burgeoned at that time. But occasionally there were tensions and it was my misfortune at one stage to get caught in their crossfire. Although they had both gone down by the time I joined the Footlights, I had met them both at Cambridge and David also came to Edinburgh and visited The Sphinx. He was looking for material, for *TW3* and for his nightclub act. He particularly fancied my Richard Dimbleby Royal Barge sketch, which he duly broadcast on the show and, after protracted negotiations, he bought the UK rights to perform the sketch in his nightclub and cabaret acts.

It had become quite notorious by then. In those days the Lord Chamberlain, head of the Queen's Household, was responsible for vetting all material to be performed in theatres; Lord Cobbold, then holder of that office, had banned the sketch from public performance of the Footlights Revue as it mentioned the Queen. The producer of a new London revue named *See You Inside*, which was to be put on at the Duchess Theatre, wanted to include it along with other material of mine in this show. I had warned him that it had already been banned, but that of course was the whole point as he saw it, because it had by now been seen by some eleven million people on television yet could not be seen in a London theatre. What a scandal!

Sure enough, the Lord Chamberlain, whose writ did not run to television or nightclubs, banned it again, as he had to do, and there ensued massive publicity for *See You Inside*. 'BLUE-PENCILLED – THAT TV SKETCH' shrieked the top, front-page banner headline in the London *Evening Standard*. That newspaper's Londoner's Diary, under the heading 'Ridiculous', wrote:

> It seems almost incredible that Lord Cobbold, the Lord Chamberlain, should ban from the stage the television sketch on a Royal departure.
>
> But perhaps it is for the best in the long run. One or two more similar decisions should ensure that the whole ridiculous business of stage censorship will be swept away in a gale of ridicule.

Other newspapers pitched in. In the *Daily Mail*, Bernard Levin began his regular fulminating column thus:

> Every court must have its jester, and that of Queen Elizabeth II is no exception. The present incumbent is Lord Cobbold, formerly Governor of the Bank of England. Yesterday, cap and bells dancing in the breeze, stuffed eelskin at the ready, he was following the precedent of his distinguished forerunner Yorick and setting the table on a roar. Allow me, therefore, to pour a flagon of Rhenish upon his head.

The poor Lord Chamberlain really had no discretion in the matter, constrained as he was by a statute enacted in 1737 at the hand of Sir Robert Walpole. The defence put out by his office – 'the fact that a thing appears on TV does not mean that it can go on the stage and, I suppose, vice versa' – did not really help matters. In due course his censorship role was indeed swept away, doubtless to the relief of his successors.

Three years later, ironically, the tables were turned when David Frost performed the sketch on stage, at a Royal Gala Performance, in the presence of the Duke of Edinburgh. The Duke, reported the *Daily Telegraph*, 'clearly enjoyed the item', but it was cut from the televised version of the show, along with a reading from the *Kama Sutra*, allegedly because of a time overrun. 'Ho Ho! Very satirical!' as Frost would have said.

At the time of the original row, however, whilst I was rapidly becoming famous – for fifteen minutes – it was not a comfortable experience, stuck as I was in Scotland and frustratingly far from the mainstream. But when, despite the sketch's increasing familiarity, a letter arrived from Peter Cook, who had seen me perform it in a Footlights Smoker, asking if he might use it at the Strollers Theatre Club in New York, my cup overflowed. Here were the two kings of the satire jungle, both wanting to use my material. So Frost could use it in the United Kingdom and Cook in the United States. I explained to each what was agreed with the other, which they both accepted, so everything was fine and dandy.

Except that it wasn't. A few months later a furious row broke out between them over who was or wasn't and who should or shouldn't use on which continent a modest little sketch that I had knocked up in an hour at Cambridge a couple of years earlier. It became quite vicious, with Cook describing Frost in *Private Eye* as 'the bubonic plagiarist'. It would be pointless now to apportion blame but, although neither of them blamed me for their spat, at the time it took the edge off my appetite.

The Royal Barge sketch itself was a comparatively gentle piece. Its opening line was: 'Good morning from the Pool of London where, on a cold, wet and windy morning, we are all eagerly awaiting the departure of the Queen.' Hardly treason and quite unlike the vicious diatribes some of *TW3*'s writers were serving up. For example, they were cruelly unfair in their sustained attacks on the then Home Secretary, Henry Brooke. I took the view – expressed, I think by George Bernard Shaw – that satire was most effective when there was an underlying respect, even affection, for the object of the satire. Anyway, the Royal Barge piece did seem to catch the mood of the times and, more importantly, to make people laugh. Indeed, long afterwards I found that many people remembered it clearly; it even characterised for them the whole satire scene. David Frost certainly continued to use it, almost as his cabaret signature tune, for years afterwards.

I hadn't performed it myself since my Cambridge days, having sold the rights, and had stopped doing cabarets altogether. I found it increasingly difficult, away from the stimulus of the Footlights hothouse, to write entertaining material. The frustration of being out of things was made worse by finding my material quoted from time to time in such magazines as *Time* and *Life*. This was often followed by a flustered letter, and sometimes a cheque, from some ex-Footlights friend or other who had found himself obliged to fall back on my old stuff to help him out in venues that ranged from the *Ed Sullivan Show* to Madison Square Garden. I once received a cheque from the BBC for repeat fees for some of my sketches, broadcast in Yugoslavia and Brazil, in the sum of £1.6s.8d. I still wonder what they made of them.

There was to be an echo of all this more recently, during the 1992 and 1996 American presidential elections. In a speech during our general election of 1992 I had made one of those fatuous remarks that occasionally reach the columns of the press, describing Neil Kinnock as 'not the comeback kid. He's the karaoke kid: press the button and he'll sing any song you want.' Several months later President George Bush was quoted making the same remark of Governor Bill Clinton. In 1996 a remark I made about loving my job as President of the Board of Trade – 'I sleep like a baby: I wake every four hours and cry' – made its way into a newspaper diary piece. Soon afterwards Senator Bob Dole was quoted as saying he loved being a presidential candidate, he slept like a baby …

I'm sorry that my involuntary help did neither candidate much good.

After I had gone down from university, my former Footlights colleagues had continued the Cambridge idyll, riding the satire craze. Their 1963 revue *Cambridge Circus* was staged in London and then went on tour to America and elsewhere. I discussed with Tim Brooke-Taylor the possibility that I might join them on this tour and he encouraged me to do so, but in the end I decided that would be frivolous so early in my business career. From that springboard, many of them then went on to fame and fortune in the world of comedy show business.

There have been several generations of good comedians and comic actors thrown up by the universities, usually in pairs, since my Footlights days. Many of them have been highly talented; and literate comedy has become established as a major sector of the entertainment industry – something none of us foresaw in the early 1960s. One can trace the thread of comic development down the years and the subtlety and creativity of some of today's performers is impressive. They have escaped the tyranny of the punchline, with a mixture of the deadpan, the surreal, the absurd and sharp social observation, only slightly exaggerated.

For some years I regretted my decision not to join my Footlights friends as they drifted into professional status, reinforced by reading occasional interviews in the press in which they said kind things about me. But in truth, my career in comedy hadn't really amounted to all that much. My good year at Cambridge had been a year too soon. My talent was limited and I had come to the dull, Presbyterian conclusion that there was more to life than trying to make people laugh. Looking back now, I sometimes think: 'What the hell: I should have stuck to comedy.' But at the time, I decided it was not enough just to knock and mock. I felt I wanted to do something more positive, more constructive. It was really the wrong way round, but youthful cynicism and a strong sense of irony were beginning to give way to a kind of idealism. I was becoming interested in politics.

THREE

Into Politics

After the razzmatazz of the fringes of show business, Scottish politics was pretty dull stuff to start with. It took a year or two to get on to the candidates list and a couple more before I was selected for a constituency. Reginald Maudling once said that we lived in a Conservative country that voted Labour from time to time. In Scotland it was the other way round: Conservative support had already begun the inexorable decline that was to lead, despite the rallies of 1970, 1979 and 1992, from a majority position in 1955 to oblivion in 1997.

I suppose I became a politician by default. In part it was a reaction to the negativism of satire, in part a wish to get back into the mainstream and, in part, a search for fulfilment that I was not finding in insurance broking. But there was, too, an emerging sense of purpose, a crystallization of ideals that began to turn my instinctive conservatism into something more considered. I did not suddenly become an ideologue; there was no Damascene conversion. Rather, the principles that I believed in – freedom, the rule of law, the rights of the individual, free enterprise and so on – began to engage me intellectually as well as intuitively. I suppose having read history at Cambridge helped. But mine was the kind of conservatism that was against things, such as nationalisation or penal taxation, rather than a positive force. It was quite simple, really: I detested socialism, which I rated a close cousin of Communism, with a passionate contempt. I abhorred its arrogance and its incompetence and the stultifying damage it was doing to our national life. Centralisation, nationalisation, subservience to trade union demagogues, the controls, the bureaucracy, the cronyism and the casual deceptions of its slippery-lipped leaders – all those things steeled me with a determination to play a part, however small, in the battle to destroy that sterile doctrine.

My history supervisor at Cambridge, Raymond Smail, had always emphasised the human element in the triumphs and tragedies of history and I began to sense that our progress through life need not be preordained and dull. One could become involved and make a difference.

Above even my hatred of socialism and all its works, I had a deeply imbued respect for our democratic process whose development I had studied at Cambridge. I know it is a cliché and an excuse to cover baser instincts in politicians, but I did feel – perhaps on top of those baser instincts – a growing wish to serve and to help to carry the democratic torch through my generation. To say that, I know, invites disbelief but I aver that it was true. Politics gradually became my vocation.

It was to be twelve years before I was to reach Westminster and have the chance to start to live out those high-flown ideals. In the meantime, to gain experience, I joined The Empirical Society, a debating group run by Andrew Strang, the doughty secretary of the Scottish Conservative and Unionist Association, which met sporadically in the cavernous rooms of the old Glasgow Conservative Club. The first constituency I went for was the one in which I lived, Central Ayrshire, and in 1967 the party chose me as its candidate. I don't suppose there was much competition as, in those less volatile times, it was rated a safe Labour seat. It got me started, however, and it also gave me something I still badly needed: experience of public speaking.

Rural politics in the 1960s still retained some of the charm of the old hustings. There were over twenty branches in the constituency and I spent many an evening and weekend getting around them. Whist drives, coffee mornings, brains trusts and the like became my political diet, under the inspirational leadership of the association chairman, Colonel Bryce Knox. He organised my campaign along military lines. Bryce's ringing voice would have sounded more at home at Ascot or Henley than in the old mining villages of Ayrshire, but he gave me staunch support and much sound advice and I admired him greatly. It was said of him, perhaps apocryphally, that when he had lined up his men of the Ayrshire Yeomanry to lead them off to war, he asked them why they were going to fight Hitler. He swept aside their standard replies with: 'Nonsense. We're going to fight so that I can go on fox-hunting.' His men revered him and so did I.

On one occasion, at a large whist drive in the little town of Kilbirnie, I was asked to do the customary five-minute speech during the interval. 'Nothing too political', said Bryce as I headed for the stage. 'Tell them a joke; make them laugh.' I struggled quickly to think of one, but the only one that sprang to mind was the story of Noël Coward, touring Australia, where his clipped English tones had caused a stir. In a farewell interview at the end of his visit, he had been asked to treat his audience to a word in 'Strine' (or Australian). 'Certainly,' said Coward, clipped as ever. 'Kangaroo'. In the silence that followed, echoing round that large hall, several farmers' wives gave me a look of blank incomprehension, while others started to shuffle and deal out the cards. Despite that, in due course I got the Labour majority down from 6,400 to under 5,000 in June 1970.

The campaign itself was lively enough and I gained some useful experience, not least in how to seem calm and unruffled whilst privately terrified. At Dreghorn, an old coal-mining village, where I had been warned that in previous elections they had either stormed the stage or thrown stones on to the corrugated iron roof of the hall, no-one at all turned up. Lunchtime factory meetings were livelier. At Scottish Aviation Ltd in Prestwick they banged their metal trays on the table to drown out my speech, so I went round individual tables instead, which quickly thinned down the numbers present. In Irvine, at Ayrshire Metal Ltd, the whole workforce of around eighty assembled at the gates to await my arrival and barracked me loudly. Instead of trying to shout them down, I walked right up to them and started speaking, quietly. It worked for a few minutes, as they fell silent until their local union leaders mobilised them to disperse noisily. I was to discover later that the same technique, of dropping one's voice, works in the Commons Chamber as well.

The Scottish Conservative Party had – and still has – its own central office and its own annual conference and all the usual paraphernalia of politics and, on top of constituency activity, I had plunged into all of that, never feeling the need to get involved in the larger show in the south. At our 1968 conference, whilst I was still a raw candidate, I was sitting in the audience for the Foreign Affairs debate to which Sir Alec Douglas-Home was to respond, when John Mitchell, one of the mandarins from Central Office, passed me a note. 'We are a bit short of speakers for this debate', it said. 'You will be called next but one.' Panic. I had not yet spoken at a conference; now I had to face an audience of 800 people, with nothing prepared. Mercifully, I had recently written an article on the Royal Navy for a newspaper and, with a bit of extempore tweaking, I regurgitated the essence of that and had a useful lesson in public speaking.

I began to take an interest in particular subjects – defence, foreign affairs and constitutional issues, in particular. Readers of the *Glasgow Herald* were treated to my views in articles on the need for reform of the House of Lords and on Britain's duty to intervene to end the horrific Biafran civil war. The latter led to an affable correspondence with the writer Auberon Waugh, who shared my horror at the genocide taking place in Nigeria and was campaigning furiously to stop it. Our cause may have been a just one but the timing of my intervention was poor: the war ended with defeat for the Biafrans, almost as soon as I spoke up on their behalf. But I still believe we were wrong to stay on the sidelines whilst many hundreds of thousands of citizens died violently in what was still a young Commonwealth country.

Housing was another issue in which I developed an interest. At the 1973 conference I was chosen to move the motion on housing asked for debate. At that time Scotland had the worst housing in Europe and four-fifths of all new houses built in the previous fifty years had been for public ownership. Official policy on this issue was weak. It called on local council housing authorities to consider the interests of their tenants in framing policy and it encouraged them to consider selling council houses to sitting tenants at a discount of up to 30 per cent. In my speech, I called for council house sales to be made compulsory to those tenants who wanted to buy them. So far as I know, such a proposal had not been made before and it was six years before it was to appear as official policy in our party's manifesto, but when it did, although I've no doubt others had also proposed it, I felt a proprietorial glow of satisfaction.

In 1974 I fought the first general election of that year – the 'Who governs?' election – in Glasgow Pollok, a seat that Labour had won back from us in 1979 after an earlier, famous by-election victory by Professor Esmond Wright. The Labour majority was only 600, but by then the tide that had swept Ted Heath into government in 1970 had turned. The clear-eyed policies of Selsdon Man had been abandoned and, following several U-turns, our industrial and economic policies were in tatters. Encouraged by this, trade union militancy, particularly in the coal mines, had brought about the three-day week. The outcome of the election Ted eventually called that February, belatedly seeking a mandate to stand firm, was almost a dead heat, but it was Harold Wilson who ended up back in No. 10. In Scotland we lost two seats but our share of the vote fell by almost 15 per cent and Labour's majority in Pollok increased to over 3,000. It was an augury.

That summer, I was interviewed for the seat of Galloway, in the south-west, not far from where I lived. It was a beautiful part of rural Scotland, where the sitting MP, John Brewis, had decided to retire, leaving a 4,000 Conservative majority. I was certainly attracted to it, despite the huge size of the constituency, and I made it on to the short list of three, notwith-standing I had declined, courteously but firmly, to move to the constituency, if elected. I lived twenty miles from its boundary and knew I could handle constituency duties from there. Moreover, I had bought a house only two years earlier in Ayrshire, where my wife Sandy and I were bringing up our two little daughters, Venetia and Lucy. We were not prepared, on top of the unsettling impact that the life of an MP would bring, to uproot them in such uncertain times. The Scottish National Party bandwagon was rolling again and there was no knowing what the future held. So when the Chairman of the Association telephoned me to tell me I had been shortlisted and had a strong chance of being selected, but that I would need to promise at the next round to move to Galloway if elected, I decided that I could not change my position. She was adamant: unless I did, I would not be chosen. So I withdrew from the contest – probably wrongly. I should have gone to the final interview to plead my case again.

To give up the prospect of a safe seat like that, after several years of hard grind on the candidate circuit, caused me no little anguish. There is all the difference in the world between being a parliamentary candidate, still uncertain of eventual success and obliged to hold on to an alternative career, and being an elected Member of Parliament. I began to think I might never make it to Westminster. I was thirty-four and had already fought two seats: to fight and lose any more would take the edge off my marketability. So instead of standing again as a candidate, I seized the opportunity, in the autumn election of 1974, to be personal assistant to George Younger, the Chairman of the Party in Scotland and my own local MP.

We had a lot of fun on the campaign trail as we traversed the country, but the outcome of the election was dismal. Labour scraped home again nationally; and in Scotland Conservative fortunes sank again, losing five more seats, both to Labour and to the SNP. It was to me a poignant experience to note that Galloway had gone to the SNP, by thirty votes.

I decided to have a break from active politics for a year or two. I still wanted to be an MP: indeed, I felt more than ever that this was my vocation. But the demands of my career and family life were growing and the chances of finding a seat I could win and hold were few. We only held sixteen of the seventy-one constituencies in Scotland; and the Conservative share of the Scottish vote had fallen in twenty years from over half to less than a quarter.

Hoping that a bit of intellectual stimulus might be good for my jaded political appetite, I set out to write a pamphlet of the 'whither Conservatism?' variety with Barry Henderson, who had been briefly an MP between February and October 1974. Our aim was to refocus the Scottish Conservative Party on its nature and purpose and to motivate it to win back support in those turbulent times. Scotland now had four-party politics, with Labour running scared of the SNP, who had just failed to penetrate their heartlands. The Liberals had clung on in their rural corners and we had been everyone's kicking-boy.

The pamphlet, optimistically entitled *The Scottish Conservatives – A Past and a Future*, was published just before our new leader, Margaret Thatcher, was due to attend her first Scottish Party Conference. Its central message was: 'We must be seen as Scots who are Conservative rather than Conservatives who happen to be Scots.' It was well received by the press: Barry and I were 'the angry young men of a torn party', according to the *Scottish Daily News*. Alas, it transpired that Scottish Central Office had done a clever deal with a national newsagent chain to display it on their shelves throughout Scotland. The entire print run was sent to them, from whom, months later, most of it was returned, but not a single copy was available where it was most wanted – at the Conservative Party Conference in Dundee. The shelf-life of a pamphlet is short and by the time the many unsold copies had been returned to the party, events had moved on and people had lost interest. As the Conservative Political Centre had published the pamphlet, one could hardly claim that this was part of a subtle plot to suppress our polemic. I fear the explanation is more straightforward.

Over the next year or two, Margaret Thatcher began to go back to basics and spell out a clearer, crisper Conservatism; and my political enthusiasm revived. The Labour government under James Callaghan and Denis Healey was heading for the rocks and our chances nationally picked up. But in Scotland the picture was more clouded, with Conservatives and Labour each having reversed their former stance on devolution and the SNP seeming to prosper on the base of the eleven seats they had won in 1974.

In 1977 I developed a mystery illness, which put me in bed for three months. It followed a bout of 'flu and left me weak and exhausted, but despite extensive tests it remained undefined. The collective view was that it was some kind of post-viral stress syndrome, akin to what is now called ME. At any rate, my recovery was slow, and for years after I was elected to Westminster its symptoms were to continue to dog me. I had to try to ration my energy, and whenever the symptoms hit me – pain at the back of the neck and internal pressure at the top of my lungs – rest was the only cure.

In September that year, whilst I was still having to spend half the day in bed, I was telephoned by Scottish Central Office. David Mitchell, the Vice President of the Party, told me that Galloway needed a new candidate and wanted to talk to me again. I told him of my previous experience with them. 'That will not be an issue this time.' I told him I had been ill. 'I know and so do they. But I gather you are getting better.' I said I would think about it.

My doctor, unexpectedly, was robust. 'Go for it', he said. 'You are on the mend and it may be just the stimulus you need.' 'Should I tell them that I'm still not sure I can cope?' 'I think you will find you can cope, so long as you pace yourself. And, anyway, you will find out quickly.' I knew I would not get a better chance of a seat in Scotland. I felt that I was, indeed, recovering and I was about to start work again on a part-time basis. Above all, I was convinced that I could win in Galloway and that this was my last chance to have a political career. So my hat went into the ring.

On the sunny day when I drove south through the autumn colours of the Galloway hills to the first selection meeting, I had to stop in a lay-by to sleep for twenty minutes before completing the journey. But my long illness and convalescence had relaxed me and I felt no nerves at all, either then or at the final. I felt, rather, a sense of the pre-ordained: I was going to be chosen and then I was going to win the seat. If not ineluctable, it was, at least in my view, a racing certainty.

And so it proved. The support of several hundred party members at my adoption meeting was exhilarating. Here was a natural Tory seat that had gone wrong and there was massive determination to win it back. They did me the honour of choosing me as their standard-bearer and so developed a bond that was to last for the next twenty years.

I loved Galloway and my feeling that I had become a part of it endured throughout that time. It was almost as though Galloway was another country, detached from the rest of Scotland. Even its name sounded ancient and romantic, and its scenery was the Scottish idyll. Its people were strong and self-reliant and true. The sense of community was palpable, both across the constituency and in each of its many old towns and villages. There seemed to be a vibrancy and confidence in its own identity which embraced you. Any countryside that has water running through it has an immediate advantage and Galloway has several fine rivers, but it also has woods and hills and glens, wild moorland and gentle grassland, all laid out criss-crossed by its famous drystone dykes, almost like some great landscaped park. Every aspect pleased the eye and, in the years to come, it never failed to lift my spirits after a week at Westminster.

Pacing myself discreetly, I set about getting around the constituency. It is a large one; laid across southern England, it would stretch from London to the Isle of Wight. It had four local newspapers and covered two and a half counties. Our own party organisation had around fifty branches. All of that worked to my advantage, as it helped me get close to people in every part of Galloway. Once, when Gordon Reece, Margaret Thatcher's image guru, spent a weekend with me whilst the Leader of the Opposition was staying privately in Scotland, I took him on one of my Saturday tours. At the end he said: 'I think your agent wants you to meet every voter in the constituency.' We certainly met a lot of them, and in particular I tried to meet all the local opinion-formers. I was indeed getting over my illness and was well enough by the following summer to climb to the top of Mullwharchar, almost the highest granite hill in the area, where the UK Atomic Energy Authority were threatening to dump spent nuclear fuel – something we eventually succeeded in stopping.

In all my activities I was guided and sustained by my agent, David Bell. David was a Galloway man born and bred who, after a career as a feed salesman to the farming community, had trained as a political agent. He knew everyone, and all their secrets, and he was to give me wise advice for many years to come, until he retired to be succeeded by an equally dedicated successor, Ian Mackie. I was fortunate in the loyalty and friendship I had from them both. By the time the general election came, I had made many friends in Galloway. It was a happy and exciting time. In eighteen months I had got to know the area well and my local profile was high and positive. The local papers were full of photographs, press releases and comment. Not a sparrow fell ...

I was helped by the referendum campaign in March 1979, over the issue of setting up a Scottish Assembly. The Labour Government had reversed its steadfast opposition to devolution a few years earlier, out of a mixture of opportunism and panic at the threat from the SNP to their central Scotland heartland. I can think of few Labour MPs – though Donald Dewar was one

– who genuinely and consistently believed in it. But Willie Ross had retired as Secretary of State for Scotland and the pass had been sold.

The unfolding story of devolution is addressed elsewhere in this book, but what mattered most at this stage was that the referendum stopped it in its tracks. Far from being the obsession of the Scots that its supporters claimed, it secured the support of less than a third of those eligible to vote. In consequence, the measure fell; and so did the Government, when the SNP abandoned Labour in Parliament. Appeasement had blown up in their faces. In Dumfries and Galloway, our resistance was rewarded by a huge majority against the proposed assembly.

It was a marvellous prelude to the election, which followed a month later. I worked flat out every day of the campaign, holding no fewer than fifty-four public meetings in three weeks and canvassing in every town and village. Buoyed up by the enthusiasm throughout our organisation, which was admirably led by its determined chairman James Wilson Walker, I became increasingly convinced we were going to win. My confidence grew with every speech; fluency and an ability to recall and marshal facts and figures emerged as new talents I did not know I possessed. Above all, a feeling of rapport with my audiences, on the doorstep and in the village hall, and a determination to have done with the socialist rabble at Westminster, added to the momentum for victory. We were further cheered by visits from such luminaries as Michael Heseltine and Geoffrey Howe, the latter revealing to a startled audience in Newton Stewart that, as a young naval officer, he had had his first proper grown-up kiss on the cliffs at Portpatrick. In due course we romped home by a margin of nearly 3,000 votes. Six other Conservative seats were won back in Scotland that day from the SNP, who lost nine of their eleven MPs. Margaret Thatcher became Prime Minister and I became a Member of Parliament.

It was another rite of passage, but it brought a special kind of euphoria: something to do with fulfilment and participation in the processes of parliamentary democracy that I so respected.

FOUR

Into Westminster

T HE HOUSE OF COMMONS that assembled in early May of that hot summer of 1979 was abuzz with anticipation and a sense of change. Perhaps I exaggerate because, for me and for the large new generation of MPs, it did indeed mark a great turning point in our lives. However our personal fortunes were to fare, nothing would ever be quite the same again. But politically, too, there was a feeling that the general election had marked a watershed. We had taken power after a period of governmental meltdown. James Callaghan's Labour Government had collapsed in ignominious failure and socialism itself stood utterly discredited. It was a time for new departures.

As I stood with Malcolm Rifkind in the bustling Members' Lobby that first day, the heroine of the hour suddenly emerged through the throng, her new parliamentary private secretary Ian Gow glued to her side. She congratulated Malcolm on his appointment as a junior minister at the Scottish Office – odd, I thought, since it was she who had appointed him – then fixed her gaze upon me. 'And how are things in Galloway, Ian?' I was amazed. We had met a couple of times in the past few years, but for her to recognise me, and to remember both name and constituency, with all the preoccupations and burdens she now carried, was startling. 'They're fine, Mrs … Prime Minister,' I stammered. But she was gone, off to dazzle some other new member.

This sense of what might now be called inclusiveness, of embracing the gauche newcomers into the team, of sharing in our commitment to change things and make life better, came as a great relief to those of us who walked in wonder at the new responsibilities we now carried, to serve in the Mother of Parliaments and support our new government. As I sat in the Aye lobby next to the Chamber, writing a letter to my daughter Venetia, describing the scene as the Queen had opened Parliament, another distant hero, Keith Joseph, breezed up and introduced himself. It was the same in the dining room, in the smoking room and the tea room: everyone in the party, old and young alike, was keen to meet, to help, to advise and thus to create a strong and united team for the battles ahead to restore our country. Christian names, with these political giants, were *de rigueur*.

Of course, this mood of idealism would take a battering in the months and years ahead, but bliss was it in that dawn.

The first business of the House was the re-election of the Speaker, George Thomas was a wily Welshman, who ran the House as Speaker with a fierce discipline, laced with wit. I was surprised at the silky eloquence with which James Callaghan, whom I had always considered to be smug and insensitive, spoke in this debate. Indeed, he always treated Margaret Thatcher with an unexpected courtesy. One sensed that with George Thomas, however, this fellow Welsh MP had unsettled scores to settle. After referring to an awkward incident in George Thomas's past when he had unknowingly bought and worn an Old Etonian tie, Callaghan moved on to tell the story of how the Speaker's predilection for indulging his skills as a lay preacher had once taken him to the southern states of America. There, in a little white clapboard church, before an all-black congregation, he had preached a sermon of such fire and brimstone that the Hallelujahs had echoed around the rafters and, as George tottered from the pulpit, drenched and exhausted, the presiding pastor had stepped forward to proclaim: 'My friends, Mr Speaker Thomas has jes' given us de great sermon. Mr Speaker Thomas may have de white skin, but underneath, his heart am as black as yo's an' mine.'

It was a surprise to me to learn just how much direct power the Speaker of the House of Commons could exercise. George Thomas's skill lay in making each of us new members feel that we had a special personal relationship with him. He also had a talent for defusing tense situations in the Chamber. It was said that once, in the last parliament, a row had broken out when the Scottish Nationalist MP Winnie Ewing had been ranting away in her strong Scottish accent. A Labour MP from Yorkshire intervened to protest, in his own equally impenetrable tones, that he couldn't understand a single word the honourable lady was saying. Bedlam ensued. The nationalist MPs all leapt to their feet clutching with glee at this new grievance to nurse. But Speaker Thomas was quick to impose his command. With his lilting Welsh cadences scaling new heights he poured oil on troubled waters. 'There are many accents in this place. It's part of its charm. You know, I sometimes wish I had one myself.'

That story served me well when, years later, as Secretary of State for Scotland, I was taking part in the BBC's radio programme *Any Questions?*, broadcast from Glasgow University. It was the usual arrangement, representing the BBC's idea of balance: three to one, plus the question master, against me, the same proportions in the audience and a 'light-hearted' final question chosen with care to discomfort me. Did the panel agree that a Scottish accent was an advantage to a Scottish politician? The other three panellists each giggled with relish as they took their pious turn to roughen their vowels at my expense, but the memory of George Thomas's wit came to my rescue.

We were a mixed bunch in the 1979 intake, but with Chris Patten, William Waldegrave and John Patten reckoned to be the emerging new stars, there was the hope of an intellectual injection to Conservatism such as had last happened in the early 1950s, when Iain MacLeod, Enoch Powell and Edward Heath had first made their mark as members of the 'One Nation' group. Another feature of the intake was the new Scottish cohort. After twenty years of decline, our numbers rose to twenty-two, many of them new MPs.

But whilst the new boys began to make their presence felt, there were still plenty of the old guard to nudge them gently into their place in the herd. I remember being in the Chamber during a division one evening that summer, when one dapper new MP strode in wearing a white tuxedo. A knight of the shire, Sir Walter Clegg, turned to his equally distinguished colleague Sir Albert Costain and said, in a loud stage whisper, 'I see the band is taking a break.'

By then we had all taken the oath and become fully fledged MPs, salary £6,800 per annum. Working conditions in the House, it has to be said, were appalling. Designed before the days when constituents wrote letters to their MPs, office accommodation was cramped and limited, and the authorities took weeks to allocate desks to new members. We were all itching to get on with the job and had hundreds of letters to deal with. Eventually I suggested to Peter Fraser, newly elected MP for South Angus, that he and I should take possession of a room I had found, vacated by two colleagues who had just become ministers. So we squatted there and notified the authorities, who in due course confirmed our rights of possession.

We also had to find ourselves somewhere to stay in London. For several years I was to be a tenant in Cowley Street, first of Tam Galbraith, one of the grand old Scottish Tory MPs, and then, after Tam's premature death, of his son Thomas, later to be Lord Strathclyde and our leader in the House of Lords. It was conveniently close to Parliament: on one occasion I was in my bath when the Commons division bell rang – I still made it into the Aye lobby within the eight-minute time limit allowed.

One by one, we found a chance to make our maiden speeches and get on with the business of being an MP. One's maiden speech was for most of us a daunting prospect, but it had to be done so one just took a deep breath and got on with it. I chose the Second Reading debate on the Bill to repeal the Scotland Act. That ill-considered measure to create a devolved assembly in Scotland had failed to secure enough popular support in the referendum a few months earlier, thus triggering the downfall of the Callaghan government. My speech contained the usual, though heartfelt, tributes to the charms of my constituency and a robust defence of the constitutional integrity of the United Kingdom and of 'One Nation' politics.

To a newcomer, the general mood at this time was one of unity and optimism. There was little visible sign of Cabinet rifts or ideological divisions, though we had heard that they existed. We, like the whole country, were just hugely relieved to have got rid of socialism. The economy we had inherited was in a terrible state, with high inflation and rising unemployment against a background of massive fiscal deficits, industrial anarchy and appalling productivity levels, especially in the nationalised industries. It has been rightly said of Margaret Thatcher that she set a fine example at this time of tough leadership and firmness of purpose. So she did, but in truth she had an open goal, with the Labour Party in tatters. She also had a secure parliamentary majority. So stark were the failures of recent years that the political agenda set itself and the entire Conservative Party rallied behind it.

We were glad to be back in power, where we belonged; and 'doing the right thing' – the instinctive application by Conservatives of the principles of our philosophy to the needs of the times – was rationale enough. Sound money was common sense and had not yet been elevated to the status of a political creed, though the beat of the mantra could be faintly heard. Denationalisation was simply the undoing of harmful socialist confiscation and the restoration of human rights. It had not yet become the creed of 'privatisation' and small government. As for strikes, we had been presented by the trade unions, who had so overplayed their hand, with the perfect opportunity to step in at last and clip their wings; and we were all determined to do so. Nevertheless, Margaret Thatcher seized the day with flair and determination. There were dragons to slay and she knew the dangers of losing momentum. She also knew that things would get worse before they got better and that her strong resolve would be tested as she asserted the overriding importance of a strict monetarist stance.

As a Scottish MP, I did not need to choose my priorities and interests in Parliament. Westminster was not just the Parliament of the whole United Kingdom, it also made provision for the separate needs of the nations that comprised it. For Scotland, with our distinctively different traditions and needs, that meant separate legislation on most domestic issues, separate Scottish Committees to study Scottish Bills and Scottish matters, a separate Scottish Question Time and, once the new Select Committee system was established as a check on the executive, a separate Scottish Select Committee.

All of these had to be manned, and most of us new MPs found ourselves heavily committed to the passage of Bills on Scottish housing, Scottish education, Scottish criminal justice, Scottish health, and so on. We spent long hours, often late into the night or even all night, fighting to give Scottish council tenants the right to buy their council homes and Scottish parents a say in their children's education. Scottish MPs did work very hard on Scotland's behalf in those days, something that was later to be obscured by the devolution debate.

There were quite a few dining clubs in the Party at this time, usually centred around members of similar political attitudes. Nick's Diner was one, run by Nick Scott. One Nation was another. They flourished and faded with the careers of their founders and leading members, but as Conservatism began to take on a distinctively Thatcherite stamp, and the strains of government, during a recession, began to show, they came into their own in the early 1980s. I did not join either club. Indeed, they didn't invite me to. I didn't like the labels that membership of such clubs tended to bestow. But my Groucho Marx tendency dissolved when some of my friends asked me to join a particularly strong new club, called The Blue Chips. Founded and attended solely by members of the 1979 intake, its stamp was convivial rather than conviction politics, despite the membership of such luminaries as William Waldegrave, Chris Patten and Robert Cranborne. The driving force was Tristan Garel-Jones, the new MP for Watford and a man with a passion for the intrigue and undercurrents of politics, who was later to be one of the best whips of recent years before becoming a minister with a panache that must have startled his Foreign Office mandarins. His favourite saying there, when problems became intractable, was 'Thank God it's only a game.'

Maligned as he was later to be by the Eurosceptic right, Tristan was in fact a loyal and objective minister. Had Margaret Thatcher listened more carefully to his warnings and advice in 1990 – 'The assassins are out there, Prime Minister. They are out to get you' – she might have survived the leadership contest that brought her down.

The Blue Chips met and dined at Tristan's house in Catherine Place, a house steeped in politics, formerly the home both of Maurice Macmillan and of Randolph Churchill – two famous scions. In April 1981, after positive vetting by William Waldegrave and John Patten over lunch at the Travellers' Club, I was elected to membership. Before accepting, I asked William for reassurance that it was not simply a 'nursery of sedition'. 'Don't worry', he replied 'we just relax over an agreeable dinner.' If this was true – and it was, thanks to Tristan's wife Catali – it was not to remain the whole truth, because almost at once we decided to write a book, appraising the emerging Thatcherism of Margaret Thatcher and suggesting its future course.

William and Chris were both old hands at works of this kind but we carved up the research and early drafting between us. Michael Ancram and I were to prepare a chapter on social policy. Much work ensued, culminating in a brainstorming session in mid-July, at which we all produced and debated our chapters. Then William was appointed to write up the finished version of what was by now reduced to a pamphlet, its planned title modified from *Change Gear* to *Changing Gear*.

The year 1981 had been a rough one for the Government, with the recession still raging and a robust monetarist budget from Geoffrey Howe. Creative writing of any sort by a group of backbenchers was bound to attract suspicion at a time when the press were looking for signs of disunity and, as William's draft did not reach us until the House had broken up for the summer and close to the printer's deadline, we had almost no chance to amend it.

I did not recognise all I read from our July discussion and disagreed with a number of its sentiments, but we were all tied in as joint authors of *Changing Gear*, which was published just before the Party Conference in October. Much of what it proposed was what would soon be regarded as mainstream Conservatism: renewed zeal for denationalisation, tougher action against the closed shop and on unfair dismissal, flexibility on pensions and on the retirement age, better training for young people, more emphasis on energy conservation and so on.

Its opening sentence, however, read: 'Conservatives should never become too entangled with a particular economic theory.' I suspect that those in the party who thought that all thinking should come only from the top may have read no further. Anyway, a wholly disproportionate row erupted and the pamphlet was pounced on as evidence of sedition of the worst possible kind. William and I had both become members of the Government by then and there were calls for our instant dismissal, though I was at a parliamentary conference in Fiji at the time so missed all the excitement. By the time I got home it had all blown over and, a couple of years later, when we analysed what we had written, we discovered that many of our proposals had by then been adopted as

Government policy. Others, such as the radical reform of the House of Lords, have only recently become part of the party's agenda. But perhaps its most important message, the foolhardiness of preaching fundamentalism whilst practising more conventional politics, was never accepted, with sad and avoidable long-term consequences.

Changing Gear apart, membership of the Blue Chips was indeed agreeable, the more so when a couple of years later we invited John Major, Douglas Hogg, Nicholas Soames and Matthew Parris to join us. Over time, the Chips have provided their party and the country with one Prime Minister, six Cabinet Ministers and two Chairmen of the party.

By the time he joined us, Matthew had abandoned his parliamentary career for journalism. Many will share my view that he a sublime journalist. Less well known, perhaps, is the tale that did the rounds when he was still an MP. I haven't checked the facts, because it would spoil the story, but if they are incorrect I apologise to anyone wronged. Matthew, it is said, was planning to be in his West Derbyshire constituency one Friday, to address his Ladies' Lunch Club. Unfortunately, there was Government business in the House that day and by chance the Chief Whip, Michael Jopling, asked him to stay in London to speak in the Second Reading debate of the Non-Imprisonment of Prostitutes Bill. This was a controversial issue at the time. I understand that during the debate the Rev. Dr Ian Paisley MP was to proclaim: 'It's time we showed the red light to prostitution!'

It was also around the time when a certain madam, Mrs Cynthia Payne by name, was alleged to be engaged in the provision of services in exchange for luncheon vouchers. A special offer was said to have been devised for MPs: £25 for a two-course lunch and a bottle of wine, to be served by the waitress of one's choice. This prompted the observation from one of the knights of the shires, the late Sir Brandon Rhys Williams MP, that 'it can't be a very good wine'.

Matthew Parris, being a keen new member, agreed to the Chief Whip's request to stay at the House of Commons to speak in the debate on the

Non-Imprisonment of Prostitutes and is said to have sent a telegram (in the days when one could) to his Ladies' Luncheon Club which read: 'Sorry not to be with you. Am representing your interests at Westminster.'

My own constituency work was a constant preoccupation. I enjoyed the routine and ritual of being a constituency MP and had quickly established a rota of surgeries, which I held on Saturdays in nine different locations, three each time, around the area. From time to time one won small victories over officialdom for constituents to whom their MP was often the last hope of success in their battles with the system. To win was rewarding, but often their difficulties were beyond solution and I would return home after a day of listening to other people's problems feeling drained, rather as I suspect a faith healer must feel after a day of laying on of hands.

At Westminster, I saw my role essentially as supporting the Government under whose banner I had been elected. But there was one – and only one – occasion when I felt unable to go into the Government lobby. It arose when, in his 1981 Budget at the depths of the recession that had dogged us for two years, the Chancellor Geoffrey Howe proposed to raise petrol duty by 20p.

In Galloway, as in every other remote area, that caused fury. I and several other rural MPs rebelled and sought a meeting with Geoffrey, threatening to abstain or worse when the measure came to the vote in the Commons. The Chancellor listened courteously but conceded nothing and so twenty Conservatives, myself among them, abstained when the vote came.

Later, the increase on derv was halved, which was a figleaf to show our constituents, but four of us from Scotland – Peter Fraser, Alex Pollock, John Mackay and I – decided to form a pressure group which we called 'The Petrol Patrol', to lean on the oil companies to moderate their transport charges and price structure for fuel in rural areas. They would not agree to revise these, but we noticed soon afterwards that the price differential did narrow. The following year, as the Scottish Whip, I had an opportunity to make representations to Geoffrey Howe ahead of his Budget. His speech, when delivered, contained several sympathetic references to the interests of Scotland – so perhaps rebellion, however muted, does occasionally pay.

By then, however, I was no longer a backbencher. Promotion from the large 1979 intake of MPs had been slow. By the time of the reshuffle of July 1981, only five of us had joined the Government. But during the summer recess that year I had an unexpected call from the Chief Whip, inviting me to join the Whips' Office. Thus I became the most junior member of Margaret Thatcher's administration and embarked on the most enjoyable period of my political career.

Enoch Powell, who like most of the whipping system's critics had never been a whip, once observed that 'Parliament needs its whips as a city needs it sewers'. I think that was too disparaging; whips are needed to maintain party cohesion and to gather and disseminate information. I was to find my five years in the Whips' Office, when one had no public profile and made no speeches in Parliament, enormously rewarding. One was on the inside track of government and had a direct input into the decision-making process. Also, in the collegiate nature of the Whips' Office, as in an officer's mess, one made strong and enduring friendships – something rather rare in politics.

As Scottish Whip, I had to make sure that the extensive Scottish programme of debates, Bills, regulations, statements, committees and question sessions ran smoothly. The arrival in 1983 of a strong new intake that included Gerry Malone, Micky Hirst and Michael Forsyth helped me, on the whole, in this task. They certainly had minds of their own, however, which whips do not really regard as a good thing.

My memories mainly come in snapshot form. I was the duty whip on the front bench when a fresh-faced Tony Blair made his maiden speech in July 1983. I thought it very well constructed and delivered, though his version of a rational and moral socialism was not one I recognised. Afterwards in the smoking room I congratulated him on it, the only time I ever did so to an opposition MP. At the beginning of that year, we had discussed in the Whips' Office who should join us to fill a vacancy. The Prime Minister would of course make the appointment, but she tended to rely on the Whips to choose their colleagues. My suggestion was John Major. I did not know him well but he was clearly very bright and articulate and, with his gregarious nature, was well liked in the Party. In due course he was appointed and was soon a dominant member of the Office.

I remember our periodic meetings with the Prime Minister – notably the occasion when the Whips' photograph was being taken on the soggy lawn of No. 10's garden and all the chairs sank into the mud, but the PM was more concerned not to disturb a duck that was nesting in a trough full of hyacinths. Then she came into the Whips' Office in No. 12 for a drink and, to our astonishment, told us the date on which she planned to hold the 1983 general election, still over two months away. She talked of other world leaders, saying at one stage: 'There's Reagan, Kohl and myself. We are the trinity.' I remember the Whips' Dinner at which she chose to misunderstand comments of John Major's when he tried to tell her that the Government was not getting its message across. A row ensued in which he held his ground, thinking afterwards he had ruined his career. I told him what was obvious: that it would be the making of him.

When the row reached its height, one of the House of Lords whips, Lady Trumpington, intervened bravely to try to deflect the Prime Minister's attention. 'Oh, Prime Minister, that was wonderful. The whole world should be told.' 'Told what, Jean?' 'What you said just now.' 'But what did I say?' 'Er . . . I can't remember, Prime Minister.' It certainly helped to defuse the situation. On another occasion, when Jean Trumpington arrived at a party event as guest speaker, there was no one waiting to greet her so she started chatting to the members. Eventually the Chairman appeared. 'Hello,' said Jean, 'I'm mingling.' 'How do you do, Mrs Mingling,' said the Chairman, 'how nice to meet you.'

Above all, I remember Margaret Thatcher during the Falklands War. On the Monday in April just after it had started, despite the pressures upon her, she held two separate briefings for groups of junior ministers. We crowded into her room at the House, where she sat on a low sofa stool to tell us what was happening. She was formidably on top of events and dealt with questions with a forthrightness that left us in no doubt as to her intentions. Example: to a question from one unfortunate colleague about whether or not we had enough ships – 'The world is full of ships. Next question.'

The mood was quite different on the evening of Monday 14 June, when news came through of the Argentinian surrender. After an ecstatic reception for her statement to the House, she came into the Whips' Office with her husband, Denis, and Ian Gow, to thank us for our small contribution in trying to steady the party during some of the more fraught moments of the previous three months. Champagne was produced and the Chief Whip, Michael Jopling, proposed a toast. Then, while the crowds waited in Downing Street to cheer her, she sat on the sofa, between David Hunt and me, kicked off her shoes and chatted. She pulled from her handbag and showed to us the statement she had just made, written in her own hand on five sheets of House of Commons writing paper, and also the notes from which she had carefully prepared it. Then she quoted Enoch Powell's remark, made at the outset of the crisis, about how we would now find out of what metal the Iron Lady was made. Now we all knew. She was at her apogee.

The Falklands War left little doubt as to the likely outcome of the next general election. But when, after the most careful and thorough considera-tion, it was eventually called for 9 June 1983, I very nearly ruined everything.

It was on Tuesday 10 May, when the election had already been announced and we were finishing off a batch of outstanding Bills in time for the dissolution of Parliament by the end of the week. The Chief Whip was negotiating with his Shadow which parts of the Finance Bill would be dropped and which agreed to. At five o'clock, when I came on to the bench to do my one-hour stint, it looked as though there was enough

business to fill the rest of the day and to enable the Finance Bill negotiations to be concluded.

Suddenly, though, things started to accelerate. 'Keep the business
going', Michael Jopling had said, 'but don't be seen to delay it.' The
Importation of Milk Bill was finishing and Geoffrey Finsberg was present
to handle the remains of the Dentists Bill. He said it would only take
between five and ten minutes. I left the Chamber briefly to summon
William Waldegrave for the Education (Fees and Awards) Bill and David
Mellor for the Marriage Bill. But where was John Mackay for the Mental
Health (Amendment) (Scotland) Bill? I had to dash back into the
Chamber in time to move various procedural points which arose at the
conclusion of each Bill. Mellor was there but Waldegrave had come in
and gone out again. Finsberg didn't take ten minutes: his Bill went
through on the nod. Panic. Mellor's Bill had no amendments, so he
would not be able to delay it. Waldegrave and Mackay appeared: each
said they could talk for a bit on theirs.

I had to find the backbench MPs – Joan Lestor and Janet Fookes – who
had tabled adjournment debates, which would come at the end of
business, but I could not leave the Chamber. There was no one in the
Whips' Office to summon to my aid. They, like the ministers, were busy
clearing their desks and preparing their election addresses. The Bills were
going through so quickly that opposition spokesmen were not reaching
the Chamber in time to move their amendments. It was like the bathwater
that accelerates as its spirals down the plughole. Mackay moved his amendments in a block and Martin O'Neill, for the Opposition, had almost
nothing to say. In a flash, Mental Health had gone through and we were
into Education. Alan Beith, the Liberal MP, did not arrive in time to move
his amendments: collapse of debate, the Bill nodded through.

We had tabled a second adjournment debate and John Cope, the Deputy
Whip whom I had managed to catch a little earlier, was scouring the building
to find Janet Fookes, who was to move it. Only one more piece of govern-

ment business remained, the Litter Bill. John Biffen, the Leader of the House, was in his place to move it, but under Standing Orders he could only do so formally, so no debate to be had there. I looked round our otherwise empty benches – no backbencher within reach to table quickly a third adjournment debate. No Labour MPs at all present, except Willie Hamilton, who was fuming because he had arrived too late for Mental Health.

The moment of truth arrived. The clerk signalled to me to move the adjournment motion. I prevaricated. He scowled. I got to my feet slowly and moved the motion. 'Miss Joan Lestor!', called the Deputy Speaker. Not present. 'Miss Janet Fookes!' Not present. 'The House stands adjourned.' As the fateful words echoed around the empty Chamber I sat down quivering in trepidation at what I had done. In fact, in less than twenty minutes I had safely delivered six Bills and a Money Resolution through all their remaining stages and had had the right minister in his place for each measure. Objectively, I had played a blinder. But – and it was a big 'but' – what was worrying me was that if the Finance Bill nego-tiations had not been concluded, if – worse – the next day's business had not yet been tabled, as it had to be before the adjournment of the House, then the carefully constructed plan for the election would have been destroyed. The House could not be dissolved on time; the requisite number of days between dissolution and election would not be available. The general election would have to be delayed by a week.

As I limped back to the Whips' Office to learn the worst, fellow whips – so absent when I had needed them – appeared from every direction. The Chief Whip materialised like a Kansas tornado and I wished I could dema-terialise. The story had a less unhappy ending, however. It transpired that he had indeed finished his negotiations over the Finance Bill and the next day's business had indeed been tabled in time. The next day he vented his spleen at the whole Whips' Office, rejected my proffered resignation and confided in me – best news of all – that he had decided there had been no need to tell the Prime Minister. She went on to win her greatest election triumph.

In 1984, by then exalting in the title of Lord Commissioner of the Treasury but really still a whip, I added to my Scottish duties the role of Defence Whip. One of its pleasures was to attend the morning 'prayer meetings' that Michael Heseltine held in his office at the Ministry of Defence. He would sprawl on a chaise-longue, always wearing a navy blue sweater, and in a stream of consciousness put the world to rights for his attentive audience of junior defence ministers, whip and parliamentary private secretary. He had an impressive grip on defence issues and I believe it was only thanks to his determination, sustained over years, that the new, multi-national European Fighter Aircraft got off the drawing board and, eventually, into service.

The shadow of Westland and its helicopters began to loom, however, and I suddenly found myself deep in discussion with him in December 1985 at, of all places, Jeffrey Archer's Christmas party of champagne and shepherd's pie. The previous July, Michael had been relaxed when the crisis first blew up: let the company go bust and then pick up the pieces. Not now. He had become manic. He spoke calmly but very earnestly, his eyes almost glazed. As we talked, journalist guests of Jeffrey's began to swim past like sharks. Later on, he came into the Whips' Office at the House and talked obsessively about it whilst waiting for the Chief Whip, who had to be summoned from his home to come and see him.

It came as less of a surprise, therefore, when Michael resigned from the Cabinet the following month. For me the consequence, through a knock-on chain of events, was promotion out of the Whips' Office and into the Department of Employment, in succession to Alan Clark. My main reaction was one of relief at having escaped the fate of most Scottish Conservatives of a career confined to the Scottish Office, coupled with anxiety that, after five years of monastic silence, I would now have to learn to speak in the House and in the media again, and face the terrors of the despatch box.

Employment was a small department, but it had at that time two cabinet ministers, Lord Young as Secretary of State and Ken Clarke, whose title was Paymaster General. They were an immensely stimulating pair to work for. David, who had come into politics late, from business, was full of positive ideas and drive, and Ken was buccaneering and assertive – but brilliant. I was put in charge of a whole range of training and employment schemes which were being developed to tackle the unemployment that was still painfully high after the post-socialist shake-out. David had already mapped out the broad strategy, but I was able to contribute to the detailed design of some of them and to the brigading of our array of schemes under the campaign 'Action for Jobs'.

'Enterprise – Training – Jobs' read the sub-heading on our campaign literature; and I was in no doubt that enterprise was what mattered. Our commitment to stimulate and encourage it was what distinguished us from the other political parties. As I toured the country setting up job clubs and publicising all our schemes it became clear that, along with the Government's macroeconomic policy, they were beginning to have a marked effect. At last, unemployment was on the turn and about to begin its long fall, as the Thatcher revolution took hold.

We had all been amused by the story of how one of David Young's predecessors, Norman Tebbit, when first appointed had leapt from his car outside his new department and swept through the entrance of Barclays Bank, next door, instead of the new department. Unfortunately, I managed to do the same. Soon, though, I became comfortable both with the public speaking and the endless seminars and conferences and with the red box life of a junior minister. I got to know parts of England I had never been to, including a particularly enjoyable visit to Chesterfield at the invitation of Tony Benn, to debate employment issues with him at a public meeting. He was the only Labour MP who took the trouble to find out what we were trying to do to help.

My sojourn in the mainstream of British politics was shortlived. In the autumn, only eight months after I had joined the department, a problem arose in Scotland and I was telephoned by the Prime Minister with the challenging news that I was needed there.

FIVE

Moving up the Field

Although in one sense I was coming home when I moved to the Scottish Office, it was quite a culture shock. Politically, the ground was of course familiar, though it was depressing after just six months of freedom in a wider world to find oneself once again engulfed in the parochialism, the petty wrangling and the entrenched anti-Toryism of this smaller, inward-looking political arena.

The first change I noticed, however, was in the frugal, even Calvinist, approach of the Scottish Office Civil Service. The Department of Employment had not been extravagant, but under the quiet urbanity of Sir Michael Quinlan there had always been enough resources to enable ministers' needs to be met with efficiency and ease. I had had a private staff of four next to my office there. In the Scottish Office I had just a private secretary and half a girl down the corridor, to help me handle the large flow of paperwork and diary engagements that were now my daily diet. The Permanent Secretary was Sir William Kerr Fraser, a figure of remote grandeur held in awe by most of his staff, and a man before whose frosty stare I had often quaked when attached to the department as

Scottish Whip. Over time, and with promotion, I was to discover the warmth and geniality that he normally kept hidden. Later, when I was Secretary of State, his wife Marion was to have a great success as the first woman, other than royalty, to serve as Lord High Commissioner to the General Assembly of the Church of Scotland.

Despite the pressures, I was very well served over the next few years by a succession of very bright private secretaries. Peter Ritchie, Ian Jardine, Donald Henderson and Ken Thomson were followed, when I became Secretary of State, by Jim Gallagher, Alan Fraser and Mike Foulis. All of them did their best to smooth my path and worked even harder than I did. On one occasion, when Donald Henderson and I returned to our Glasgow office from a lunchtime engagement to find eighteen messages on his telephone answering machine, I plucked up the courage to ask Kerr Fraser whether we might follow the lead of other government departments and install car phones (this was before the days of the mobile telephone). Good heavens, what a suggestion! If I had one they'd all want one and it would cost £35,000: but in due course he yielded.

I had a similar experience at Dover House, the Scottish Office's Whitehall base. I had a beautiful room on the ground floor, with grey-painted wooden panels bearing still their original eighteenth-century Adam designs; but it was rather dark, so I asked for another standard lamp. Again, the Permanent Secretary paid me a visit. He had had this costed. Did I not realise that it would cost over £600 to match the existing, rather battered, lamp? The next day I went to Peter Jones and found an almost perfect match for £29.95. Perhaps he was just teasing, or testing, me.

It was a while before I decided to chance my arm again, but one day I wanted to write some notes for a speech and it suddenly struck me that, whilst oceans of printed verbiage washed daily across my desk, there was never any plain, blank paper within reach. I opened every drawer – empty. So I rang through to my private secretary: could I have some plain paper, please? He rushed in. Was there some kind of problem? No, I just wanted to write something so I needed some paper. He went out and came back after a pause, holding in front of him like a dead rat, one single sheet of plain white paper, which he solemnly laid on the desk. After an apprehensive glance at me he left and I suddenly realised how civil servants controlled their masters: always keep them supplied with an endless supply of neatly prepared memoranda. Never give them time to think for themselves. Above all, never give them paper with nothing on it.

Certainly at the Scottish Office there was never any dearth of written material. When I was Secretary of State my private office, which by then did number four again, carried out a count and informed me that a thousand different items passed through their office each week, of which I saw seven hundred – an average of one hundred a day, every day of the week. Some of these would be short acknowledgements or items of information; others would be long detailed submissions, often with several complex appendices, requiring sensitive and detailed decisions. No matter how much of this flow of paper I managed to deal with during the day, there was always enough to fill a red box to send home with me. Ministers must be spared the evening distractions of the real world, as well as the chance to think for themselves.

After five years as the Scottish Whip I was now to serve in the Scottish Office for the next nine years, comfortably breaking the record as the longest continuously serving minister in its entire history. Over time, it became quite wearing. When I arrived at the department in the autumn of 1986 though, I was a humble joint parliamentary under-secretary of state with responsibility for industry and home affairs and the first thing I did was to leave the country.

As Industry minister, I undertook my first duty, leading a trade delegation to Los Angeles. My first ministerial engagement there was an official visit to Disneyland: was this a metaphor for my new job? More appropriately, the emphasis of my whole visit was on inward investment and that was a theme I was to focus on strongly, first as minister and then as Secretary of State. The need for new jobs, in bulk, to replace the declining industries was urgent. Also, I was determined to try to help Scotland's industrial base become broader with the attraction of sunrise industries – foreign-owned, probably, but better to have companies owned by foreign entrepreneurs whose horizons were global than owned by the state and run by Whitehall, whose vision was confined to the limits on public expenditure. It was high time Scotland started to look to wider horizons again. To have a future we had to compete in the global market-place, and these new businesses would play to the strengths of our university research base and generate indigenous jobs and skills around them.

Our man on the ground in California (from the Scottish Development Agency) had had some business cards hurriedly printed for me and it was only after I had distributed a couple of dozen of these around the chief executives of our key target companies to attract to Scotland, that I discovered that my name and title had been printed on the back of cards that already bore the legend 'The Neva Dance Ensemble' and a Moscow address and telephone number. These were still the days of 'the evil empire'.

When I got home I set to work on appraising the state of Scottish industry – its strengths and weaknesses, opportunities and threats – and considering how I as industry minister could best help it. Already, Scotland's economy had improved dramatically from the appalling state of our 1979 inheritance. It is perhaps forgotten these days exactly how bad things were when we took over. Inflation had doubled in just five years. So had unemployment; and it was to continue on its upward trend for some time, as we fought our way through an oil-induced world recession and as the subsidised jobs in overmanned industries, particularly in the state sector, finally came face to face with reality. Industrial output in Scotland had failed to grow over the previous five years, and productivity growth had collapsed – the UK had fallen from second place to bottom in the league of G7 nations.

Scotland had a disproportionately large number of jobs in the old heavy industries of steel-making, coal-mining and ship-building. Like all nationalised industries, they had been starved of funds for investment but bloated with subsidy to maintain job levels, so it is unsurprising that it took us twice as long to make a tonne of steel as it did in the rest of the EEC. British Shipbuilders had just revealed that the average shipyard worker only worked five hours of an eight-hour shift.

The Labour Government's mismanagement of the economy and its surrender to the trade unions was partly to blame for this, but so too was their commitment to nationalisation. This crippling socialist icon had done untold damage in Scotland. All her major industries had felt its dead hand. Her successful public companies had been consumed by it, an entire management class wiped out and the decision-making and head office functions taken south to civil servants in London. Over the years, almost four hundred Scottish companies had suffered that fate, ranging across ships, steel, gas, electricity, transport and coal. I suppose my passionate commitment to denationalisation was coloured in part by the fact that my own family had seen our marine engineering interests on the Clyde snatched from us on confiscatory terms, but I also felt strongly that centralisation and state ownership were wrong in principle and could only destroy enterprise. I always preferred to talk of denationalisation rather than 'privatisation' because it had long been a policy central to Conservatism – it was not invented in 1979 – and involved undoing the folly of nationalisation, rather than introducing some wholly new concept. Over the next decade or so I was glad to be able to play a direct part in restoring the steel, electricity, nuclear and other industries to the private sector. That, like council house sales and reductions in direct taxation, was devolution – of power and ownership – of a kind that could benefit my fellow Scots directly.

Of course, the ship-building industry, like others, was in trouble before nationalisation because of the militancy of the trade unions and the endless disputes over pay, conditions and demarcation that so damaged their productivity. All the groupings and manoeuvrings, involving the Fairfields Experiment, Upper Clyde Shipbuilders and later Govan Shipbuilders could not, despite the heroic efforts of Sir Iain Stewart and others, overcome that fundamental lack of international competitiveness.

The 1960s and 1970s had been a time of artificial restructuring of business, of state planning and direction that sought to head off and deflect change instead of embracing it. There was the Toothill Report, with its emphasis on growth points; then there was the Nicoll Report that laid a matrix across Scotland in the shape of a saltire cross – one axis running from east to west across the central belt, the other from north-east to south-west. They meant well and they did identify some assets and areas in which government could help to foster enterprise, but it was not until Margaret Thatcher's government confronted union militancy and the control of the money supply head-on that realism came into play. Then Scotland's economy began at last to grow and prosper.

By 1986, when I became industry minister, we had lost many of the heavy industry manufacturing jobs which in truth had been put beyond recovery in the 1970s and were now like so many dead leaves clinging to the branch. Our productivity, however, had at last begun to recover, and thanks to our efficient private sector manufacturers our exports were now breaking records. Industrial relations were the best for half a century. Self-employment had increased by 50 per cent and unemployment had begun to fall. It was to continue to fall, almost without interruption, throughout our remaining years in government and for some time afterwards. By 1987 we were exporting 30 per cent more per head from Scotland than from the rest of the United Kingdom.

The Thatcher magic had worked, but many Scots could not reconcile themselves to it. Was it because her success troubled their complacency? I have heard it suggested that some in Scotland simply could not forgive her for being right and could not forgive her for being a woman, above all an

English woman and one who knew her own mind. Certainly, despite the welcome that had greeted her succession to Ted Heath in 1975, something turned many Scots against her: perhaps it was her didactic authoritarianism. It was sad, because she liked and admired many Scottish characteristics, but she never really got on to the Scottish wavelength.

By 1988 productivity was growing faster in Scotland than in any other major industrial country in the world. Productivity in the coal mines was up by 60 per cent on 1979 levels; and British Steel, which had been losing £5 million per day in 1979, was making annual profits of over £400 million. By 1989, Scottish unemployment was falling at a faster rate than in the rest of the United Kingdom. But this was not the story that was being portrayed on Scottish television screens or in Scottish newspapers. Bad news made better copy; and most of the media's leading figures were paid-up members of the Labour Party. Always preferring Flodden to Bannockburn, they chose to dwell on the old heavy industries, whose decline had been under way for years and was now almost beyond redemption. So, with Malcolm Rifkind's agreement as Secretary of State, I decided to publish an economic profile of Scotland to try to dispel the myths.

My officials did an excellent job and *Scotland – An Economic Profile*, the first edition of which was published in 1988, was packed with information, laid out in an accessible way. It covered population and employment trends; the structure of economic development, by area and by industry; incomes and expenditure; training and assistance schemes and many more matters. The picture it revealed was of a country where economic development and living standards were forging ahead, where new industries – diverse and often technology-based – were taking root and where, although manufacturing still accounted for 23 per cent of employment, two thirds of jobs were in the fast growing service sector. The interest of the media in this document was, however, ephemeral and once they had filleted it to extract what could be portrayed as bad news, they ignored it. But its preparation was a useful exercise for me and, I believe, the Scottish Office. It confirmed my instincts as to where and how government's role should be directed and where it should be constrained.

I had long been convinced that it would be fruitless and harmful to prop up the declining heavy industries; they had suffered too much under state ownership. The British Steel Corporation (BSC), under the rigorous, free-enterprise chairmanship of Sir Ian MacGregor, had improved its performance by leaps and bounds and, slimmed down and rationalised, had a chance to prosper in the private sector. I was later to enjoy taking the denationalisation bill through its committee stage in Parliament. Before that stage, however, in 1987, the management wanted to close Ravenscraig, the major steel plant directed to Lanarkshire by Harold Macmillan's government twenty years earlier but soon absorbed into the subsidy culture of all nationalised industries and beatified as an icon of socialist mythology. Many in the Government now wanted to close the hot-strip mill immediately and the rest of the plant in two or three years, to increase the proceeds of selling the company. But this was to ignore the politics. It was never understood in the south how the steel industry held a very special place in the hearts of the Scottish electorate. It epitomised Scotland's great days as a world economic power and although employment in metal manufacturing was now below 2 per cent of the total, to many Scots the country's white-hot steel furnaces represented the beating heart of Scotland. If they went cold the heartbeat of Scottish industry would die.

Already the alleged heartlessness of Thatcherism had been rebuffed in Scotland at the general election earlier in the year, when we had lost eleven MPs – more than half our number, including such able colleagues and good friends as Michael Ancram, Peter Fraser, John Mackay and Alex Pollock. I felt like a survivor of the Battle of the Somme, disorientated and vaguely guilty. They had all become good friends as well as colleagues and, had they survived, I am certain that I would have been spared subsequent high office. But that painful electoral outcome in Scotland had made only a limited impression on our otherwise triumphant English colleagues. They regarded all Scots as whingers, because that was how the Scottish opposition MPs at Westminster behaved. Where the political need was for sensitivity and careful handling, they tended to treat Scotland as a spoiled and recalcitrant child that should be punished for failing to absorb the lessons of monetarism and the market. After all, wasn't Adam Smith a Scot?

There were plenty of new English members and, over time, I got to know many of them. One morning, spotting one of the new, woman members approaching the Members' Entrance to the House, I said, in my smoothest tones: 'Hello. We haven't met yet, but I've heard all about you. You're Teresa Gorman.' 'No', she replied coolly. 'I'm Gillian Shephard.'

For those of us from Scotland who had survived the electoral rout, it was a traumatic time. Insouciance became the order of the day, with none better at it than Malcolm Rifkind. Scottish business in the House of Commons took on the air of Custer's last stand but, as Malcolm cheerily pointed out, unlike General Custer we had the Gatling gun in the shape of our overall parliamentary majority. None the less, for a private sector company to close Ravenscraig was one thing; but for the Government to do it in order the better to sell off the company – and at a time when its improved performance was already breaking new records – would in Malcolm's view be a step too far, given our weakened position in Scotland. Without actually threatening to resign, he let it be known that he could not accept closure by government and, as his industry minister, I told the Whips that if he went I would go too. I was a strong supporter of the Government's economic policies, but I never believed that ideology should be allowed to overrule common sense.

For three weeks a crisis raged within government, which we managed to keep entirely secret. Even when it was over, not a word of it was to reach the press. Malcolm and I had meetings with Ken Clarke from the Department of Trade and Industry, the leading advocate of closure, and with Sir Ian MacGregor, to try to find a way forward. We considered a separate Scottish industry being established, in the private sector and with various other guarantees and options for onward sale. No easy solution could be seen and we were getting word from DTI that if their proposals were not accepted in full David Young and Ken Clarke would resign. Two could play at that game.

On Tuesday 1 December, Malcolm was outnumbered thirteen to one at EA (Economic Affairs) Committee, but his dissent ensured that the issue would go to Cabinet two days later. The following morning Malcolm and I told our fellow Scottish Office ministers of the seriousness of the problem and the deadlock that had been reached. They all agreed that there was no other single issue that could so destroy our political prospects as this one. In the course of the day various discussions took place. It did not seem to me to be impossible to find a solution acceptable to all parties, that would include some guarantees for the future and would give Ravenscraig a chance to prove itself once in the private sector, whilst not constraining BSC from taking commercial decisions. By the next morning a deal had been struck. An announcement would be made to Parliament that day: denationalisation of the steel industry would go ahead during the current session, the Ravenscraig hot-strip mill would operate until at least 1989 and some steel-making would continue there for at least seven years, both on the timescale BSC had intended anyway. In addition, if and when they did decide on closure, they would first offer it for sale.

Although the opposition made a ritual fuss, this was an acceptable deal that saved the Government from a massive political own goal and which did not constrain BSC from operating commercially in the private sector. There would have been a cataclysmic fuss if we had been seen to close Ravenscraig, as an act of government, wiping out jobs in a totem industry that was actually improving its performance day by day, simply to put more money in the coffers of the Treasury in Whitehall when the industry was denationalised. The man in Whitehall did not, in my view, know best; and now Ravenscraig could take its chance in the real world and its new owners would be accountable for its fate. That, it seemed to me, was better politics. More importantly, it was the right thing to do.

All Scottish secretaries of state faced from time to time a dilemma over whether to play the Scottish card or the Unionist one – it is a dilemma that even first ministers in the new Scottish Parliament will not escape, unless they are nationalists. But this was not a Scottish card issue; nor was it a free market issue, since steel was still a state industry. Rather, it was an issue of good politics and common sense; and it challenged the unionism of our English government colleagues. We won the argument on this occasion, but only just.

Throughout these years I sought to remove the iconic status of the steel industry and dissolve its mystique. Producing *Scotland – An Economic Profile* was part of that exercise. After BSC joined the private sector I intensified my efforts. The acid test of success was to come not in 1989 – for British Steel prospered in the private sector – but in 1992. Just before Christmas in 1991 I was telephoned, as Secretary of State, by Sir Robert ('Black Bob') Scholey, the new Chairman, to tell me in confidence that he would be announcing early in the new year that the stripmill at Ravenscraig was to close and that production at some of the other steel-making plants would also be cut back.

We were about to head into a general election and we were badly behind in the polls. The timing was not ideal, to put it mildly, but this was a market-driven decision taken by a private sector company in the interests of its shareholders. I was determined not to challenge it. I asked for more information, I asked for sensitive handling of the redundancies, and I asked for help both with retraining and with environmental work at the site, to all of which Bob Scholey readily agreed. Then I braced myself for the row ahead when the announcement was made.

It started with a loud bang. The ritual rhetoric of socialism was cranked up but then, like a soufflé, it slowly subsided and it began to seem that our message had finally got through. Scotland's economy was riding high and steel had at last begun to lose its sex appeal. Labour, too, had a problem with the announcement. As the *Herald* journalist Murray Ritchie perceptively told me as soon as the news broke: 'This is bad news for Labour.' He was right. Even Neil Kinnock had begun to abandon cheque-book socialism and felt unable to promise renationalisation; and a vicious internal battle was triggered within the Labour Party, which the Kinnock modernisers won. Only the SNP could address the closure with cynical glee. But by the time of the election, just two months later, the issue had sunk below the political horizon.

What the travails of the steel industry did do was underline again the clear need to help Scotland develop a broader and more diverse industrial base, preferably in the sunrise industries. George Younger had recognised this and had set up 'Locate in Scotland' as an inward investment bureau, run jointly by the Scottish Office Industry Department and the Scottish Development Agency. Malcolm Rifkind also valued it and, as his industry minister, I had resolved to make it one of my priorities. Over the next nine years, five of them as Secretary of State, I was to visit Japan and the United States almost every year to seek to persuade mobile high-tech companies to make Scotland their European base.

Purists would argue that the inducements we offered were a distortion of market forces. I had no such qualms. Others in the market – such as Germany, France and Ireland – all offered grants and assistance. Our main selling points were the use of the English language, the quality of our academic institutions and the vast improvements in our deregulated workforce, with the trade unions finally tamed. Unlike in France, where it was almost impossible to reduce the workforce when times were hard, we were removing the workplace burdens on business. In consequence, many more companies chose Britain. Why Scotland? Because we worked hard at it: because our labour was available in large numbers and close to new, custom-built factories; because that labour force proved to be

adaptable and quickly trained; because the social and transport infrastructure was in place and because we were able to offer regional assistance.

In 1988 we abolished the previous government's regional development
grant, which had been automatic and indiscriminate and thus enormously wasteful. The Opposition said the world would come to an end,
but it didn't. The regional selective assistance scheme, although still
confined to the creation of manufacturing jobs, allowed much more
discretion in the awarding of grants and was therefore more productive
in costs per job created. English colleagues complained that Scotland (and
Wales) were uniquely favoured by this scheme. They were wrong to do
so: the rules were applied absolutely even-handedly across the United
Kingdom. It was just that, because of a greater dereliction from the
decline of the nationalised industries, a higher proportion of the Scottish
and Welsh populations were in areas eligible for grant. In parts of the
north-west and north-east of England the use of such grants was as
intensive as it was in central Scotland.

The Treasury, in its hand-to-mouth, myopic way, thought the grants
were wasteful, displacing existing jobs, moving jobs around the UK and
funding jobs that would have come anyway. The scheme had rules
though, which were rigorously applied to ensure that any such wastage
was kept to a minimum and much of the grant created jobs that would
otherwise have gone elsewhere in Europe. The grant involved was only a
very few thousand pounds per job, which was rapidly recouped by the
Treasury in taxes. Indigenous industry complained that foreign
companies were uniquely favoured, but this, too, was wrong. The rules
were fair: it was just that foreign companies brought whole factories
creating thousands of jobs. Domestic companies tended to have less
ambitious plans and their announcements therefore made less impact in
the media.

Where the assistance schemes could have been improved was in
modifying the rule that restricted grants to the creation of jobs which

could only be defined as manufacturing. Apart from the anomalies in definition that this threw up in an economy where manufacturers out-sourced much of their work (such as carriage), what we really wanted was to attract more research work. Good though our universities were, they were not always a sufficient inducement to research-centred projects that would create self-sustaining centres of excellence in our country, instead of branch assembly plants, reporting to a head office in, say, Massachusetts. A scheme that recognised the economic benefits of intel-lectual property would have been much more effective.

Nevertheless, our inward investment drive was a great success. It trans-formed the face of Scotland, enriched the Treasury and created a bigger, more diverse market place. In 1981, the first year of Locate in Scotland, some £234 million of investment from abroad was announced, creating or safeguarding over 7,000 jobs. By the end of the decade, the figures were £853 million and 12,300 jobs, respectively; and, cumulatively, job numbers linked to inward investment had by then exceeded 70,000. These were jobs in electronics, healthcare and biotechnology, engineering, chemicals and in textiles, and although most of them came from the United States we were also attracting growing investment from Japan, Korea, and the rest of Europe.

These companies were following in a tradition that had brought the Singer Sewing Machine Company to Clydebank early in the twentieth century and in the 1950s and 1960s such giants as Motorola and IBM, the latter to build its huge plant in Spango Valley behind Greenock, on boggy land where I can remember shooting pheasants and snipe in my youth. Several such companies have brought successive generations of investment to Scotland. Not all, of course, would survive indefinitely. But the net gain for Scotland, as for the United Kingdom as a whole, has been incalculable and has balanced the massive investment that we as a nation have made abroad, tying us into the global market place and forcing us to sharpen up our act accordingly.

Inward investment, with its rejection of trade unionism, also reinforced our industrial relations legislation in the 1980s, helping to break the malign hold of the trade unions on the workplace. The appallingly destructive behaviour of the Transport and General Workers' Union, which in 1988 frightened the Ford Motor Company away from its planned location of Dundee to Spain, where it was to prosper greatly, was a sad reminder of an age that had almost passed. I and my officials in the Scottish Office and in Locate in Scotland had spent months winning Ford for Scotland and we were bitterly disappointed to see our work and thousands of jobs prospects destroyed by atavistic socialism. I think it was the only occasion on which I lost my temper on live television, when interviewed by Kirsty Wark alongside Bill Morris of the TGWU, who blithely excused his union's wanton destruction of job prospects for the Dundee area in a new growth sector.

Despite that débâcle, I constantly sought as industry minister to establish a rapport with the unions, in the hope of begetting a little understanding. I thought the Government's policy of pretending unions did not exist was silly. I had a friendly relationship with Campbell Christie, the sensible and realistic general secretary of the Scottish TUC, and so I asked him if I might attend their annual conference in Perth in 1987. I was the first Conservative minister to do so. Of course, the unions would not go so far as to let me address the conference; but as I sat and listened to the rhetoric and sentiments expressed in their debates, a language that came from another epoch completely detached from the real world, I was glad that the growing number of our multinational investors in Scotland were not there to hear it.

As well as seeking significant employment from the investment we attracted, we strove constantly to raise the quality of the jobs secured and to derive spin-off benefits for the domestic economy. At one stage my officials claimed to me, on grounds I regarded as shaky, that half of all the inward investment we had brought in had a research component attached to it. At any rate we did have some successes in that respect, rather more than we did in our other initiatives to help local supply chains to develop and to enable an indigenous, high-tech industry to become established as a spin-off. I always felt that Scottish business missed opportunities there, but, over time, some progress has been made.

One of the useful selling points for Scotland, in our inward investment missions, was the existence of five well-developed New Towns, offering attractive factory locations and good access to labour and transport facilities. These towns, at East Kilbride, Glenrothes, Cumbernauld, Livingston and Irvine, had been developed during the two decades after the Second World War, partly to relieve the appalling housing problems and population density in Scotland's central belt, but partly too to contribute to earlier attempts to diversify Scotland's industrial base. They had been a success and they were well run, but they were costly and it seemed to me that they had become institutionalised. They were also mature towns now, except for Irvine which had only been designated in 1966, and I felt that they could be given a new lease of life by ending their privileged status and liberating them into the world of free enterprise. In short, I wanted to sell off their state-owned assets and wind up their bureaucracies.

I asked Malcolm Rifkind if I might develop plans to achieve this and, with his agreement, in May 1989 published a Green Paper entitled *Maintaining the Momentum*, setting out my proposals for consultation. My objective was to involve the private sector as fully as possible and, to take over the economic role of the New Town organisations, I wanted to create new local development companies based in the private sector – rejecting the New Town Commissions that had been established to handle such wind-ups in England, which had proved expensive and slow-moving. After a year's consultation, this was the central proposal I included in the White Paper that we published in 1989 to announce our conclusions. So far as the industrial property was concerned, some of this would be sold off, but a residue would be held for a while by the Scottish Development Agency to meet the needs of inward investors. Housing was already largely privately owned and we did everything we could to encourage more private sales as wind-up proceeded.

The Opposition railed at all this, unable to imagine that the New Towns could continue to prosper outside the embrace of public sector bureaucracy. But I pressed on with my plans. We passed the necessary legislation and in the private sector the five towns went on from strength to strength, though my plans for private development companies were to be superseded by the later establishment, all over Scotland, of Local Enterprise Companies.

The main instrument of economic development and regeneration across Scotland was the Scottish Development Agency (with the Highlands being covered by the Highlands and Islands Development Board). Set up by a former Labour Secretary of State, Willie Ross, the SDA had become a powerful and in many ways effective body, funded by government and with a remit set by government. But by the end of the 1980s its corporatist ethos and self-aggrandising objectives were undermining and even displacing enterprise, where it should have been helping to establish it. I proposed a number of changes to rectify this. I made it sell off many of its shareholdings in Scottish companies. Taken originally to help such companies become established, these shares had been retained as a kind of nationalisation portfolio. Government resources should be more productively recycled. I also required it to dispose of the large majority of its factories and commercial properties: it had become the biggest landlord in Scotland. In addition, to emphasise that Locate in Scotland was not part of the SDA, but a separate body, run jointly by them and my industry department in the Scottish Office, I asked Malcolm Rifkind to agree to the setting up of a Supervisory Board, which I would chair and which would produce and publish an annual report on our inward investment performance.

These measures helped a little to counter the perception that all good economic news in Scotland was thanks to the SDA and all bad news could be blamed on the Government. But a bigger change was afoot. Bill Hughes, the Chairman of the Scottish CBI and, incidentally, a hard-working Conservative supporter, suggested to Margaret Thatcher that delivery of the Government's training schemes in Scotland should be combined with the enterprise role of the SDA and delivered at local level, by newly created branches of the SDA and with the involvement of the private sector. It was an idea whose time had come. She took to it at once at a conference convened at Chequers in September 1988 and Malcolm Rifkind and Norman Fowler, as Secretary of State for Employment, were asked to develop the idea. They quickly agreed on the broad principles and that Scotland's share of the Training Agency's budget would be devolved to the new body.

When Malcolm first told me what had been agreed and was now to go ahead I was not wildly enthusiastic. I was concerned that the Local Enterprise Companies, as they were in time to be called, would be dominated by Scottish Office and SDA bureaucrats and by local councillors. But Malcolm gave me the task of working up the details, so I had the chance to ensure that my own fears would not be realised. I soon became enthused. I was already fully familiar with the Government's training and enterprise schemes from my days in the Department of Employment and could see how the Youth Training Scheme, Employment Training and the rest could benefit from a more flexible local delivery. This I set out to give them.

After some to-ing and fro-ing with the SDA, I decided on thirteen local enterprise companies, rather fewer than Bill Hughes had envisaged, which private sector consortia would bid to operate on a commercial basis. We had already encouraged the Agency to set up seven regional offices to deliver its services more locally and the network of LECs, as they came to be called, built on this. Each company board would draw two thirds of its members from the private sector. The initial rule-book, drawn up by my officials, was almost two inches thick. I sent it back and asked for another one, less than a quarter as thick. I also resolved early on that, in order to benefit from local input and give the LECs a chance to prove themselves, at least three quarters of the SDA's budget must be delivered through them and not from its head office in Glasgow.

We were immensely fortunate to have Sir David Nickson as Chairman of the SDA at the time, who achieved everything we asked of him and more, with efficiency and enthusiasm. Malcolm and I launched our detailed proposals at a conference of businessmen at Dunblane in September 1989, and in due course I took the necessary legislation through Parliament. Scottish Enterprise, as the SDA would now be called, was born and in April 1991, by which time I had become Secretary of State, it started to operate in its new form. It rapidly settled down and I believe it did have a beneficial effect both on the efficient delivery of government training and enterprise schemes – the one-door approach – and, more importantly, in the stimulus of enterprise at a local level. The first task of each LEC, to carry out an economic audit of its area, was itself a highly beneficial exercise. By the time Michael Heseltine launched his later Business Links scheme from DTI in 1995 (which was a pale imitation of what we had done) I was already reaching the view that it was time to rein in the LECs and give Scottish Enterprise a more narrowly focused role, so successfully had enterprise again taken root around Scotland.

In the early 1980s, whilst still in the Whips Office, I had found myself contributing, almost by accident, to Margaret Thatcher's conference speeches. It began after the Brighton bomb drama. I had been staying in the Grand Hotel for that conference, but had left on the day before the explosion: I was expected in Dumfries for a party in honour of my neighbour Sir Hector Monro's celebration of twenty-one years as the local

MP. Among those murdered by the IRA was Muriel Maclean, whose husband Donald was President of the Scottish Conservative and Unionist Association (SCUA), the voluntary wing of the party in Scotland.

I was vice-chairman of the Party at the time and, in case the need for a tribute to Donald might be overlooked in the Prime Minister's speech the following May, I sent a short form of words to Michael Alison, her parliamentary private secretary. Before I knew it I was writing first the introductory paragraphs and then more substantive parts of her annual speech to the Scottish faithful and occasionally contributing to the Blackpool, Brighton and Bournemouth speeches as well.

A speech-writing discussion with Margaret Thatcher was like a session on the psychiatrist's couch, though I'm unsure who was the patient and who the psychiatrist. One would sit, usually with others, in her study at No. 10, pen poised over notepad, hanging on her every word. Phrases, themes, single words would be scribbled down as one tried to identify – from the stream of consciousness, often inchoate, that poured from her, brow furrowed and with that penetrating gaze turned inward – some thread from which to form sentences and paragraphs. One could sense the specks of gold in the ore, but it was agonisingly difficult to capture them as she darted quickly from subject to subject and theme to theme. More than once I came away, my pad covered with a bewildering jumble of words and phrases covering everything in the political lexicon, but having failed to grasp the thrust of what she truly, deeply wanted to say. I felt as the scribe to the ailing Delius or the dying Mozart must have felt, desperate to capture the tumbling cascade of genius and transmute it to ink marks on paper. But it didn't really matter, because there was always a last-minute rewrite by others and often only snatches of what I had submitted would survive.

Sometimes, though, longer sections got through to the final version. I remember particularly, in 1986, a section on caring, which she delivered in her Perth conference speech. I had long been concerned that we did not, as a party, explain clearly enough that it was precisely because we cared, not because of adherence to some abstract theory, that we had taken so tough a stance on inflation and public expenditure; it was because we cared that we had fought the trade unions to a standstill and so transformed our economic performance; because we cared about housing that we had forced councils to sell to tenants their homes; because we cared that we had doubled the widows' allowance, the attendance allowance, the mobility allowance and so on. It was not commonly realised that under Margaret Thatcher the budget for health and welfare payments had increased by more in real terms than it had done under any previous Labour prime minister, indeed under any prime minister at all. Margaret Thatcher did not like saying she cared. She said it was like proclaiming, 'I am a modest man.' In her view, it should be a given that everyone in politics cared and the debate should only be about means, not ends. But that was to ignore the vicious attacks on her and the Conservative Party that were, by default, taking root in the electorate's mind.

She was also driven by an admirable determination to move the centre of gravity in British politics to the right and to break the dependency culture, so she never took enough credit for what she had done in the social field. As a result she was never recognised by the electorate as having delivered, by her deeds, compassionate help to those in need on an unprecedented scale, while her opponents had only ever talked about it. It is an attitude that has hardened the image of the Conservative Party over the years since and has continued to harm us substantially at the polls.

On this occasion, however, my text got through the sifting process and she spoke at some length, and with force and conviction, on how much she did care, concluding:

I am in politics because I care. And so are we all. We care about the future of our country and the welfare of its people. We care about its laws and

its traditions. Its freedoms. We care enough about our country to be
willing to defend it. It is because we care that we don't care for socialism.
It is because we care that we are Conservatives.

It went down well in the hall and got laudatory front-page headlines the
next day, but it was a one-off, not followed through.

It has not often been remarked of Margaret Thatcher either, that she
was one of the politest people in politics; but it is true. She was a stickler
for the social proprieties, courteous and sympathetic in her private
dealings away from the political arena, punctual, considerate and scrupulously deferential to the status of others, whether to her monarch (to
whom she always curtsied low) or to the local mayor or church minister.
She always wrote a kind letter of thanks for help with her speeches,
however tenuous that help had been. It was a beguiling trait in her
character.

On another speech-writing occasion when just Andrew Dunlop, her
adviser on Scottish issues, and I were present, there had recently been a
fuss over her comment that 'there is no such thing as society'. In the
intimacy of her study I thought I could (uncharacteristically) risk a
confrontation with her by challenging that claim, which I thought wrong
as well as politically inept. I expected a fusillade, and hoped at least for
some kind of revelation as to her thinking that I could use for the speech.
Instead, she didn't bristle; she didn't claim she had been misquoted. She
said 'It's an interesting subject. Just wait here' – and disappeared from the
room. While I sat tensely tapping my pen on my pad, the Prime Minister
of the United Kingdom climbed the stairs to her private apartment to
find and bring down to me, one of her junior ministers, the answer to
my challenge. After some minutes, she reappeared holding a book
through which she was searching in vain for a quotation.

'Society is a socialist concept,' she intoned, whilst she scanned the
pages, 'community is Christian.' I quickly wrote that down. She did not

tell me the title of the book (though I think it was *Persons in Relation*, which has an interesting chapter on community and society) but she mentioned the name of its author, Professor John Macmurray. It was a name that meant nothing to me at the time but it was to re-emerge years later as the name of the guru allegedly claimed by Tony Blair, the new leader of the Labour Party. In her memoirs, she says more clearly what she had really thought and meant to say on this subject – and, of course, quoted in full and with her explanation, it makes more sense, with its emphasis on individual responsibility within the community, but on that occasion the words I found afterwards on my notepad were even less help than usual.

A crisper success I had in a Thatcher speech was when she came to her last Scottish conference, in Aberdeen in 1990. As an ice-breaker I had written about how good it was to be back in Aberdeen, adding: 'Denis has his Scottish favourites, too: St Andrews, Carnoustie, Turnberry …'. That got a laugh, but a later hand had added: '… Glenlivet, Glenfiddich, Glenfarclas'. That got a bigger one.

There were many other events to vary the life of a junior Scottish Office minister. With Law and Order responsibilities I had to cope with a prison riot and hostage drama almost as soon as I started in the department. Would I send in the SAS?, I was asked by an eager official. 'Perhaps, but not yet', was my reply. The riot ended peacefully soon afterwards. Responsibility for the Glasgow Garden Festival, as industry minister, was one of the more enjoyable and successful events. Responsibility, when I became Local Government minister, for the aftermath of the Lockerbie Pan-Am disaster in December 1988 was another, utterly harrowing, one.

It began when John Home Robertson MP approached me in the Members' Dining Room in the House of Commons, having just seen on the tapes the news of an aircraft disaster over Dumfriesshire. He was looking for Sir Hector Monro, the local member. We could not find Hector at that point, but the Prime Minister was in the dining room that evening and I suggested that John should tell her PPS Mark Lennox-Boyd the news, which he did.

The morning after the event I attended my first ever Cabinet meeting, Malcolm Rifkind having flown straight to the disaster area to report on the latest developments. The mood of the meeting was sombre, Margaret Thatcher sensitive and subdued, the business despatched with quiet efficiency. My abiding memory of successive visits thereafter to Lockerbie, which was next door to my own constituency, was of the dedicated competence of the police, army and local government personnel and of the sustained leadership qualities displayed by Sir Hector Monro, whose tireless pastoral work continued long after the story had faded from the headlines. He was always a good friend and colleague to all of us in Parliament and a devoted servant of his constituents. Typically, he was to agree to come back into harness as a Scottish Office minister in 1992, when we needed his wise counsel.

Over my years as Scottish Whip and junior minister, which lasted almost a decade, I had the task of helping to steer almost every piece of Scottish legislation that went through the parliamentary process safely on to the statute book. This involved long hours in the Committee Rooms, requiring meticulous attention to detail and many late nights. I have not checked the records, but I am almost certain that I handled more legislation during this period than any other Member of Parliament.

No Bill was more hard fought than that to abolish domestic rates and bring in the community charge, or poll tax. At the beginning of that drama I was still the Scottish Whip and as such was not involved in the policy decisions or the drafting of the legislation. I had watched the row that developed over the 1985 property revaluation, which threw up large rate increases for some householders. Like everyone else, I could see the injustice of so large a burden falling on a small proportion of the population, regardless of individual means – a burden, moreover, that was increasing hugely year by year as ratepayers bore the cost of high-spending local authorities at a time when central government rate support grant was tightly controlled.

But at the same time, I wondered whether the hysteria was not perhaps being overdone. After all, the revaluation redistributed the existing burden – most unfairly, in some cases – but it did not increase it overall. When Sir James Goold, chairman of the party in Scotland, sought a meeting with George Younger to tell him something should be done, I asked to sit in on the meeting and noted that George, too, was cautious about climbing aboard this emotional bandwagon.

But the row mounted, until it became clear that something had to be done. I was cautious of any new miracle cure, especially one that brought a large number of new contributors into the local rate-paying net. So I was at best agnostic about the merits of the community charge. It was certainly a fairer system than rates, but its introduction just ahead of a general election seemed politically foolhardy and I argued, strongly but in vain, that it would be a mistake for Scotland – the guinea-pig – to proceed ahead of England, where the absence of revaluations had created greater unfairness but less of a political problem.

This was the high noon of Thatcherism and caution was for wimps. So no sooner had I joined the Scottish Office a few months later, than I found myself put on the Committee for the Bill, to help Michael Ancram get it on to the statute book ahead of the election. I agreed to do so on condition that my role was confined to the reform of business rates which, to me, was the best part of the legislation; Michael could enjoy single-handed the glory of bringing salvation to domestic ratepayers.

It was not to be. The unhappy ratepayers had not enjoyed the promised relief by the time of the election, but everyone else could see a new tax burden heading their way. As one of the few survivors of the Scottish Conservative cull of 1987, I then found myself having not only to defend

87

the merits of the newly enacted legislation, but also to put its provisions into effect – and to try to do so, moreover, without fomenting civil unrest. Although the rallies and marches and civil disobedience and non-payment campaigns were sustained and wearing – so, too, were the endless debates in Parliament as we brought through the various regula-tions that were needed – we gradually made progress and by 1990 the worst was over. The new system was slowly taking root.

By then, however, the English had galloped up, all gung-ho, behind us. Instead of phasing in the new system over several years, they went for a quick changeover and they did so when the cost of the new charge *per capita* was soaring away from original estimates and the Treasury, seeing a black hole ahead, was warning of impending disaster. I suggested to them, from my Scottish experience, some eight or ten modifications – affecting pensioners, students, second homes, etc. – that might have made the new tax more acceptable, some of which I had managed to introduce in Scotland. All were ignored. The result was the poll tax riots and, although there were other contributory factors, the fall of Margaret Thatcher.

On the business rates front in Scotland, however, I did have some success, though not without having to resort to the arts of Machiavelli. Business rates in Scotland were quite a bit higher than in England, despite the more substantial level of rate support grant, because of higher local council spending levels. In bringing in a Uniform Business Rate, as the corollary to the changes for domestic ratepayers, it seemed to me that logically this should apply on a United Kingdom basis. There were no spare resources in Scotland to level the playing field and neither the Treasury nor the English Department of Environment under Nicholas Ridley were showing any enthusiasm to ease our plight. But the Scottish business community had persuaded themselves that this was indeed what would now happen and I had the task of squaring the circle.

Malcolm Rifkind was on holiday in France that August, when I called in the local government correspondents of the *Scotsman* and the *Herald* and in the course of a long interview tossed in the grenade of ' *If* business rates are harmonised...', rather than '*When* business rates are harmonised...' Publication in both newspapers duly generated the predictable outburst in business quarters, to which my innocent reaction was that I had only stated accurately the Government's position.

Margaret Thatcher was due to attend the Scottish CBI Conference in September, by which time business had mobilised. She got the message from them rather than from her ministers, and when she said to Malcolm and me – and subsequently to Nick Ridley and the Treasury – that something must be done, all we had to do was to nod wisely in agreement. The Treasury duly augmented the Scottish spending block and Scotland got its Uniform Business Rates, at the same level as England.

As a sad postscript, I have to record that the Uniform Business Rate at a United Kingdom level has been abandoned post-devolution and is under threat even on an all-Scotland basis. My other small achievement on the rating front, the abolition of sporting rates (a levy on field sports and fishing from which Wales and England were already exempt), has also been reversed. This will doubtless appease the gods of socialism; it will do little for rural employment or the environment.

Local government finance generally was a thorn in our side throughout our years in power. The reason was simple: local councils could increase their spending levels above that planned by central government, but when central government held the level of its grant, the extra burden fell on ratepayers. As ratepayers contributed only around 15 per cent of the total cost of services, the gearing effect of any overall increase was therefore penal. Somehow, though, local government won local praise for its profligacy and we in central government bore the blame for the painful costs of it that ratepayers had to bear.

We were accused of centralising power from councils when we capped their spending, but we did so only to protect ratepayers and we used powers that had been enacted by the previous Labour government. Certainly, we devolved power from councils to tenants who became owners and to parents who joined school boards, but that was not central-isation; indeed, in the social work sphere, substantial new powers, and funding, were transferred to local councils from central government.

The irony for me was that, having implemented a local tax system that I did not much care for but which was designed to give more power to local people to control council spending, and which was just beginning to do that, the first thing I had to do on joining the Cabinet was to help repeal the poll tax and design and implement the new council tax. The latter was closer to what I would have done in the first place, but less effi-cacious than the poll tax might have become, had it survived.

SIX

Taken at the Flood

As I left the platform at the Party Conference at Bournemouth on the morning of Thursday 11 October 1990, to make room for the senior colleagues who would occupy the seats for the next debate, I met three figures waiting in the darkened wings. There was no one else there and as I brushed past them in the cramped space each said, 'Hello, Ian,' in their own unmistakably distinctive tones.

They were Margaret Thatcher, John Major and Geoffrey Howe. I wished John good luck with his first Conference speech as Chancellor, just a week after we had joined the Exchange Rate Mechanism, and went on my way. Behind me I heard the applause break out as the Prime Minister, her Chancellor of the Exchequer and her Leader of the House stepped into the bright lights to make their entrance, stage right. The drama was about to unfold.

'Have you heard that Geoffrey Howe has resigned?' The question was asked coolly by Charles Humfrey as we sped into Tokyo from Narita

Airport in the back of the Ambassador's Jaguar. Charles was the Economic Counsellor at the Embassy and he had just come out to meet me off a flight from London. I had arrived for the second time within four days, the earlier journey having been followed by an immediate return to London less than two hours after landing, to help the Government defeat an anticipated House of Lords amendment to the Environment Protection Bill, in favour of dog registration. In the event, the amendment had been defeated by their Lordships themselves just before I had got back to Heathrow, rendering my return trip unnecessary, but that is another story.

No, I hadn't heard. What did I think it portended? My brain was not at its sharpest after so much air travel but I cautiously suggested that it might have far-reaching implications. That was the sort of comment diplomats liked.

It was the beginning of November, and when I returned to London on the eigth the immediate novelty of Geoffrey's resignation had worn off. But already the subterranean movements were at work that would soon provoke an eruption. The resignation of the Leader of the House, former Foreign Secretary and before that Chancellor, the staunchest ally of Margaret Thatcher's heroic early days who alone remained of her 1979 Cabinet, had come just after the House had been prorogued at the end of the 1989–90 session. It had been triggered by an unguarded performance at the Despatch Box by the Prime Minister, reporting on a European Summit in Rome. In fact, rumours of festering discontent had been building up for some weeks. More significantly, it came just at the beginning of open season for the leadership election, though until now there had been no speculation about a repeat of the 'stalking donkey' challenge of Anthony Meyer the year before.

Suddenly it all looked a bit different. Michael Heseltine, who had been champing at the bit for some time, looking for a pretext to mount a challenge, wrote an open letter to his constituency chairman. Rather to his surprise, his chairman replied. The letter had been a rather pious homily on the true nature of Conservatism, clearly compiled from an undelivered speech. The reply was a brief declaration of loyalty to the Prime Minister. Both were fully reported in the Japanese edition of the *Financial Times*.

The State Opening of Parliament on 7 November had gone as smoothly as ever but the tension at Westminster was clear to see. On Monday 12 November I was invited to one of the Prime Minister's periodic lunches for senior ministers and I was placed at her right hand side, in the small dining room. Lynda Chalker, Michael Howard, Tony Newton and Tim Renton were there, as were Ken Baker, the Chairman of the Party, and Peter Morrison, her PPS. When she came into the drawing room, where we had gathered for drinks, she made a bee-line for me to ask how things were in Scotland, after that 'artificial row' in the summer. At the end of that 'artificial row', she had had to dismiss Michael Forsyth as Chairman of the Scottish party, but had immediately promoted him to Minister of State. She paid little attention to my reply.

The lunch passed off well enough – I told her about my Japanese trip and we talked about such exotic subjects as regional assistance, Scottish Enterprise and the need to reduce local government – but the jokes about Michael Heseltine were a little edgy.

Geoffrey Howe picked his moment. He delivered his resignation statement at the beginning of the last day of the Queen's Speech Debate. The House was packed and the atmosphere electric. He started in his well-known dull, dulcet tones; but elegantly constructed phrases and sentences, gently delivered, gradually developed into a sustained and deadly assault on the Prime Minister. She had to sit and listen to it, transfixed. As he left the Chamber afterwards Michael Heseltine was heard to say: 'That's it. That's the catalyst.' Malcolm Rifkind said to me behind the Speaker's Chair that it was the most momentous parliamentary performance he had ever heard.

Two days later, nominations closed for the leadership contest. The Prime Minister had brought forward the timing of this in the hope of catching potential contenders off balance. There were two nominees – herself, proposed and seconded by Douglas Hurd and John Major, and Michael Heseltine. George Younger was to lead a team of senior colleagues, including John Moore and Michael Jopling, in running the Prime Minister's campaign. The Heseltine camp was led by Michael Mates, Tony Nelson and Keith Hampson. I always had the feeling that his active supporters were a small dedicated band. He was not a House of Commons tearoom man and had never courted personal popularity amongst colleagues.

Neither campaign seemed to get off the ground. The overall effect was muffled and unreal, in part because the Prime Minister spent half of the campaign in Paris at a meeting convened to sign the Disarmament Treaties negotiated with the Russians. However, it did begin to seem possible that she might not achieve enough support to head off a second round. She needed a really convincing victory to avoid lasting damage and that seemed increasingly unlikely. But George Younger, who had led her campaign to an easier victory the year before, was busily taking over the Chairmanship of the Royal Bank of Scotland and had agreed to act as nominal chairman only; and both John Moore and Michael Jopling had been unwell and seemed uncertain what posture and profile to strike. I was never sounded out by anybody on her behalf and saw no sign whatever of an active campaign. I decided to revive my dormant journal for the next few weeks. What follows was written up later from notes kept at the time.

Wednesday 14 November

Heseltine lobbied me behind the Speaker's Chair at the ten o'clock division. I told him that, as a member of the Government, I felt obligated to the Prime Minister. He said he understood but that it was not a universally held view.

Saturday 17 November

After getting home from a constituency surgery I rang Robert Atkins [fellow Blue Chip and MP for South Ribble], who I knew was in regular contact with John Major, to make it clear that I would be in John's corner should he decide in due course to enter the fray. We agreed that that should not happen so long as the Prime Minister remained in contention. John was at home in Great Stukeley after an operation to remove two wisdom teeth, but Robert gave me his new telephone number and urged me to ring him. We were all rather feeling our way. Would the Prime Minister survive? If not, would John run? Would anyone support him? Who else might stand? Everything was in flux. We had no idea what the next few weeks would bring, but it began to look like the beginning of interesting times.

Sunday 18 November

I rang John, who was still a bit groggy from the general anaesthetic, and made it clear that he could count on my support and help, should the time come.

Tuesday 20 November

I voted for Margaret Thatcher just before lunch and told the hordes of journalists waiting outside Committee Room 12, what I had done.

She had been told by Peter Morrison that she would win easily, but speculation was growing that the 'nightmare scenario' might develop – a wounded Prime Minister going on to the second ballot, having failed to obtain the required majority (50 per cent of the votes of the parliamentary party plus 15 per cent, i.e. 208). In the event, at 6.32 p.m. the result was announced: 204 to 152, with 16 abstentions – the nightmare scenario, precisely.

Had her campaign team been at all active she might have avoided the follow-on, but she would still have been wounded by Heseltine's strong showing. As it was, my immediate instinctive reaction was that she was doomed. I remembered a distant echo from Neville Chamberlain: 'I have friends in the House . . .'

Sitting in my flat, I watched fascinated as, soon after 7.00, she emerged from the Embassy in Paris, during a live television news broadcast, to announce that she would go on to the second ballot. She was clearly trying to head off speculation that she should stand down. Half an hour later Douglas Hurd appeared, to express his continuing support. Then they sped off to a Versailles banquet, in the Hall of Mirrors.

At 7.45 p.m. I rang John Major. He had not seen the Hurd statement. I advised him to put out a statement of support and although he said a senior backbench colleague had given him contrary advice, he seemed minded to do so – and an hour later did so.

I already felt that she might reconsider her decision to stand again, since her vote could only fall in the second ballot, now that she was seen to be badly wounded. Therefore it was important that those who might later enter the contest should not be seen to be grudging in their support for her at this stage.

John asked me to keep my ears open and to keep in touch. Later in the House there was quite a buzz. I bumped into Michael Heseltine in the Members' Lobby just before the division. He was very chirpy, but backed off, joking: 'You'd better not be seen talking to me!' He was actively canvassing, both before and after the division.

Wednesday 21 November

I rang John early – too early – at 7.45, clearly waking the household. Norma was tactful. John professed to be awake and thinking. I told him what I had seen of Heseltine the previous evening and of the rumour that

Douglas Hurd was not keen to have to run, but that two thirds of the Cabinet were said to be sliding towards him. For John himself I reported press speculation, considerable warmth amongst colleagues, but no sign of a bandwagon. There were some views that it was too soon for him: he was not yet ready. I sensed that he felt that, too, but that in the absence of a credible excuse not to run, he thought he might have to.

At the Scottish Office an hour later I had a quiet chat with Malcolm Rifkind, who clearly thought that the Prime Minister should stand down. He asked me my view. I said I thought so too, but that if she did not I would vote for her again. A little later, as we were starting our routine Ministers' Meeting, Malcolm was called out to talk to John MacGregor, the new Leader of the House, who was ringing round to take soundings from colleagues as to their junior ministers' views. After that meeting, I rang Alastair Goodlad, the Deputy Chief Whip, to tell him my view. I said that if a compromise candidate were to emerge to unite the Party it would probably have to be Douglas Hurd, though my own preference in an open contest would be John Major.

For the rest of the morning I was stuck at the Scottish Office, negotiating over our public expenditure programme for the forthcoming year. At lunchtime I went over to the House. It was awash with rumours. In the seething Members' Lobby, Andrew Marr of the *Economist* told me the word was that she would be out by 2.30. But towards the end of Scottish Questions, just before half past three, she came quietly into the Chamber and sat on the Front Bench between me and Michael Forsyth, waiting to make her statement on the European Security Treaty. She was subdued, composed, but seemed isolated and strangely vulnerable. I felt a sudden wave of sympathy and even affection for her, trapped as she now was in an epic tragedy. As ever, she rose to the occasion when her turn came to take over at the Despatch Box.

While this was going on several ministers, mainly of Cabinet rank, were forming in groups in the corridor behind the Chamber. I met Robert

Atkins there, who said half the Cabinet were forming up to tell her to resign. A meeting of ministers, including Malcolm Rifkind and Norman Lamont, had taken place in Tristan Garel-Jones's house last night and had decided to force the issue. On her way from No. 10 to the House, however, the Prime Minister had announced to the press: 'I fight on. I fight to win.' Clearly these groups – I saw Norman Lamont, John Gummer, William Waldegrave and John Wakeham in one group, Michael Howard, Peter Lilley, Ken Clarke and Tony Newton in others – thought differently.

Up in my room, dictating constituency letters, I looked out of the window and across Star Chamber Court into another office. There I saw the familiar leonine mane of Michael Heseltine, who was talking on the telephone. The drama seemed to be everywhere.

I went back to my flat at 5.30 and rang John Major again from there. I told him that he should stay at home: he was far better off away from things at this stage. He replied that others had advised him to come to London at once, and that he had again agreed to sign Margaret Thatcher's nomination papers. She had virtually ordered him to do so, which appeared to have rankled.

The mood against the Prime Minister I reported as focusing on her quick decision to continue, which had aroused resentment, and on the fact that a number of colleagues, whilst wary of whom they would support, felt that they had now done their duty by her in the first ballot. She was mortally wounded in my view and her majority in the second ballot could only fall, but I still intended to support her myself.

Against Heseltine, I reported strong resentment for triggering the contest and that a lot of colleagues, including some who had voted for him, did not want him as Prime Minister. The 1922 Committee were active, sounding opinion. The No Turning Back Group were out and about, twisting arms pretty viciously to try to hold the Prime Minister's support together. The Heseltine troops were buoyant. Despite reports of the Cabinet forming up to her there was no sign yet, apart from the corridor cabals, of a change of heart on her part. There was no sign of a draft Hurd movement – this, it seemed to me, was the most significant point.

Finally, on John's own position, I reported that some contemporaries were said to be jealous, conscious of the threat he would pose to their own long-term prospects: Douglas Hurd by contrast was over sixty. Older colleagues, such as Philip Goodhart, thought it was too soon for John. Nevertheless there was a lot of speculation, continuing warmth and no hostility. John told me his PPS Graham Bright had been approached by 98 colleagues asking his intentions. Their tone was supportive. John remained sceptical.

Thursday 22 November

The Cabinet convened early, at 9 o'clock, against continuing speculation in the media, but no hard overnight news. Then, just before 10 o'clock, my Private Secretary Ken Thomson came into my room at Dover House to tell me that the Prime Minister had announced her resignation. I was able to watch a few minutes of television coverage outside No. 10, before I had to break off for a rather distracted meeting with Professor Stephen Littlechild, the Director General of Electricity Regulation. As soon as I could decently dispose of him I rang John Major's home. No reply. I tried Robert Atkins: not available, but his PS took a message. I tried Tristan Garel-Jones at the Foreign Office, reported in yesterday's media to be leading John Major's campaign. He was there and we spoke. He had with him William Waldegrave and John Patten. To my surprise, he told me that they were working for Douglas Hurd and I was welcome to join them. I explained that I found myself on another side in this particular battle and we rang off.

At this stage, with the deadline for nominations closing at noon, I was still uncertain if John even wanted a campaign. He had made no commitment, even privately and, apart from Robert Atkins and Graham Bright, I knew of no active supporters. Like me, everyone still seemed to be working for him below the surface. From this feverish haze of uncertainty I departed for the calm of Westminster Abbey, for the Memorial Service to Lady Home, where I found myself seated directly in front of a preoccupied-looking Michael Heseltine. Afterwards, I had promised lunch at the House to my daughter Venetia and a friend of hers, Jess Williams, but before meeting them there was time to look in at the Chancellor's room in the House. There I found Robert Atkins, sprawled at John's desk, giving instructions to Anthony Coombs.

He told me that John had decided to take the plunge. He had been nominated by Norman Lamont and John Gummer – the latter had been sensibly substituted, at Robert's insistence, for Peter Lilley, giving the ticket a broad appeal. John had been telephoned at around 7.00 a.m. by Peter Morrison to tell him the Prime Minister was going to resign and was now on his way up from Huntingdon. He would be here shortly. We agreed to keep in touch and I went off to meet the girls.

Jess was waiting in Central Lobby, but there was no sign of Venetia, so I went off to do a round of the corridors to see what was happening. Outside the Members' Dining Room I bumped into Robert Atkins and Gillian Shephard with a pale-looking John Major, still suffering from his wisdom tooth operation. They were just about to brave the dining room and asked me to come in with them to make up a table. I explained about the girls but agreed to help them get in and settled. Our entry caused a stir in a busier and more talkative than usual dining room, but we managed to find a table, near the meat trolley.

I just had time to make three quick points to John. Firstly, it should be a bright, cheerful, open campaign. Secondly, the No Turning Back group or those of them who supported him should be kept under wraps so as not to frighten off the rest of the party, and, thirdly, was he definitely playing to win, because win was what he was going to do? He reassured me on all three points. Giles Shaw came in then and I asked him to take over my place at the table so that I could give lunch in the canteen to my guests. It was only later that I discovered that Giles was a leading campaigner in the Hurd camp!

After finding Venetia struggling through the crowds outside St Stephen's entrance, and giving her and Jess lunch, I put them in the Strangers' Gallery for what promised to be a memorable day: Prime Minister's Questions followed by a motion of no confidence in which the Prime Minister would make her valedictory speech at the Despatch Box. She received a standing ovation from our side when she came in – I don't know when, if ever, that has happened before in the Chamber.

During Business Questions, before the debate started, I went to John's room again and he called me in to a meeting he was having to discuss tactics and lines to take on various issues. Seated around his table were Norman Lamont, Michael Howard, Peter Lilley and special adviser Andrew Tyrie. They were discussing the community charge and John asked my view. I suggested that he should promise, like Michael Heseltine though less fundamentally, to review the tax. That way he covered the Heseltine position whilst giving no hostages. Michael Howard disagreed and said he should promise a complete overhaul of the charge and the whole local government structure, effectively outbidding Heseltine. I said I thought that would be too sudden a change to be credible with colleagues, coming from a senior Cabinet Minister, though it might have its attractions later. The whole Government had, after all, been robustly defending it for several years. The discussion broke off because Norman Tebbit was coming to see John; and the press were getting restless and demanding a lobby. But I was glad to see that John later confined himself to promising a review: it did the trick. He also asked me at the meeting if I would do high-profile canvassing and media for him, to which I readily agreed.

Finally, the debate got under way and, as ever, Margaret Thatcher rose to the occasion. It must have taken all her legendary courage. Like the final speech in a Shakespearian tragedy, hers seemed to transcend anything she had done in the Chamber before. She had the self-discipline and the technique to summon up eloquence in adversity – there had been many occasions in the past decade when it had been necessary. But this was something luminously different. Her performance took on a kind of nobility. As I looked down from one of the galleries, having failed to find a seat in the packed Chamber, it seemed as though everyone below, on all sides, was willing her on. The Labour MP Dennis Skinner, the best heckler in the House and her tormentor over the years, intervened to suggest sarcastically that she should become Governor of the European Central Bank. 'What a good idea. I hadn't thought of that ... Now where were we? I'm enjoying this!' And at that moment it seemed that she was; and so was the House. But it was a glorious dying fall.

After the main speeches in the Chamber our Major campaign got going in earnest. I did as much lobbying as I could, in the tearoom and around the corridors. After the division at ten o'clock, a crowded meeting in John's room at which Francis Maude, Richard Ryder and Terence Higgins were prominent. I fed in my ten or twelve names of committed colleagues, including seven out of the ten Scottish MPs, and then went home, having arranged to keep in touch from Scotland over the next couple of days. I had several unbreakable diary commitments there, but it would also be a good opportunity to take soundings and to see the campaign from the outside.

Friday 23 November

A flying visit to the Paisley double by-election, on a wet, cold day. Two Labour MPs, Norman Buchan and Allan Adams, had both died recently; and I took a press conference in a local hotel with our candidates. The questions were mainly about the community charge review and attempts by the media, who were there in force, to persuade the candidates to declare their leadership candidate. My choice was of course already known and I did a few interviews afterwards.

On to Babcocks, with STV in tow. A good photo-opportunity for them with some very large power station equipment as a backdrop. Morale in the campaign was high (to be justified the following Thursday with our best by-election result for nearly twenty years).

Later in the day, after a series of Scottish Office meetings in Edinburgh, I heard that our Major team had put out a claim to have 123 declared votes, almost certainly an understatement, to keep the team – and the candidate – on their toes.

The evening was spent at Bute House, where I played host at a dinner in honour of prominent Scandinavian businessmen in Scotland. They were all delightful company but my mind was not really on the evening's activities. I stayed overnight at Bute House and the next morning drove in glorious sunshine to Perth, to open a conference of Scottish Conservative Business Groups in the Station Hotel. It was a good chance to take soundings and I was pleased to discover almost unanimous, unprompted, support for John.

At 11 o'clock I set off south by car for Castle Douglas to attend the Christmas Fair, the main event of my constituency Conservative Association's year. I reached it in time for a quick lunch and a tour of the stalls as it opened. Two hours and a lot of fast canvassing later I was on my way home. From the car I rang Angie Bray who was handling our campaign's media affairs, but there were no media pressures at this stage. I reported on the support I had found, which was clearly being reflected in other reports coming in.

After a very quick stop at home, to repack and collect the mail, I drove on to Glasgow Airport to rejoin the rest of the family in London.

En route to my flat, I called in at our campaign headquarters at 18 Gayfere Street, the little house off Smith Square owned by Alan Duncan, a prospective candidate for a safe seat, which had been offered at very short notice the previous Thursday. Norman Lamont, who was leading John's campaign, Francis Maude, one of his deputies, and William Hague had taken the house over and had six telephones installed. By the time I got there for the first time, at around 9 o'clock, it was already running remarkably smoothly, with instant junk food and endless amounts of wine readily available.

The nerve centre was the basement dining room, where one meeting or another went on almost continuously throughout the campaign. It was from here that the presiding duo of Francis Maude and Richard Ryder controlled virtually all aspects of the campaign. Working almost around the clock, Francis endlessly flicking his worry beads, they were the main reason why John Major's campaign ran with such apparently effortless efficiency.

I had called in ostensibly for ten minutes, but in the event I stayed for an hour and a half, to review progress and plans. At every subsequent visit, more new faces were to appear of colleagues working on the campaign – David Maclean, Rob Hayward, Michael Jack, David Davis and journalist Bruce Anderson amongst others. It quickly became known as the Bunker.

Sunday 25 November

Richard Ryder rang me before breakfast to see if I could do some media events. We agreed to meet at Gayfere Street at 9 o'clock. When I got there it was still quiet except for Richard, Michael Howard and, briefly, David Mellor, who was going off to do television. The good news was that we now had 150 committed votes and intended to announce it later. Richard and David had already drafted a statement which Michael and I commented upon, making a number of amendments. As we finished this, crammed into the small bedroom, Norman Lamont arrived to clear it and I headed off with Michael, leaving growing chaos in the Bunker and kitchen, for a 10 o' clock meeting with John at No. 11 Downing Street.

Upstairs in the drawing room at the Chancellor's official residence there was a circle of sofas and armchairs. Peter Lilley, Gordon Reece and Francis

Maude were there – Gordon's presence being comforting evidence of the Prime Minister's support, now becoming clear, for John Major. After a few minutes, John appeared in blazer and flannels to occupy the central armchair.

We speculated on what Michael Heseltine might do and what our reaction should be. The general view, advanced by Norman, was that he would claim victory, as an attempt to stem the erosion that we were now convinced was taking place in John's favour. We agreed that 'He would say that, wouldn't he?' would be our public reaction. (In the event – and perhaps significantly – he made no such claim.) John suggested he might challenge Michael to stand down after this ballot if he were wrong.

At 11 o'clock Norman and I and Terence Higgins and others stepped out into Downing Street to make our 150-vote announcement to the phalanx of cameras and reporters whilst John went off to do more television and press interviews.

Back to Gayfere Street, where eight or ten colleagues were ringing around and checking endless lists. I fed in my information and made a few more calls – some fellow MPs out in the country were getting a bit fed up being lobbied; others were enjoying the unaccustomed attention. Then I went back to the flat to do some work on my box – the country still had to be governed!

At 2 o'clock, back again to 18 Gayfere Street for a photo-call with John, who was paying his first visit to the HQ. This was probably the most successful photo-call of the campaign. John walked down the street with Graham Bright and talked to the press with Norman, Terence, William Hague, Bob Hughes, Michael Jack and myself outside the front door. It featured on all the news bulletins that night and in the following day's papers. My daughters Venetia and Lucy and their cousin Poppy Fraser had come along by taxi from a family lunch in Kensington and watched the whole event from an opposite doorway.

There wasn't much left to do at Gayfere Street, so I went back to the flat to do some more telephoning and get on with my box.

Monday 26 November

At 8.30 a.m. I attended a large campaign meeting in the drawing room
at No. 11. John, Norman, Francis, Richard, Michael Howard, John
Gummer, Gillian Shephard and Robert Atkins were also present, as well
as a few backbenchers, including James Arbuthnot and Bob Hughes. This
was the last full day of our short, intensive campaign. It was suggested
that we should squeeze the Hurd vote, as it was now clear that he was
running a poor third. But John said he did not want to see Douglas
humiliated. It was important that his credibility as Foreign Secretary
should not be undermined.

Later, at 11.30, a smaller group of us met again downstairs to go
through our lists and decide our tactics for the remainder of the
campaign. We decided that overkill was the main danger – there was too
much canvassing going on – so we agreed that each wavering MP should
be approached by one of us only. As the afternoon advanced I moved
round the House, finding colleagues returning from their constituencies
with a clear pro-Major message from their constituents. But there also
seemed to be some evidence of a hardening of the Heseltine vote. The
press polls were firming up nicely in our favour and when I looked in at
Gayfere Street at around 9.30 there was little left to do.

Tuesday 27 November – Election Day

I was up early to do a live radio interview for LBC with Angela Rippon
at 7 o'clock from their radio car outside my flat. It went smoothly but I
had been very nervous because of the tensions of the day and the fear that
I might drop a brick at this critical stage in our campaign.

The press and media all had John coming through as the man to win.
At our 8.30 meeting in 11 Downing Street there was confidence but not
a little tension. Our line on Heseltine was clear: the balloon has burst.

But Margaret Thatcher had generated some concern by saying that she would be a backseat driver. [In fact it was not directly to do with the leadership campaign, but a comment on President George Bush and the Gulf War, but it was most unhelpful and would cause John to have to distance himself from her later, more than he would have liked.] We agreed on the line to rebut this if it started to run, then John thanked us all for a first-class campaign and the meeting broke up.

After doing a little work at the Scottish Office I went to the Crypt Chapel for the service to mark the annual visit to Westminster of the Moderator of the General Assembly of the Church of Scotland. Then, in case I forgot later, I went up to the Committee corridor to cast my vote, before going on to the usual Moderator's lunch at Dover House.

I spent the afternoon at the House trying to find something useful to do as the hours dragged by. After listening to Margaret Thatcher's last Question Time I toured the tearoom and smoking room. There was no canvassing left to do, but the first edition of the *Evening Standard*, with a favourable headline – 'Heseltine's Balloon Bursts' – had been followed by a less helpful second edition suggesting that John Major would be a puppet. Robert Atkins and I decided that the earlier edition copies deserved a wider audience, so we did a little re-cycling. Later from my room in the House I saw Michael Heseltine in the office he was using across the courtyard. He was interviewing waverers or potential recruits, shepherded in by his team of supporters, but there were long gaps between these encounters, during which he seemed to gaze into space.

At 6 o'clock, when the polls closed, I was on College Green in the temporary studio set up by Channel 4 to do a live interview into their evening news programme. It was crowded and a bit chaotic, but I got back to my car after the interview and sat in a traffic jam in Parliament Square as my driver Frank tried to get me to Downing Street. We made it to No. 11 just after 6.15 and I wandered upstairs, thinking I would have twenty minutes or so to kill before the result would come through.

There were about a dozen people in the drawing room, chatting and watching a flickering portable television set perched on a stool at one end of the room. John was standing in the middle in his shirtsleeves. I had poured myself a drink and said a few hellos when suddenly, just after 6.20, a call for quiet went up. The result was about to come through. John shouted for Norma, who hurried in from the corridor and we all crowded round the set.

A gasp and then a suppressed cheer went up as we heard Cranley Onslow's voice in the Grand Committee Room announcing the Heseltine vote: 131, down by over 20 from the first ballot. Then an immediate whoop of delight as John's 185 was announced. A momentary pause followed as we agonised briefly over the fact that he had failed by two votes to secure an overall majority, but it was instantly clear that he had won – Michael could not conceivably overtake him on the third ballot.

The calmest man in the room in the rather emotional moments that followed was John himself. A handshake and a hug for him and a kiss and hug for Norma, then we all moved around congratulating each other. Another huge cheer as his victory was confirmed by the dignified withdrawal speeches of Michael Heseltine and Douglas Hurd.

A few minutes later Margaret Thatcher, still Prime Minister, arrived to congratulate her successor through a small door in the corner of the drawing-room that connected with No. 10. She was accompanied by the Cabinet Secretary, Robin Butler, and her Private Secretary, Andrew Turnbull, and also by her son Mark. She shook John's hand as we all applauded, then turned to wish Norma well. As she turned back to John he was already going into a huddle with Turnbull and Butler. Power was visibly passing.

I went off to the kitchen to ring BBC Radio Scotland to do a promised interview. As I got through, John came in looking for the line on which his daughter Elizabeth was waiting to congratulate him. Then he went off to put on his jacket whilst some of the team started to draft a short speech for him to make to the huge press crowd in Downing Street. I did my interview live into the news programme: 'I'm speaking to you now from the kitchen of No. 11 Downing Street ...', which I heard later went down rather well.

Back in the drawing room people were coming down to earth, some whips arrived (they had had to remain neutral during the campaign) and some of the No. 10 staff filled the stairs. I heard Margaret Thatcher say to no one in particular, 'It's the cause that's important; and that goes on.' The she went off to the front of the house to look out of the window into Downing Street. We saw this on television.

I muttered something in exasperation and Mark, who had been sitting on the floor watching it, went off to try to dissuade her. But she was not to be dissuaded.

I had promised to do some television interviews so I slipped out of the front door of No. 11 just before John was due to emerge and went off to do them on the Green. There was total pandemonium there and afterwards I headed back to the flat, feeling drained. I could not face the celebration party at Gayfere Street until I had had a break and some food. By the time I looked in at 9.00 on my way back to the House, the party was over, so I had a quiet word with the girls there who had helped with food, typing, etc., and thanked them for all they had done.

At the 10 o'clock vote John came into the 'No' lobby during the division and made a little impromptu speech which was very well received. He got a great cheer as he entered the Chamber and Neil Kinnock came across to congratulate him.

In the smoking room afterwards Michael Heseltine was dispensing champagne to a noisy crowd led by Teresa Gorman and they all sang 'For He's a Jolly Good Fellow'. It was a very professional rapprochement with the party he had riven and I joined the others making their peace with him.

A more-or-less normal working morning during which one could at least concentrate on work again and start looking ahead. I paid a short visit, as Scottish Tourism Minister, to the Tourism Fair at Olympia then to the Institute of Directors, for lunch with three old school friends: Michael Fowle, George Mathieson and Robert Rendel (I hadn't seen the latter since 1958). My private office had insisted I take a large portable telephone with me, but I carefully explained to my lunch partners why no call was likely to come through on it.

At 3.15, when I was working at my desk overlooking Horseguards Parade, my Private Secretary Ken Thomson came in looking intense. I was to go to No. 10 at 3.35. My reaction was genuine astonishment and a pang of fear. It had not occurred to me that, with so few Scottish Conservative MPs, there was scope to promote Malcolm away from the Scottish Office. (Madsen Pirie was to tell me later that Margaret Thatcher, watching the announcement of my promotion on television that evening, whisky glass in hand, had complained that she had been told it couldn't be done.)

Clutching a chair for support, I asked Ken if it meant what I thought it did. He replied that Malcolm Rifkind was already on his way to No. 10. As I left for Downing Street, Jim Gallagher, Malcolm's Private Secretary, and Russell Hillhouse, the Permanent Secretary, were hovering benevolently on the landing. 'This wasn't in the script', I murmured as I headed down the grand staircase of Dover House.

I was feeling shaken: it is one thing to be a government minister, quite another to be in the Cabinet with overall responsibility for a whole country of five million people.

It was wet as my car drew up at No. 10 and a barrage of flashlights went off. I went through the hall, down the long corridor and upstairs to the first floor, where I was met by Dominic Morris, one of the No. 10 staff, who told me Malcolm was in with the Prime Minister and left me waiting in the lobby. Next door in the white drawing room Jean Rook of the *Daily Express* was interviewing Norma Major whilst camera lights were flashing. I lurked for what seemed an age.

Eventually Malcolm came out and strode purposefully off and I was summoned into the Prime Minister's study. He was alone with Andrew Turnbull, his new Private Secretary. I congratulated John again, for the first time as Prime Minister, and we sat down in wing armchairs on either side of the fireplace. By then I was feeling a little more composed.

He came straight to the point, offering me the Scottish Office. I replied, 'If you can cope with all this, I suppose I can cope with Scotland.' This did not seem to be a sufficiently clear acceptance and as he repeated the offer in different words I saw Andrew Turnbull's pen poised above his notepad. My second answer seemed to suffice.

We discussed the political position in Scotland and agreed that we both wanted Michael Forsyth to stay and Allan Stewart to join the team. He said he would like to visit Scotland soon. Thereupon he wished me luck and I braved the barrage of cameras to return to Dover House and my new responsibilities.

The announcement went out at 5.45 and bedlam ensued. A series of interviews in the QE2 Conference Centre and on St Stephen's Green followed. As a joint interview with Malcolm to an audience in Scotland began, the sound failed and apparently we were seen throughout the country gazing silently into the camera for some thirty seconds. Next came a wave of congratulations in the division lobby at 8 o'clock. Then a family dinner in the Strangers' Dining Room and home to Vincent Square, with a new Red Box.

Thursday 29 November

First Cabinet at 10.00. My place was between Peter Brooke and David Mellor, second from the end on the Prime Minister's left. I was asked to wind up the forthcoming debate the following week, which Michael Heseltine would open, on the future of the community charge. In at the deep end.

Photo session with the family and more media interviews.

Friday 30 November

To Buckingham Palace at 9.30 a.m. to be sworn a member of the Privy Council in the small ground-floor room to the right, off the central drawing room that opened on to the garden.

Apart from the Queen, others present included the Prime Minister, John MacGregor, Kenneth Baker, Michael Heseltine, David Waddington and David Mellor. I managed the elaborate procedure of bowing, kneeling, walking backwards, etc., even in that illustrious company.

I then returned to Scotland to fulfil my first engagement there since becoming Secretary of State: opening the BBC's new studios in Queen Street, Edinburgh. The Chairman, Duke Hussey, was inordinately proud that they had managed to have the commemorative glass plaque re-engraved in time, to show my name instead of Malcolm's.

Thursday 6 December

The Prime Minister congratulated Michael Heseltine and me at the start of Cabinet on the success of our speeches in the community charge debate. We little knew what problems lay ahead in deciding on its successor.

Friday 7 December

Sworn in as Secretary of State and Lord Keeper of the Great Seal of Scotland in the High Court in Edinburgh, before the Lord President of the Council and seventeen judges, arranged in wigs and robes – a formidable sight, like a row of Raeburn portraits. The ceremony was unpublicised, by tradition, but the courtroom was packed, with my parents and sister Patricia looking on from the witness box as I signed the aged scroll, below the names of all my predecessors.

Just before the ceremony started, I was confronted in the corridor outside by one of the judges, Lord Marnoch, who took me to task over changes that were being made to the law affecting stake-net fishing in Scotland. I stammered through what I understood to be the official 'line to take', whereupon he bowed, smiled seraphically and said: 'I expect you will feel better for having told me all that.' [This proved to be one of the more elegant put-downs I was to encounter during my Cabinet career.]

Early in the week following the ceremony I observed the convention whereby incoming Cabinet Ministers presented a book to the No. 10 library. I chose the bicentennial history of my family's firm, written by John Hume and Michael Moss. Its title, *A Bed of Nails*, seemed appropriate.

SEVEN

O Caledonia!

As I sat at the Secretary of State's desk, beneath the portrait of the Old Pretender, looking out of the tall windows across Horseguards Parade to St James's Park, I began to reflect on the nature of the job I had just taken on.

I already knew the department well. Even the curtains on those windows were familiar. Transferred from the identical office I had occupied as Minister of State, they were the product of another altercation with officials. Plans had been made a month or two earlier to install new curtains in the same pattern throughout the interlinked rooms of the Secretary of State, the Permanent Secretary and the Minister of State, but so extravagantly expensive were they that I had rebelled and chosen another material at one fifth of the price. This had prompted a continuing internal correspondence in the department under the heading 'Curtains for Mr Lang'.

But although I had been Scottish Whip for over four years and a junior Scottish Office minister for almost five, there were still areas of the department about which I knew little, and as I considered the range of subjects that came together under the Secretary of State's responsibility I began to realise the sheer scale and diversity of my new role. I was responsible, in Scotland, for the equivalent of about nine different departments in England. I was, with a few exceptions that were handled on a UK basis, Scotland's Home Secretary, Secretary of State for Education, for Health, for Industry, for the Environment, for Agriculture; and I also had responsibilities for local government, transport, the arts, and for forestry throughout the UK. One almost felt like a prime minister of Scotland.

Because the job no longer exists in that form and no other job affecting Scotland now brings together such powers, it is worth recording what great advantages I and my predecessors enjoyed in being able to coordinate the development and delivery of government policy in Scotland. As such, it was one of the best jobs in government. Not only did it give its incumbent the opportunity to prioritise areas of activity and generate synergy through the interaction of, say, education and training or industry and transport, but it also had a clear hierarchical structure, replicated in its civil service back-up, that brought together the levers of power in the hands of the Secretary of State, at the top of an efficient pyramid. It is ironic that the Labour government of 1997 that made so much of 'joined-up government' should have destroyed the Cabinet job that best embodied it. But then, in politics, the paradox predominates. Certainly, Scotland's new First Minister retains the majority of those roles, but cut off from the rest of the UK, with all of its continuing functions that are so relevant to Scotland.

Another advantage was that, because of the range of departmental interests embodied within the Scottish Office, I would be involved in the decision-making processes of many of the Whitehall departments, gaining a wider perspective than most of my Cabinet colleagues. At the same time, although it was clearly desirable that government policy in Scotland should be harmonised, in broad terms, with that of the United Kingdom, it was widely acknowledged – and stressed by successive

Secretaries of State – that Scotland was different and had to be able to pursue different policies when circumstances and the country's different traditions dictated it. This was no mere theoretical difference; it could and did regularly happen. So being Secretary of State for Scotland combined the advantages of the collegiate nature of British Cabinet government with a high degree of autonomy in the Scottish fiefdom.

The position was, though, a demanding one. Quite apart from the endless round of departmental meetings, media interviews and outside visits around Scotland, I was also a member of about a dozen of the influential Whitehall ministerial committees, including all the economic and social ones, that did so much to shape and agree national policies. There were, too, the ever-present demands of my far-flung constituents, which filled many weekends. My constituency secretary Stella Walsh did wonders in reading my mind and so lightening the burden of my Galloway correspondence, but in spite of that there were times when I longed to work less than a seventy-hour week.

In this, as I fear in other ways, I differed from my immediate predecessor. Malcolm Rifkind never showed the slightest indication that the administrative side of the job of Secretary of State was other than easy and quickly disposed of. His desk was always tidy, his in-tray always empty. In this, he reminded me of John Major, whose desk had been back-to-back with mine in the Whips' Office. While mine had heaved with papers and other documents to be read, re-read or filed, John's was always clear and gleaming. He – and Malcolm – seemed to file everything in their heads. Malcolm was the same in public. He spoke effortlessly, fluently and without notes at the Despatch Box, even under intense duress, and was never fazed or outwitted in argument. Some thought him cold and dispassionate, so efficient and analytical was the marshalling of his arguments, but to me he was a joy to work for, a warm and considerate friend, always happy to delegate responsibility and give me my head. He reminded me of the military strategist Basil Liddell Hart's definition of leadership, as exemplified by Marlborough: the capacity to inspire affection whilst communicating energy.

My other exemplar was George Younger, who had come into office with the Thatcher victory of 1979 and had the delicate task, which he accomplished with calm aplomb, of delivering the Thatcher revolution to an unreceptive Scotland. George's charm was legendary, and it was a necessary attribute at that time. But it also disguised the essential steel within and his ability to achieve his major objectives by a mixture of guile and steady determination. He had an instinct for the core of any issue. In another life he could have been an enormously successful army general; he had all the attributes – but a Wavell, I think, rather than a Montgomery.

Following those two in this role that covered the whole political diaspora – one that combined something of the viceroy with something of the bovver boy – would stretch me to my limits and beyond. I had not sought it, had succeeded to it unexpectedly and by the accident of the 1987 electoral rout, but I now relished it and felt ready for the challenge. As Browning put it: 'But a man's reach should exceed his grasp, or what's a heaven for?' As for my shortcomings, others were never slow to identify them, and my thin skin and often weary spirit quickly learned to shelter behind a languorous outward calm that I rarely felt.

One thing could be guaranteed: saturation media coverage in Scotland, though rather less elsewhere. I therefore took the view that to over-project oneself would not be sensible. Those who live by the press in politics usually die by the press. So, whilst I never shrank from interviews and news conferences – on some occasions I did between fifteen and twenty in a day – I did not seek to create some kind of artificial persona, saying and doing things just for effect. I sensed that I might be in the job for some years and I preferred to play the long game, seeking to persuade people by informed, courteous argument and to be judged by results. We were after all a minority government in Scotland, with the need to win the electorate's support – a subtlety that occasionally eluded some of my southern colleagues.

One fault I admit to was a reluctance to delegate. I had four junior ministers: Michael Forsyth, Allan Stewart, Lord James Douglas-Hamilton and Lord Strathclyde. They combined a broad range of skills and outlook and there were some areas where they had considerably more experience of their subject than I did. For example, Michael had already spent some time bringing his penetrating powers to bear on education and health; and Thomas Strathclyde quickly demonstrated an effortless mastery of agricultural and forestry matters, as well as great political sensitivity and maturity in handling his duties as our new minister in the House of Lords. Allan brought robust good sense to bear on most problems, though dogged by ill-health; and James was the most diligent and agreeable of colleagues. On one occasion when others were jockeying for position in the reallocation of ministerial duties, James's reaction was utterly equable, so long as he could keep responsibility for Ancient Monuments. Perhaps I should have just left them all to it, but I needed to take a strong hands-on role myself in order to master all my new responsibilities. Also, a general election could be called within the next year, so I had to ensure that we presented a united team.

The custom of employing special advisers – those hybrid figures chosen on a party political basis but employed as civil servants – was not long established in government. Graeme Carter chose to move on when Malcolm Rifkind went to the Department of Transport so I decided to look around for a new one, but meantime Alan Young, Graeme's assistant, could help out. Very soon I was to discover that I had inherited an adviser of quite exceptional qualities and promoted him to the main job.

Quite by chance I had met Alan several years earlier when, as a schoolboy at the Douglas Ewart High School in Newton Stewart, he had come with two friends to my constituency surgery in Galloway to discuss politics. I think he was already a Conservative then, so I cannot claim credit for converting him, but I was to benefit enormously during my term as Secretary of State from his breadth of knowledge, his shrewd political instincts, his capacity for hard work and his steadiness when we came under pressure. The first thing I asked him to do as my special adviser was to help me to look at all our policies across the spectrum, to test them, to challenge them and, if necessary, to change them.

My broad strategy was already clear in my mind. Economic progress in Scotland was the key to electoral success, so that was my top priority, continuing the role I had already played for five years as Industry Minister. For the rest, it was too late in the parliament to develop major new policy initiatives so I set out to identify and defuse trouble spots and where possible create an atmosphere of calm and, hopefully, efficient government.

Margaret Thatcher had been the best friend Scotland's economy had ever had. It was her clear-eyed recognition of Britain's deep-rooted economic and industrial problems and her unflinching determination to solve them that turned the country from near-terminal decline to a new era of prosperity. Reinforced by John Major's seven-year term of office, that era continued to blossom long after their departure. Scotland had suffered Britain's problems, but to a more intense degree and has benefited correspondingly more. I and the other Secretaries of State during that period sought to manage a transition that was inevitably more painful, given the dominance of nationalised industries that were in some cases dead on their feet, and at the same time, as a minority government within Scotland, to persuade a correspondingly more resistant electorate of the new economic realities.

It was always my view that these new realities, which were really the old verities that socialism had smothered, would find a better reception if accompanied by the visible signs of their efficacy. Hence the priority I attached, not to preaching at people, but to delivering the new jobs and new industries that were the fruits of our policies.

With this in mind, I did what I could during the annual public expenditure rounds to increase our help to industry, in particular the resources of Scottish Enterprise and Highlands & Islands Enterprise and to ensure that they remained focused on supporting the development of self-sustaining enterprise around Scotland, with as much as possible of the decision-making process devolved to local level. I was fortunate in the quality of the Chairmen of these bodies. First, David Nickson and then Donald McKay responded positively to my priorities and so did Fraser Morrison and his predecessor, Mike Joughin, in the Highlands. For the local enterprise companies I considered it vital to have a majority of businessmen and women on their boards and a minority of local government and trade union officials. Sadly that objective has been undermined since 1997, but in my view the whole concept is, anyway, now due for fundamental review, in the light of the dramatic improvements that have come about.

Transport, too, was vital to economic progress. The rail network had suffered over the years since nationalisation from chronic under-investment, to the detriment of Scottish industry as well as the travelling public. That was an area outside my responsibility, but I fought to ensure that Scottish interests would be fully taken into account in planning the links with the new Channel Tunnel.

I had an opportunity to influence more directly our transport links with markets through the roads budget and this, like Scottish Enterprise's budget, I sought to enlarge. When I had been responsible under Malcolm Rifkind for roads as well as industry, we had given top priority to the upgrading of the A74 between Carlisle and Glasgow, insisting on three lanes in each direction, so that our manufacturers in central Scotland could speed their goods by continuous motorway into their English and European markets. Completion of that long stretch of new road was a

My grandparents Peter and Margaret Lang (at the back) enjoying a day's yachting on the Clyde with friends, *circa* 1910.

My parents Jim and Maudie Lang at a wedding in the 1930s.

On the beach at Nairn in August 1942 with my mother and brother Ronald.

Un homme d'affaires, aged three or four.

Performing the cabaret with Nic Ullett at a May Ball, Cambridge 1962.

Prospective candidate for Central Ayrshire with Ted Heath,
then Leader of the Opposition, September 1969.

A visit from Michael Heseltine when canvassing in Galloway during the 1979 general election.

A happy family outing to a constituency summer fête!

Cartoon by PC Nuttall of the Government Whips' Wednesday morning meeting at their office in 12 Downing Street, 1984. Standing (left to right): Michael Newbert, Tim Sainsbury, Archie Hamilton, Donald Thompson and Murdo Maclean (Chief Whip's Private Secretary). Seated (left to right): John Cope, Tristan Garel-Jones, Alastair Goodlad, David Hunt, John Major, the author, Douglas Hogg, Bob Boscawen, Carol Mather and John Wakeham (the Chief Whip).

The Blue Chips after dinner, March 1987.
Back row (left to right): Alex Pollock, Douglas Hogg, Nicholas Lyell, Robert Atkins, Robert Cranborne, Tristan Garel-Jones. Front row (left to right): Michael Ancram, Peter Fraser, William Waldegrave, Chris Patten, John Major, the author.

With Margaret Thatcher in the garden of 10 Downing Street, April 1983.

Advertising, at great personal risk, the Glasgow Garden Festival, for which I had
ministerial responsibility, Spring 1988.

massive undertaking, which occupied most of my years in the Scottish Office, but I am sure it has helped Scottish industry to improve its competitiveness. We were still able, however, to complete many other bypasses and road improvements across the rest of Scotland. Our roads were the envy of English colleagues, but vital to a sparsely populated country (and to a densely populated central belt), remote from the main markets for its goods.

Although my inclination was always to reduce the number of official bodies operating at the taxpayer's expense, I could occasionally be persuaded, if benefits could be demonstrated, of the need to set up new ones. Scotland Europa was one such, located in Brussels, to help Scottish companies find their way through the morass of the EU. Scottish Trade International was another, through which I aimed mainly to assist our exporters, but also to help Scotland link in to the global marketplace and, through such means as technology transfer, to improve competitiveness and trading opportunities. Some years later our example was followed with the establishment in England of British Trade International.

Scotland had benefited from all the major British denationalisations such as gas, telephones, airlines and steel. With Malcolm Rifkind I had worked up plans to send electricity in Scotland down the same route. There was a strong lobby in Scotland, supported by Scottish Office officials and the Chairman of the old South of Scotland Electricity Board, Donald Miller, for setting up just one large company. Fortunately, Malcolm and I both took the view that this was unnecessary and anti-competitive. We also rejected an alternative proposal of setting up four or five smaller companies, which would have been unable to survive in the market place, and we chose instead two vertically integrated companies, one serving the Highlands, as successor to the much-loved North of Scotland Hydro-Electric Board and the other covering the rest of Scotland. This broadly replicated the existing state companies. With Michael Spicer, the junior energy minister, I had already taken the legislation through its parliamentary committee stage. Our opposite numbers then were Tony Blair and Bryan Gould, though we saw little of Blair, who spent much of his time in the committee corridor, briefing the press rather then debating the Bill. Now, as Malcolm's successor, it fell to me to handle the actual flotation as well.

The English flotation had already gone ahead a few months earlier and, with the benefit of that experience and a firm stock market, I felt we could secure substantially more for the Scottish industry. I had to engage in some fairly firm discussions with some of the participants but, in the end, everything fell into place as I wanted it. I finally set the flotation share price in a telephone call from my car, parked in a lay-by *en route* to my constituency, on the edge of the mobile telephone reception area. To add to the problems of communication, I had to speak in code because the line was not secure. However, the message got through and all went well a few days later. The issue was described by the City as 'tightly priced', but in the event, two major new Scottish companies were successfully launched – Scottish Power plc and Hydro-Electric plc. The offer, heavily angled towards Scottish consumers, was oversubscribed and raised nearly £3 billion for taxpayers, much more proportionately than had been secured south of the border. Our 10 per cent of the total national supply raised 25 per cent of the total proceeds of electricity privatisation.

Not everything went so smoothly on the industrial front, however. I had to contend with the rundown and final closure of the Ravenscraig steel mill, that great totem of a totem industry, as the reality of international competition finally struck home. I have described that experience elsewhere. There were also recurring threats to another important employer and perceived barometer of the Government's commitment to Scotland, the Rosyth Naval Dockyard. Rosyth had been threatened with closure by a MoD review soon after I had become Secretary of State. On that occasion, the defence secretary Tom King and I had reached agreement to save it, which we had then announced at a joint press conference. Rosyth was to do nuclear submarine refitting and it started to excavate a large hole in preparation for the dry dock facilities needed. In 1993, however, defence officials returned to the fray. It was now considered that Britain needed only one nuclear submarine refitting base and it was to be a choice between Devonport and Rosyth. Rosyth's massive hole in the ground was already dug, but the new recommendation was that this should be scrapped and the whole exercise should start again from scratch, at Devonport.

I was convinced that this was wrong, that Devonport would be more costly and less efficient and that the case had been artificially skewed against Rosyth. However, it was clear that I would have a battle royal on my hands. The south-west of England was an important area in parliamentary terms. I fought the matter through every stage of negotiation, culminating with Cabinet, where I argued at length, on a whole range of points, that the decision should favour Rosyth. I argued it on strategic grounds – the dispersal of defence facilities around the UK. I argued it on grounds of job distribution around the UK. I argued it on grounds of relative cost, delay, waste and radiation leak – a much greater threat to the large population nearby in Devonport – and I questioned the timescale and costings of the Devonport option.

In the end, I was in a minority of one. No one attempted to rebut my arguments. Malcolm Rifkind, nowdefence secretary, tried to be neutral, but it was clear that all our English colleagues were impervious to the merits of the case and had already decided that Devonport must win: why else had the matter been reopened? It is small consolation to have read in recent press reports that the costings used in support of Devonport have indeed had to be revised upwards, possibly by double; the project has been completed several years late; and there are local anxieties about radiation. I remain convinced that the right decision would have been to stick with Rosyth. It was not an edifying experience.

I did secure a good second prize: Rosyth would not close, though its workforce of over 6,000 would halve. Significantly, it would be favoured for all non-nuclear naval refits. However, the Scottish media had built the issue up into such a major impending catastrophe over the preceding weeks, based on the expectation of complete closure, that this less bad outcome, which might eventually yield more secure employment for Rosyth than the nuclear work, was something they declined to comprehend. They continued to put Scotland into national mourning for several weeks.

At least when the Rosyth/Devonport battle came to Cabinet I knew in advance that this would be the case. More often, issues would arise there – and decisions be taken – with no advance warning and no paper circulated. I always found this difficult. It was never an ideal forum for debate, with each member having the opportunity of only a short contribution. Given the wide-ranging preoccupations of my own department, I never felt as assured on the broader issues of the day as I would have liked, without some advance notice to let me put my thoughts in order.

The mood of Cabinet meetings varied widely. I suppose the most serious was in 1996 when the scientists who had been categorically and repeatedly assuring us for years that BSE could not be transmitted to humans came to tell us that they had changed their minds and that tens of thousands of people might die over the next decade or so. The day in July 1993 when we approached the final votes on Maastricht was also particularly tense. We had three Cabinet meetings in one day and resolved that if we lost in the division lobbies we would table a motion of confidence linked to ratification of Maastricht and, if defeated in that, would hold a general election. The rebels duly voted down their own government, but their idealism stopped short of bringing an early end to their own careers.

Another, quite different, mood I recall was when the Foreign Secretary, Douglas Hurd, gave one of his regular reports to Cabinet in January 1991. Fiddling as usual with the little silver horse's head on his key-ring, he began his report with the words: 'The collapse of the Soviet Union continues apace.' No one around the Cabinet table batted an eyelid at this comment which would have been thought mad just a year or so earlier. A year later I passed a note to Peter Brooke, my neighbour at the Cabinet table which said: 'The Cabinet has spent its first half-hour today discussing fox-hunting. 1992 or 1892?' His reply read: '1792. You will recall Professor Parkinson's view/aphorism that the nuclear device goes through on the nod and you then get down to discussing the bicycle shed.' Peter could always be relied upon to raise the tone of Cabinet meetings, and to keep the Prime Minister on his toes on the detail of Test matches fought decades before. Another quotation he once passed to me, after a discussion on environmental matters, read: 'There is only one thing on which I insist and that is that every garden, however small, should contain at least two acres of rough woodland – Leo de Rothschild.'

Returning to Scotland, a reaction similar to that over the Rosyth saga greeted my proposals to rationalise the water and sewage industry. I would have liked to have been in a position to privatise it, but that issue was academic at this stage as it was so disparate and uncoordinated an industry, in the hands of local authorities, that we were categorically advised that the requisite three-year commercial record needed for flotation could not be constructed. So we did not contemplate moving it to the private sector. All that was proposed was to set up three publicly owned companies to operate the industry in a commercial way and to undertake the upgrading of the infrastructure that had been so neglected for many years. Scotland went mad, however. Campaigns, referenda and demonstrations were mounted by those who had convinced themselves that privatisation was afoot – and who were later to claim that they had stopped it – and much pious nonsense was talked and written. Despite this, I persevered and eventually we passed the legislation and set up the new arrangements, which have proved rather successful and have led to the long overdue investment to restore and upgrade the deteriorating Victorian infrastructure. One day I hope private ownership will follow – indeed, I am intrigued by the recent decision of the Scottish Executive to combine the three companies in one. On the face of it that is a retrograde and anti-competitive step, but it could be a precursor to the introduction of the private sector.

It was the same with almost every industrial news story. Good news – such as winning a massive British Aerospace investment at Prestwick – went almost unreported; the slightest setback or controversial proposal was proclaimed as catastrophe. But I consoled myself with the knowledge that, up and down Scotland, unemployment was falling steadily. Living standards were rising rapidly and public services were improving. More and more Scots were getting good training and qualifications and were finding their way into an ever-broadening range of skilled and well-paid jobs. There were more Scots in work than any time since records had begun, and, in particular, a vast increase in the number of women in the workforce. Scotland had a higher proportion of its population in employment than almost any other country in Europe.

My overseas visits in pursuit of more inward investment, and to help Scottish exporters, continued apace after I became Secretary of State. On one such visit to Tokyo I was in my bedroom at the Ambassador's residence, changing for a dinner, when there was an earthquake. It was as though an underground train was rattling loudly through the drawing room beneath me. The chandelier tinkled and everything shook for about thirty seconds. I waited for windows to shatter and ceilings to crack but then it stopped, as suddenly as it had begun. I grabbed the helmet, thoughtfully provided in the wardrobe, and stepped gingerly out on to the landing. There stood the ambassador's wife, a model of British sangfroid. 'Oh dear,' sighed Lady Whitehead. 'These earthquakes are such a bore. One has to go round the house afterwards, straightening all the pictures.' I slunk back into my bedroom.

On another occasion, I flew to Munich where, amongst the companies I visited one morning was Grundig, the well-known manufacturer of electrical goods. Their Chairman was there to greet me, together with a bevy of polite and efficient executives, and I was escorted into the display area to view a huge array of almost every item the company produced. We stood and talked in the television section, surrounded by some thirty to forty screens of all shapes and sizes, showing the same colourful programme, with the volume turned low.

It appeared to be a programme about the countryside, but the Chairman was more concerned to tell me about the range and quality of his products than with what they showed. Suddenly the scene on the television screens changed and, over his shoulder, I caught sight of a young couple, half-naked in a close embrace. We moved from the portable sets to the medium-sized units. I hung on his every word as my host explained their qualities. By the time we got to the large conference model, the couple were wholly naked and horizontal. Through the speakers on the new wall-hanging set I could just hear stereophonic grunting. The efficient executives were beginning to fidget; the Chairman rhapsodised about the clarity of the picture and the colour tones. 'And here we have our new prototype model,' he continued. 'It is the new wider screen for a fuller picture'. Politeness required me to turn and look at a large, wide screen, pulsating with human flesh, in various subtle shades of pink and beige. 'This will soon be all the rage.'

An executive started to mutter in the Chairman's ear. It was one of those long sentences, with all the verbs at the end. It took an age to deliver, hinting, it seemed, at sabotage. Meanwhile it was clear from the tempo and crescendo surging from forty screens that consummation was near. The Chairman turned impassively to me. 'Come,' he said, with impeccable timing. 'We shall look at our radios.'

Later that day I was due to fly by helicopter to Erlangen to take part in a seminar at its university. It was to be a memorable journey because of low cloud level, which reduced visibility to less than a hundred yards. Our party travelled in two small police helicopters and we quickly lost both our way and each other. More than once our bewildered pilot swooped down to read the road sign on the edge of some village and played leap-frog over heavy electricity cables. I had been tipped in press diary pieces at home as a suitable candidate to be the new James Bond. But when the other helicopter shot past us at high speed, just fifty yards away and heading in the opposite direction, our minders decided to abort the mission and we returned to Munich. I believe Mr Pierce Brosnan got the part.

Despite all these high jinks, the serious purpose of such foreign visits was achieved. Our inward investment effort had become the most efficient and successful in Europe. Because of that, I managed at one stage to persuade Digital, during a rationalisation process, not to close its Scottish plant. They closed their Irish one instead. On another occasion a talk with Hoover resulted in the decision to favour their Scottish plant over their French one.

It is perhaps invidious to mention individuals in what was essentially a team effort, but Robert Crawford, head of Locate in Scotland and later to head Scottish Enterprise, was exceptional. His encyclopaedic knowledge of the electronics industry, immense drive and presentational skills and his enterprising spirit made him quite outstanding. Of course, the new industries are as sensitive to obsolescence or the economic cycle as the old ones – indeed, more so. That is not an argument for not having them. It is an argument for improved competitiveness and aggressive participation in the global market place. Scotland is vastly the better for the foreign investment that has been brought to her shores over the last two decades.

One of the attractive perquisites of the post of Secretary of State for Scotland was the right to use Bute House, in Edinburgh's Charlotte

Square. This fine Adam-designed town house, part of the famous New Town, had been bequeathed to the nation by the Bute family with the request that it be made available to the Secretary of State of the day as his Scottish residence. My predecessor Malcolm Rifkind had initiated a series of occasional dinner parties there, where he mixed figures from all walks of life and all political persuasions. I continued the custom, as well as staying overnight there myself from time to time, my home being in the west. I also allowed it to be used for occasional charitable functions and for receptions during such events as the Edinburgh Festival. Guests on other occasions ranged from Mikhail Gorbachev to Billy Graham.

One of my visitors there was Cardinal Thomas Winning, the Roman Catholic Archbishop of Glasgow. I met him on a number of occasions and in a rash moment after one of them he said I was 'a man he could do business with'. This led the Free Presbyterian Church magazine to comment critically under the heading 'Fraternising with Antichrist'. I also attended the 500th anniversary of the Roman Catholic cathedral of Glasgow in 1992, after which he wrote to tell me I was the first Secretary of State for Scotland ever to attend a Roman Catholic church service. As a Protestant, there was no religious reason for me to do so. But it did seem extraordinary to me that some unwritten code seemed to subsist whereby Catholics were supposed to be Labour supporters, despite their deep differences on many political issues, whilst Protestants were Unionists, though the fierceness of the criticisms we faced from successive Moderators rather contradicted this. It had undoubtedly been true in earlier generations, when the Orange vote was a powerful pillar of my party's successes in Scotland, but I think such allegiances had long since faded. My real reason for welcoming contacts with the Catholic Church, however, was because the role of Secretary of State still had a slight flavour of the vice-regal about it and it seemed right to me to be accessible to all manner of folk in Scotland.

It is a pity to see Bute House being used now, not for the function intended by the original settlement, but as just one more office for the large Scottish Executive.

On one occasion, Chancellor Kohl came to Scotland to receive an honorary degree from Edinburgh University and deliver a lecture in the Signet Library. I was his host for the day. As I drove with him and his interpreter, Dorothy, from the airport into Edinburgh I asked him his views on events in Russia. His reply was melodramatic and, I suspect, well-honed with repetition: 'When Gorbachev came to see me at my residence in Bonn, he asked me what he should do about *perestroika* and *glasnost*. Without a word I led him down my garden to where the lawn ends on the banks of the Rhine. "Look," I said, "see the force of the waters of this great river. No power on earth can stop it on its journey towards the sea." He nodded and we returned to the house.'

I took Herr Kohl to Edinburgh Castle, to visit the war memorial to Scots killed in two world wars, and then we walked from there to Bute House, with his security guards looking anxious as we visited, on the way, a bagpipe-maker's shop, down the same close in the Lawnmarket that had once housed the Sphinx nightclub, where I had performed thirty years before.

The day went well, except that my private secretary told me afterwards that I had addressed my guest throughout the day as Herr Reichskänzler, a title that hadn't been used since the days of Adolf Hitler. The correct title was 'Bundeskänzler'. Apart from that, as I say, the day went well . . .

Alongside my earlier work as Industry Minister, I had also done an eighteen-month stint as Scottish Education Minister in 1989–90, while Michael Forsyth had left the role briefly to be Chairman of the Scottish Conservative Party. He had been an abrasive evangelist, attempting to shake the Scottish educational establishment out of their torpor with proposals for school boards, and the testing of pupils at various ages.

Michael had much personal opprobrium heaped upon him for introducing such radical measures, though in fact they were no more than the policies being brought in throughout Britain and, along with parental choice of school, the publication of schools' exam results and the issue of school reports to parents, have now become widely accepted as sensible. The assisted places scheme and opting out to self-governing status have, unfortunately, not survived. So far as money was concerned, spending per pupil had increased in real terms by almost 50 per cent in our first ten years – another Tory cut – and more pupils were staying on longer and getting better qualifications. The profession had never been better paid. But the mood in the education world had not been good. Bitterness remained from the damaging teachers' strike of the mid-1980s which, in my view, had done more even than the poll tax to harm Scottish Conservatives in the 1987 general election.

When I took over from Michael it was repeatedly explained to me, slowly and clearly because I had had the misfortune to have been educated in England – and not in the state sector – that Scottish education was different. It was broader-based and better than the English system and was widely recognised as being amongst the best in the world. The statistics told a different story, but I decided that confrontation was not the right approach at this juncture, since if education were to improve it needed the cooperation of its practitioners. In setting out to harvest the fruits of Michael's legislative battles, therefore, and carry our programme further, I decided that courtesy and communication should be my watchword.

One of the differences from England was over the school curriculum. In England a national curriculum was handed down from the centre. In Scotland the process was more democratic, with guidance from the centre, consultation through various bodies and implementation, on a grudgingly cooperative basis, at local level. In this context, that august body the Scottish Consultative Council on the Curriculum, chaired by

Sister Maire Gallagher, was about to publish a working paper on the teaching of English to five-to-fourteen-year-olds. It was a matter on which I had strong views, but by asking for sight of a draft of the paper and then feeding in my concerns before publication, I was able to steer them towards a more rigorous approach without provoking a public row.

I also inserted a foreword to the document to toughen up the recognition of the importance of grammar, spelling, punctuation and the learning of poetry. At its publication I issued a statement stressing the need to understand the structure of language and the importance of training and testing the mind and memory. When, a little later, a paper on the teaching of mathematics to the same age-group appeared, I confirmed the view the educational establishment had by now formed of me as an old-fashioned know-nothing, by insisting on including in the programme the teaching of long multiplication and long division up to two digits, and on not allowing the reliance on calculators for such exercises until pupils had already mastered the basics. Clearly I was beyond the pale so far as some in the profession were concerned: one professional educationalist described such skills as 'obsolete'. But I found that large numbers of parents agreed with me.

I took the revolutionary step of accepting an invitation to meet the Educational Institute of Scotland (EIS), whose general secretary Jim Martin turned out to be less querulous than his predecessor, John Pollock. I gave repeated, extended interviews to the press educational correspondents, whose view became that I was 'prepared to listen and argue my corner decisively, yet politely'. With the introduction of student loans and later teacher appraisal schemes, the road was far from smooth, for everything a Conservative government introduced was automatically greeted with ritual abuse and resistance, but over time the mood improved sufficiently for our changes to take root.

When I had been appointed as Scottish education minister in 1989, one thing that had struck me at once about Scottish education – even me, with my Sassenach schooling – was the poor organisation of its structure at the end of secondary school. I was surprised to find that many pupils sat 'Highers' (the Scottish broad equivalent to A levels) at sixteen, only a year or two after sitting 'Standard Grades', and then drifted for their final year with no real test or targets, other than the Certificate of Sixth Year Studies. Few pupils sat that and it was not widely recognised either by employers or universities. When I raised this with officials in the department, diffidently of course because of my own original sin, they agreed that yes, perhaps there was a problem. I thought something should be done about it. Highers had been in use for a hundred years and constituted the sacred core of Scottish education. So I was playing with fire, but I took my concerns to Malcolm Rifkind and, with his agreement, asked Professor Andrew Howie of St Andrew's University to chair a committee to investigate and make recommendations. It was to take two years before the Howie Committee reported, but the initiative was, I believe, an important one and, having arranged its conception, I was glad to be in post as Secretary of State to take delivery.

The Report was a good, professional document which more than vindicated my concerns. It criticised, as I had done, the 'two term dash' for Highers and the poor preparation for higher education. It also confirmed my sense that the famed Scottish secondary education was not all it was cracked up to be, with a slow learning pace in the early stages, low overall standards and inadequate breadth of attainment. It did so with an authority and impunity, because of the educational status of the committee's members, that such criticisms could not have had from my lips. Most encouragingly, however, it provoked a much-needed debate by proposing radical changes both to courses and examinations. It focused in particular on two new qualifications, a Scottish Certificate and a Scottish Baccalaureate. Most daring of all: it would abolish Highers.

I welcomed the principle of 'twin-tracking' because, although I did not think the Howie proposals offered the right solution, part of my concern had been the inadequacy of existing arrangements for school-leavers without Highers to gain qualifications relevant to the jobs market. It opened up the debate on this aspect too, and on the need for parity of esteem. In the subsequent consultation process the 'twin-tracking' proposals were overwhelmingly rejected, but in my view the principle of providing better vocational qualifications had been established and I asked my officials to consult with me along the way as they settled down to work up proposals on this and all the other issues for the Government's response to the Howie Committee's report.

As the ensuing weeks turned to months I became uneasy when no submissions reached me. I pressed for progress reports and submissions on individual aspects of their work, to no avail. Eventually, there landed on my desk the text of a White Paper, fully worked up and polished, together with a Statement to Parliament, a press release and full briefing, all ready for an imminent announcement. To my annoyance, however, all these documents reflected the agenda of education officials in the department, and not my own.

Where I wanted to focus on academic attainment, they were more concerned with parity of esteem. I wanted to stretch pupils, even achieve individual excellence; they wanted Group Awards and level attainment measurements. To me raising standards, academic and vocational, and bringing out quality was more important than an appraisal system that was mainly quantitative.

I immediately sent their submission back, rejected in its entirety, and told them to start again. Further delay was unattractive, but we had to get it right. My special adviser Alan Young knew a great deal about the Scottish education system, and while we had waited for the official submissions he and I had discussed the matter extensively and were of one mind as to what we wanted to do. So I set him the task of working with the department to produce a set of proposals that met our aims.

It was in March 1994, therefore, two years after the Howie Committee's

Report had been submitted, that I published my proposals in the form that I wanted, under the title *Higher Still*. This reflected my view that there had to be change, but change, to be affordable and practical, had to be introduced in an evolutionary way. It also reflected my view that it would be a mistake to scrap Highers, one of the most recognised, good features of the Scottish system. We would, however, bring in vocational courses alongside academic ones. We would extend the study time for academic courses to escape the 'two-term dash' and the uneven gradient of difficulty. I was also keen to raise the quality of Highers and to set challenges for the ablest pupils in their final year, so we introduced a new 'Advanced Higher' to stretch abilities and set new standards of excellence. Other changes included the introduction of a modular approach, a mixture of internal and external assessment and, for pupils seeking vocational exit routes, a new National Certificate. The twin-track objectives of Howie were thus met, without the massive disruption his proposals would have entailed, and by getting closer, through a single assessment system, to the equal regard for both tracks that all agreed was desirable. Other modest changes to earlier stages of secondary education aimed to create a steady line of progression for pupils throughout their schooling from age five to eighteen. It might even open up the opportunity for Scottish universities to start moving from a four-year degree to a three-year one, but this was not on my agenda, just an option for the future.

The press received the proposals favourably, which was a novel and agreeable experience. The *Times Educational Supplement* judged that: 'On the test of intellectual coherence, the package gains its own Advanced Higher.' The Glasgow *Herald* judged it 'realistic and worthy of general support', describing it as 'a bold attempt to solve the problems of upper schooling'. The *Scotsman* welcomed its radicalism. The *Economist* thought it 'a wee bit too radical'. Even the EIS, after some initial Pavlovian hostility, said that it was quite a good scenario educationally, but the *Sunday Times* said I had 'listened to the equalisers', completely missing the point. In fact the proposals were designed, above all, to identify, encourage and reward excellence: I had smuggled in élitism.

I had reluctantly agreed to a three-year phasing-in period for the reforms, which my officials, rejecting two years, promised to achieve. That was in 1994. As I write in 2002, *Higher Still* is still not fully in place, as obfuscation, wrangling and fiddling around with the proposals has been allowed to intrude. How much of what I originally envisaged will be discernible in the final package I do not know. Momentum has clearly been lost and I think it would be a great pity if the original objectives were sacrificed, but I fear they may be. In the meantime it has been interesting to watch the English Department for Education begin to feel its way towards a similar approach.

While the Howie Committee had been deliberating on their Report, I had not been idle. In 1991 I published both a Parents' Charter, setting out parents' rights – and their responsibilities – in the field of their children's education, and a White Paper on the links between education and training, which *Higher Still* was later to supplement. Before that we had reformed vocational qualifications, set up the Scottish Vocational Educational Council and established an interaction between that and the new local enterprise companies that now covered the whole of Scotland. Now we set out to strengthen the careers service, increase participation in training and improve the quality and relevance of that training, in partnership with business. We also set out to raise the performance of further education colleges, giving them corporate status and getting employers more fully involved in their governing councils. Again, there was resistance, but it was vital to meet the needs of a modern, global economy.

Perhaps the most important of the educational reforms in which I was involved were in the field of higher education. Our ancient Scottish universities, of which we had had five at a time when England had only Oxford and Cambridge, embodied more than anything else our long-established academic traditions. In 1979 fewer than one in six young Scots attended a university. By 1990 more than one in five did so; and by the time I left the Scottish Office in 1996, more than one in three. This represented a massive widening of access and opportunity for young Scottish school-leavers. Similar expansion took place among older entrants and in entry to the college sector.

The funding of universities had always been done by a University Funding Council covering the whole of the United Kingdom. Devolving responsibility in Scotland to a separate body had been looked at in the past and rejected. However, with the rapid expansion of Scottish student numbers, which was projected to continue, and the continuous demand for more local accountability, I decided in 1991 that the time had come to make a change and the Scottish Higher Education Funding Council was established to take over responsibility for funding both teaching and general research, in all eight Scottish universities.

At the same time, the English Secretary of State for Education, Ken Clarke, was considering the abolition in England of the binary line that divided universities from other higher education institutions, accompanied by a more even-handed and competitive funding process and auditing of a more robust quality. I was asked to join in this development, alongside Wales and Northern Ireland. It would mean that many of the Scottish higher education institutions, which accounted for half the student population, would seek university status, with the name and degree-awarding powers that that entailed. There would be concern in some quarters that this could dilute and debase the value of a university degree. My first instinct was to share that anxiety.

On the other hand, two of our best colleges – Napier in Edinburgh and Glasgow Polytechnic – were virtually universities already in all but name; and several others could also legitimately aspire to that status. Looking abroad at the wider range of university status that existed in other countries, one could see the consequent disadvantage to our students in an increasingly international market place. So, with the introduction of stern qualification criteria and performance appraisal processes, I decided to join my colleagues and we published a joint White Paper to announce our decisions.

It was warmly welcomed. The combined effect of establishing our own Scottish funding council and placing all our higher education institutions within one transparent framework has, I believe, been a major step forward for them, with many new universities taking root and raising their game to accommodate the needs of a larger student population.

Although some universities do offer degrees in rather bizarre subjects, without much academic content, I think that on the whole the status of a university degree has not been debased: it is still quite possible to distinguish between a good degree and a poor one.

One way and another, therefore, my involvement in education, first as minister and then as Secretary of State, was stimulating and rewarding. But although I met some wonderful and dedicated teachers over the years, it did seem that, overall, the disastrous changes of the 1960s had won the day. They were now received wisdom and inviolable. Education had seemed to be a maelstrom of rancour throughout the years since 1979. Entrenched complacency and the belief of those running the teaching profession that only they understood education, and that everything they did and said was right, still seemed to hold sway. Yet we did make changes. They were for the better; and many of them have stuck.

The Scottish Office, while permanently in the political front line, was not one of those departments, such as the Foreign Office, where physical danger was a high probability. But one day in February 1991, when I was sitting at my desk overlooking Horseguards, white under snow, briefing myself for Cabinet, we had a taste of it. Soon after ten o'clock I heard a noise – a crump that made me wonder whether a fall of snow off the roof had landed on the balcony, or whether a couple of cars had collided in Whitehall, the noise of impact muffled through the snow.

Before I could decide, there was a loud explosion from the direction of Downing Street about a hundred yards away. The window frames shook and every pane of glass shattered, falling to the floor and the balcony outside. The bomb-proof net curtains billowed in, but they caught all the splinters.

For a few seconds there was silence, then there followed two, more muffled explosions. A further silence, then alarms started to sound and I saw a policeman running across Horseguards Parade towards Downing Street. I could also see smoke rising from the No. 10 garden. Obviously a terrorist attack – my first thought was that it must be the Iraqis, rather than the IRA, who had seemed quieter of late. My private secretary put his head round the door to see if I was all right. I sent him to check on others and after a quick telephone call home, crouching beside my desk, I went to the outer office and from there started a tour of the building to make sure no one was hurt. Despite almost every window on the Horseguards side being broken, no one was injured.

I agreed with Russell Hillhouse, our Permanent Secretary, that we would vacate all the rooms on the damaged side and staff began to congregate on the main landing and in the ground floor hall. From the landing a plume of black smoke could be seen rising from Whitehall. Some of the staff who had been looking out of the windows on that side said that a van parked across the road had had its roof blown off by an explosion and was now on fire. Later it transpired that the explosions in Downing Street had been caused by mortar shells and this had been their launch pad. The mortars had gone right over the Scottish Office.

At this stage we still had no news of any injuries or damage at No. 10. Soon, though, a message reached me that Cabinet was to go ahead at eleven o'clock, but in the Privy Council building. A message from the police had been received that no one was to leave the building because a suspected bomb had been found beside the burning van, but I had their agreement to go to the Privy Council entrance some thirty yards down Whitehall from our front door.

At about 10.50, having double-checked with my private office that I was indeed to take this route and being assured that although Whitehall was deserted there was no longer a ban on leaving the building, I set off through the snow. The van was burning about thirty yards away on the other side of the street, but I didn't linger and walked quickly down to the Privy Council entrance. Despite all promises, it was closed, locked and unattended. I banged on the door. No answer. Further down Whitehall, there were a number of policemen. I was keen to get to Cabinet, to emphasise business as usual, and not keen to head back up Whitehall in the direction of the threatened further bomb, so I continued down Whitehall towards a rather agitated policeman.

I told him at once what I was trying to do and that I was there with police agreement, but his reaction was depressingly predictable. No one was meant to be in Whitehall. There was indeed still a suspected bomb and no, I could not continue into the comparative safety of Downing Street, just twenty yards away. Instead, he asked me to accompany him across Whitehall, thus fully exposed to any potential explosion, to meet his senior officer, Superintendent Campbell, who in turn said no, I could not cross back over Whitehall because it was dangerous. He said I would be escorted to Downing Street through a safer route if I would wait in safety in the lea of the Ministry of Defence building. If I wished, I could shelter from the snow in nearby Cannon Row police station.

I refrained from responding to his comment that even Cabinet Ministers could get injured and left him in a confused huddle of bemused policemen, standing bravely but pointlessly exposed to any explosion that might come.

The police station was busy, with witnesses coming and going to give their statements, but a helpful WPC gave me a telephone and a cup of tea. I was able to get a message to the Cabinet Office that I would reach Cabinet as soon as I could. Eventually a policeman arrived to escort me. In the meantime, Ken Clarke had arrived at Cannon Row as well but had been taken on in a police bus. Could I have gone on the same bus? Apparently not. Michael Brunson of ITN was lurking and joked to me that I had been arrested. He later turned that into a news story.

It was snowing heavily as I walked with my escort down the Embankment, through the Norman Shaw Building and across Whitehall – about twenty yards further away from that part of it that I had been summoned across earlier in order to be told that it was too dangerous to cross. On along Charles Street and through the Foreign Office courtyard to Downing Street, filmed *en route* by a TV crew who had somehow slipped through the cordon.

A policeman on the door of No. 10 directed me to another entrance and at last, after a series of stairs and corridors, I joined the Cabinet meeting. It was in an underground operations room, one wall covered with large maps of the Gulf. Seemingly the Cabinet Room in No. 10 was badly smashed up, but mercifully there were no casualties among the War Cabinet who had been meeting there.

Cabinet had just started, with only two or three absentees – mainly from Whitehall offices. The Prime Minister was calm and in charge. Business proceeded as normal.

Later I set off for Kensington Palace to lunch with the Prince of Wales. The traffic snarled up. Eventually I rang to cancel. Then the traffic cleared. I rang to reinstate – not quite the way to behave towards royalty. His Royal Highness was very understanding and lunch was delicious. It was, though, a slightly surreal occasion, given the other events of the day.

Another event, of a quite different nature, that sticks in my mind was the sad occasion of John Smith's death. It was impossible not to like John. He was both a tough and rumbustious politician, professional and efficient, and a gregarious party-goer who liked a drink and a gossip regardless of political colour. In some quarters it will be considered heresy, but I don't think he was one of those who truly believed in devolution. Rather, I think he saw it initially as a piece of political business to be done, that would help his party and do no harm to his own career. It was said that at one birthday party that he threw in Edinburgh, when he was taking the Government's original devolution Bill through Parliament, guests were greeted by their host with: 'Come in and have a "devolution special": not a lot of whisky, but plenty of water.'

In the same hard-headed style, he resented the way in which Tam Dalyell, that unmollified opponent of devolution, made his life so difficult during the passage of the same Bill. When, after one tetchy session, John was waiting late at night for his car at the Members' Entrance, Tam allegedly approached him in serious-minded mood to continue the argument, but was greeted with: 'Oh, push off, Tam. I've had quite enough of your Old Etonian courtesy for one night.'

Although John's miscalculation in presenting a Shadow Budget at the start of the 1992 election cost his party dear, he was a formidable Leader of the Opposition, never better than across the Despatch Box in the Commons. When he died in May 1994, it fell to me by chance to be the senior Government minister close to a television camera, at our party Conference in Inverness. So within minutes of the news breaking, I paid our party's main tribute to him outside Parliament. I was credited afterwards with delivering a generous and emotionally charged tribute. It was certainly spontaneous and heartfelt. Having two daughters of my own around the same age as John and Elizabeth's three girls, I could vividly imagine the grief they must be enduring. At the same time, I had been in a state of heightened tension all that morning, ahead of my important conference speech to a dispirited party, wracked by local government defeats and adverse opinion polls.

Some at our conference were not pleased when we decided to suspend that day's sitting, but I am sure it was the right decision. Struggling to prepare a fuller tribute to John, which I was to deliver before we dispersed, I suddenly recalled how, thirty years earlier, the then Prime Minister Sir Alec Douglas-Home had begun his spontaneous televised tribute to President John F. Kennedy on the night of his assassination: 'There are times when heart and mind stand still ...'. That seemed to me to fit the mood on the day John Smith died and the rest of my tribute flowed from that.

The next day, John Major arrived in Inverness to face the formidable task of delivering a leader's speech that would regalvanise the Party, whilst at the same time paying proper respect to the sombre national mood at the death of the man most people believed had been on a sure path to succeed him as Prime Minister. He accomplished it with sensitivity and eloquence, and largely unscripted. His moral strength shone through, reinforced by adversity, and I thought what a pity it was that the media parody was what the public saw, rather than this, the real man.

Earlier that day, he and I had walked round the garden at the Kingsmills Hotel, trying to measure the likely impact on our party's fortunes of John Smith's death. At one level it changed nothing. We were still in the depths of unpopularity and our rebels were destroying any chance we had of recovery. At another, as I put it to him, this could be turned into a new beginning. Whoever succeeded John Smith – and already we thought it would be Blair – would have the benefit of freshness but the disadvantage of inexperience. If our rebels could be brought to their senses and made to see that we could make this a new beginning for us, just as it was for Labour, we might break out of the bind we were in. Sadly, it transpired that they were not capable of even that modest leap of imagination.

We also discussed the rumours running strongly in the press that he was about to make me Party Chairman. It was not a job I coveted, nor did I think it sensible, given my remote and marginal Scottish constituency. In opposition it could be a marvellous job, but in government I preferred to do a government job. Fortunately, John agreed and I was able to relax.

With Labour's other lost leader, Donald Dewar, I always had a relationship of adversarial friendship. Away from politics I feel sure the friendship would have been unalloyed; as it was, politics always got in the way. I found him totally straight – he never betrayed a confidence – and I had a high regard for his debating skills and the force of his inquiring mind. He was a patriotic Scot, without any of the demeaning narrowness of nationalism. I would rank him highly as a parliamentarian, but less so as a politician.

On the detail of Scottish Office business his performances were variable. As a lawyer he was sure-footed on many issues and he could handle confidently subjects with a social content. On such detailed specific issues as the annual public expenditure announcement or the rate support grant, however, he never managed to master the detail and, like his successors Tom Clarke and George Robertson, he gave no trouble. But he was always agile and inventive in seeking the best political angle from which to attack.

Donald had the great disadvantage of not having served in the Scottish Office. For twelve years he shadowed, first George Younger, then Malcolm Rifkind, then me. No wonder he had became a little jaded. After the 1992 election, when in Scotland more even than in England we had confounded the pundits and held on to power, he sought me out as we entered the House of Lords to hear the first Queen's Speech of the new Parliament. He shook my hand and congratulated me warmly. I was touched because I knew how deeply disappointed he was to have lost; and he was now laying down the Scottish Office shadow brief. Five years later, as Secretary of State, he found that the pressures of office, to which his disorganised, buccaneering style was less well suited, bore heavily upon him. He was left by all his senior colleagues to carry the self-imposed burden of delivering devolution. Sadly it was to prove too much for him.

Among the more enjoyable of my roles at the Scottish Office was responsibility for the Arts and Heritage in Scotland. The National Galleries; the

National Library; the Museum of Scotland; the Scottish Arts Council; the Scottish Film Council; Scottish Opera; Scottish Ballet; Ancient Monuments; Historic Buildings: these formed only a part of the cornucopia of artistic endeavour that looked to me for support – and funds.

I had already served as Scottish Arts Minister for several years before taking on overall responsibility as Secretary of State and had already worked out my priorities. The first of these was to try to secure more money for them. There was never enough and, although we managed to increase the arts budget substantially over the years, funding crises were a recurring theme. On one occasion I was able to bail out a near bankrupt Scottish Opera with some £700,000 underspent towards the year-end in the Education Department, but any discernible gratitude from them was more than drowned out by the shrieks of resentment from Scottish Ballet, who ran their affairs rather better but were still very keen on more money. They were both organisations that produced work of quality, but it was hard for them to prosper in a small country like Scotland.

Through Historic Scotland, we funded major renovation projects at Edinburgh and Stirling Castles that have now transformed those magnificent fortresses and also restored and conserved countless other fine buildings and historic sites and monuments. The jewels in the crown, however, were the National Galleries of Scotland and the Museum of Scotland.

The National Galleries had benefited enormously from the arrival on the scene as Director of the talented Timothy Clifford in the mid-1980s. His stimulating drive and flair, combined with the canny dedication of Angus Grossart as a knowledgeable Chairman of the Trustees, had really brought them to life again. Angus and Tim were an ambitious pair on behalf of Scotland's artistic heritage and, keen though I was to help them, it was sometimes difficult to match available funds with their vaulting ambitions.

But we didn't do badly together. To their existing estate we soon added country galleries, at Paxton House in the Borders and Duff House in

Banff. Later, we added the Dean Building in Edinburgh which has been converted to a beautiful exhibition gallery. However, when they sought my support for a new Scottish Gallery to focus exclusively on Scottish artists, they stirred up a hornet's nest.

The art world was divided on the merit of brigading art in this way and separating Scottish art from its European context; and the Scottish population was divided over whether such a gallery should be located in Edinburgh or Glasgow – the supporters of the latter were later to accuse me of a 'world-class display of spinelessness'. My problem was simple. I did not want to intervene in the cultural debate, though my personal sympathies were with the objectors; and I did not want to see the Scottish National Portrait Gallery closed and its treasures transported, which was part of their plan. The main consideration was more straightforward, however. I had limited resources at my disposal and I was determined to give priority to a more important project, the upgrading of the Royal Scottish Academy building in Edinburgh's Princes Street. So I had to tell the Trustees, at a difficult meeting, that I would not be able to fund their 'Scottish' Gallery project. They later persevered with the National Heritage Memorial Fund, but it too rejected them.

The RSA building occupies one of the finest sites for an art gallery in the world. Designed by Playfair, it had long played a valuable role in the Scottish arts world, and although it actually belonged to the National Galleries, Academy members had their right of occupancy guaranteed by a parliamentary order granted in 1910. The time was long overdue to upgrade the building so that it could be used for major international exhibitions and I was keen to make the funds available for that, provided an arrangement could be reached that enabled the National Galleries to take over its management for this purpose, whilst at the same time protecting the interests of the academicians.

This was not a straightforward task. The two parties had been negotiating warily and unproductively for several years. The negotiations were getting nowhere and everyone was getting frustrated. Eventually I asked the Earl of Crawford and Balcarres to chair a committee to try to reach an agreed solution. He is the unsung hero of what is now called the Playfair Project because, after long but patient negotiation, he did break the deadlock and work was then able to get under way. The first few millions of pounds that I had earmarked for the redevelopment had to be spent on the less romantic task of underpinning the whole building, which was found to be in danger of subsiding, but at last the redevelopment itself began, with Tim Clifford's grand plans for an underground link between the RSA building and its National Gallery neighbour being duly adopted. The cost has ballooned but, to their credit, the Scottish Executive have promised £10 million. The National Lottery – that brainchild of John Major's that has made possible so many fine projects – has pledged £7 million and the rest is being raised by a well-run voluntary campaign. The final outcome will be wonderful and I am delighted that, long after my departure from office, this exciting project is now close to realisation.

The Museum of Scotland project in Edinburgh was an even more ambitious one. My predecessor Malcolm Rifkind had discovered by chance that decades before an earlier Secretary of State had given a commitment that a major extension to the existing building in Chambers Street would go ahead. A keen supporter of the museum, Malcolm had gleefully announced that this commitment would now be honoured, provided a workable and cost-effective scheme was produced. He was then reshuffled to the Department of Transport, leaving me wondering how to find the sum of over £30 million that would be needed.

I adopted the same approach as Malcolm had done: a commitment had been given – and now renewed – and it must be honoured. The vast expenditure that had been going into the renovation of the National Library of Scotland was now reaching completion, but there was still nothing in the arts budget for another major project. So, in directing new resources towards that budget I was able to fund the museum by extending the previous spending level for a few more years. With luck, the Treasury and the many other bidders for funds would not notice.

I was helped in this by the courteous but very persistent lobbying of the Chairman of the Museum's Trustees, the Marquess of Bute – another unsung hero and a great benefactor of Scotland. I told him I would find the money to let the building go ahead if he and his trustees would raise the balance needed to fit it out. This was a tall order; they would need at least £10 million. I offered to help him in that campaign. He accepted and I found myself fund-raising for the project, with many other dedicated supporters of it, in locations as far apart as New York, San Francisco and Hong Kong, as well as finding the building costs from my Scottish Office block.

In April 1993 I climbed into a large mechanical digger to turn the first sod on the derelict site, next to the existing Victorian museum building. Thereafter I watched the wonderful new building steadily grow in place. It was a special pleasure to attend the official opening by the Queen in 1998, after I had ceased to be an MP. Sadly, John Bute had died by then, after a brave battle with cancer. He had continued fighting for the new Museum until the very end. His successor Sir Robert Smith took up the torch with equal vigour.

Whilst the new Museum building required over £30 million of public funds, there were many other new developments that I was able to help, where quite a small contribution from my budget levered in funds from elsewhere or bridged the viability gap. The Dean Gallery was one, as I have mentioned, but there was also the Festival Theatre and the new Conference Centre. At this remarkable period of new build, the large new Scottish Office building in Leith also had to cross my desk. I was surprised how easily officials in the Scottish Office managed to persuade officials in the Treasury that this, their fine new home, passed all the Treasury's stringent tests for approval. To this day I do not know from what deep pocket officials produced the necessary funds, but they did not come from the Scottish block.

As Agriculture and Fisheries Minister for Scotland, I had two further industries to master. My farming constituency of Galloway had already familiarised me with the intricacies of the suckler cow premium and hill livestock compensatory allowances, but it was a complex and detailed field. So much of agriculture was dominated by the Common Agricultural Policy that my English counterpart shouldered much of that burden for the United Kingdom as a whole. However, the reverse was true in fishing, since most of the waters were Scottish. Fortunately I had able junior ministers in Thomas Strathclyde and Hector Monro, as I struggled with the subtleties of quotas, mesh sizes and total allowable catches. The essential problem was the need to increase conservation as the stocks of herring, cod, haddock, shellfish and the rest became seriously depleted, whilst trying to enable a reduced fishing fleet to earn a living.

Farming had similar problems, wrestling with milk and sheep quotas, surpluses, subsidies and set-asides. The refinements of the beef variable premium and the out-goer's scheme, the less favoured areas and the hills and uplands were a constant challenge. But I could only marvel at the stoic commitment of our dedicated farmers and fishermen as they worked so hard to earn a living in industries dogged by intervention, often wasteful and misconceived, from Brussels.

I used to visit the Royal Highland Show at Ingliston, near Edinburgh, every year when I was Secretary of State. It was an ideal opportunity to keep in touch with farmers from all over Scotland. One year, in 1993, I noticed that there were no fewer than eight policemen forming a phalanx around me as I walked around the showground, with a few obviously plain-clothes policemen lurking in the background. Now the Government was none too popular at the time, but I did think that this was an excessive show of strength. People were giving me odd looks as we passed.

It was only on my way back into Edinburgh that I learned from my private secretary what had been behind it all. It transpired that one Joseph Steele, a murderer convicted for his role in the murder of six members of the Doyle family during Glasgow's 'ice-cream wars', had escaped recently from Saughton Prison and was still at large. During an earlier escape this ingenious individual had superglued himself to the railings at Buckingham Palace to draw attention to his protestations of innocence. Now the word was that he had been planning to confront me at the Royal Highland Show to shake me warmly, and stickily, by the hand.

Farming became increasingly drawn into the debate on conserving the environment, with some of the Brussels schemes recognising the role farmers could play by protecting environmentally sensitive areas. An early legislative commitment that I inherited from Malcolm Rifkind was the implementation of the Bill to establish Scottish Natural Heritage as Scotland's main vehicle for conservation, combining, as it did, the Nature Conservancy Council for Scotland and the Countryside Commission for Scotland. We appointed Magnus Magnusson as its first chairman and gave it the task of providing a framework within which Scotland's natural heritage could be managed in a sustainable way, to reconcile its use for economic purposes with protection for future generations. Four years later I set up the Scottish Environment Protection Agency, to deal more effectively with such problems as emissions into the atmosphere, or into rivers. Professor Bill Turmeau, the former principal of Napier College, was its first trenchant and effective chairman.

There was a continuing debate around this time about whether or not National Parks were a good idea in Scotland. I took the view that they were undesirable. Scotland was so full of wonderful scenery that to try to enclose and package its wild mountains and wildernesses would be to detract from those very qualities. I had seen the honeypot effect of a

National Park in the English Lake District and considered that freedom in Scotland was preferable.

The one possible exception might be the area of Loch Lomond and the Trossachs, already a magnet for tourists, but I considered that a National Park there would add to the pressures upon it, detract from its beauty and introduce the principle that would soon spread to other areas where there was no enthusiasm for designation. We established instead a new, lighter designation of 'natural heritage area' to particularly sensitive parts of the landscape, as a means of protecting them with a light touch and with the participation of owners, occupiers and local communities. I do not believe the introduction of National Parks by our successors has been a step forward in environmental terms. Nor do I believe the land reforms of the new Scottish Parliament advance matters. They clearly owe more to social engineering than to environmental considerations. The breaking up of larger estates and the subsidised communal purchase of them, or parts of them, will soon impoverish the countryside.

Forestry was another departmental responsibility that fell upon me at the Scottish Office – and for the whole United Kingdom. Most of the forests were in Scotland and the Forestry Commission was headquartered in Edinburgh. Like so many rural matters, it was going through hard times; prices were very low and a strong pound crippled exports. With the help of two excellent chairmen, first Sir Raymond Johnstone and then Sir Peter Hutchison, I split the Commission's functions in two: the Enterprise and the Authority. The Authority would continue to handle the issue of felling licences and planting grants and generally administer the industry nationally. The Enterprise would manage the Commission's own forests, with a remit to rationalise and reduce them. Over the years, their empire had grown and spread in an almost random way. They completely dominated the market and I wanted to reduce their near-monopoly position, as well as their cost to the taxpayer, and to try to make room for a stronger private forestry sector to develop. I introduced new planting grants, both for broadleaf and conifers, and introduced measures to open up the forests more to the public.

I considered full-blown 'privatisation' of the Commission but there was strong opposition to this, not least on our own back benches and, after a long and thorough review, the benefits to be had were less obvious than in other industries. My decision to go no further was greeted with general relief.

Of the many pieces of legislation I took through Parliament over the years, in some ways the Bill to reform local government was the biggest. It was the product of widespread consultation and, although the subject of heated argument, it eventually bedded down with little controversy. We announced our intentions before the 1992 general election, and at that time our English and Welsh colleagues planned to reform their systems, too. Later, though, the English plans subsided into a morass of consultation and dither, leading to a rather obscure outcome.

In Scotland, I had no doubt that the existing two-tier structure, which dated only from 1975, was cumbersome, illogical and wasteful. Strangely, some of the top tiers were said to be estuarially based, but that irrelevant principle had been abandoned when it became clear that to draw local authority boundaries around the Forth and the Tay would split the kingdom of Fife in half. So that approach survived only around the River Clyde, where the mighty Strathclyde Regional Council was established. This monolith brought remote rural Campbeltown into the same local authority as Glasgow. Not only was there no commonality of interest, but the council found itself presiding over half the population of Scotland.

When I stood up in Parliament to announce its abolition I said: 'There is no possible justification for the size of Strathclyde. It varies from being two times to six times too big.' The Labour opposition, who regarded Strathclyde as their fiefdom, protested furiously until I pointed out that

I had been quoting John Smith. Then all the Labour benches emptied, as Tom Clarke led them on what a sketch-writer was to describe as a 'spontaneously premeditated' walk-out. They said they were off to protest to the Prime Minister at 10 Downing Street. I had to shout after them that the Prime Minister was in Japan at the time, but doubtless the policeman at the door would take a message.

Once we got down to the detail of reform it became clear that opposition was half-hearted and support for it around Scotland widespread. I wanted to introduce around two dozen single-tier, self-contained local authorities, which I felt would be more clearly understood locally and would be more accountable to their rate payers. Duplication and waste should be cut out and the dysfunctional problems of dividing local services between two different tiers of council would go. Variations in size would create diversity and the opportunity for neighbouring councils to share some services in imaginative new ways, or to become clients of each other for others. I hoped it would break up the old inefficient moulds for local service provision. It should also save money.

A further attraction was the chance to revive many of the old county names; and this duly happened. We varied the boundaries in one or two areas, such as the Borders and Argyll, in response to local consultation, but I reluctantly resisted the call from tiny counties like Caithness to break up the Highlands into smaller bodies. They simply would not be viable. However, I did make sure that our proposals provided for the local delivery of services and consultation at local level in that large but thinly populated region.

In the end the proposals went through smoothly and the new councils came into being. Allan Stewart did the detailed implementation work in Parliament as Local Government minister, and his successor George Kynoch handled efficiently their start-up year. I believe the councils are working reasonably well, if unimaginatively: I am afraid the mould proved harder to break than I had hoped, and value for money is as far

away as ever. I was conscious in setting them up that if a Scottish
Assembly were one day to be established, the top tier of Scottish local
government would be quickly abolished anyway, and its powers taken to
the Assembly. I hoped that by creating the new councils before any such
Assembly materialised I might help them to cling on to their local powers
for longer. But I hear now that the drums are beginning to beat in
Edinburgh.

Health was probably the most sensitive political issue of all those for
which I had overall responsibility in Scotland. At the same time it was,
in debating terms, the most stagnant. However large the resources we
poured into the health service – and we did increase spending year after
year after year by more than the rate of inflation – it was never enough.
Regardless of the repeated demonstration of our commitment, by word
and deed, to the maintenance of a service free at the point of delivery,
the Labour Party had only to give voice to the canard that we intended
to 'privatise' it for that to be believed. By contrast, their own poor record
when in government was cheerfully ignored by a predisposed electorate.

This puerile trench warfare was frustrating and I was glad to have two
such good health ministers, in succession, as Michael Forsyth and Peter
Fraser. I confidently left to them much of the daily grind. Their task was
a thankless one, though the record – in improved performance, new
hospitals, more doctors and nurses and shorter waiting lists – was
admirable. My own views on health were rather unfashionable. I believed
– and still do – that the sacramental nature of the NHS was eroding the
quality of health care in Britain; and the deeply prejudiced theology that
regarded private health care as some kind of élitist heresy was self-
defeating twaddle. When I was younger I used to go to my own doctor
privately as a matter of principle, not to seek favourable treatment, but
because I believed that those who could afford to pay for private

treatment should do so, easing the pressure on the NHS so that it could focus on those who needed it. Only when my doctor's practice, like others in the area, went exclusively NHS, did I have to surrender to the new religion. And only when the political bile that so discolours the debate is finally flushed out of it will there be a chance to make the real progress that depends on private and public health cohabiting, complementing and supporting each other. Then our health care will begin to catch up with that of our European neighbours.

In essence, our policies in Scotland were the same as those of our English colleagues. After all, the NHS was a nationwide institution. But we did make our own decisions according to our own priorities. Our policies often had variations to reflect Scottish circumstances and, of course, regardless of merit, their reception by voters was invariably more hostile and apocalyptic than elsewhere.

Sometimes we were at the forefront, such as when I gave approval for the new Edinburgh Royal Infirmary to be the first hospital in Britain to be built using the Private Finance Initiative, just as the Skye road bridge had, I believe, been the first road project financed by the scheme. (As roads minister, I had been asked to choose between a box girder design or a high-wire cable bridge. I chose the former, as I thought its elegant curve would detract less from the stunning setting across the Kyle of Lochalsh than a cable bridge would have done. In so doing I alienated all bridge engineers, who could only think of beauty in engineering terms.)

On other occasions we moved more slowly, as in the case of health trusts. In that, we were of course dependent on applications coming forward from individual hospitals. As luck would have it, the first to do so was from Foresterhill in Aberdeen, which landed on my desk in the autumn of 1991, just as we were embarking on the by-election campaign in the local Conservative seat of Kincardine & Deeside. The timing could not have been worse: our opponents had a field day and on every doorstep we were greeted with the charge that we were closing down the health service. I had never encountered such apparent intensity and unanimity of opinion.

We duly lost the by-election, and with a general election only months away I seriously considered putting the whole initiative on the back-burner until after polling day. But I was sure the policy was a good one – to improve patient care through committed local management of the hospitals whilst remaining four-square within the National Health Service. It would improve the use of hospital facilities, be more cost-effective and reduce waiting times. After sounding out my Scottish Office colleagues and discussing the matter with the Prime Minister, I decided we should face down our critics and press on with an initiative we knew to be right. In December 1991 I announced in the Commons that we were granting trust status to Foresterhill and the other hospitals. For the opposition, Donald Dewar fulminated. This was 'a betrayal' and 'a disgrace', which Labour would reverse 'immediately after the general election'. In the event, we turned the tide of public opinion. Applications flooded in from all over Scotland and health trusts did indeed deliver the better services they had promised. We also won back Kincardine & Deeside in the 1992 general election; and we won Aberdeen South as well.

The number of public appointments for which the Secretary of State was responsible – I was once told it exceeded 3,000 – was a constant source of sniping by our opponents, who thought this amount of patronage was excessive. They had not thought so when in power, but as a matter of fact I agreed with them. I always sought to choose the best person for any position, regardless of political party: one example of that was my appointment of Helen Liddell to the Scottish Prisons Board, after she ceased to be Secretary of the Scottish Labour Party, but there were many more. Many of the appointments required a particular professional expertise, however, so it was hardly surprising that I often appointed busi-nessmen and women rather than trade unionists or public sector workers.

However, the appointments to health trusts added a whole new tranche of alleged patronage and I decided that I should set up an Appointments Committee to take over from me the task of reviewing and renewing these positions. At the outset, I was not under any public pressure to do this; I simply thought it desirable. But it took about a year to persuade govern-ment colleagues that this was a good idea. Eventually I was able to go ahead with a broadly based committee including, for example, the Roman Catholic Bishop of Aberdeen, Mario Conti and, as chairman, Norman Irons, the SNP Lord Provost of Edinburgh. They took over the task and performed it well. Later, when Lord Nolan was asked by the Prime Minister to review the handling of public appointments, he held up our Scottish arrangements as an example of good practice.

I sometimes found that officials could be a little casual over the timing of their submissions to me on reappointments or retirals in respect of public bodies of all kinds. Sometimes they even allowed them to slip beyond the due date. I solved that problem by requiring the official responsible to telephone the waiting incumbent to apologise personally for his or her discourtesy. Though they could act quickly and efficiently in an emergency, time never seemed quite so precious to officials as it did to mere mortals. A particular source of irritation, to me as well as to the parties involved, was the time it took to complete public inquiries into controversial planning applications. Even after the Reporter had completed his Inquiry, which sometimes took a year or more, and had submitted his recommendations to the Scottish Office, it often took a further year for my officials to consider his findings and submit them to me with their recommendation. In 1994 I set up an internal review to find ways of speeding up this process, but it was still under way when I left the Department over a year later. I wonder if it has reported yet.

Another milestone in the improvement of patient care was the introduction of the Patient's Charter, which I announced in September 1991. It was, I think, the first health charter in the United Kingdom and I made sure that it included not just clear rights for patients, but also their obligations. The rights were considerable: guaranteed treatment times, a better appointments system, a simplified complaints system and undertakings to raise standards and improve choice. Performance reports would have to be published and patients would be treated with proper respect and dignity. At the same time, in *Framework for Action*, I published a series of national targets for improving the NHS's performance, in such areas as heart disease and cancer treatments, AIDS and drugs treatment and preventive campaigns on smoking, drinking and diet.

Progress in all these areas was already taking place as a result of our other initiatives and the funding increases we had achieved, but the Patient's Charter made a palpable impact on the way the service regarded its patients – as individuals. Indeed, the whole Citizen's Charter, of which it was a part, was an initiative of John Major's that deserved much wider acclaim than it got.

The opportunity for *ad hoc* initiatives is rare in such large and continuous funding programmes as health, but one project I did particularly want to help was in the rebuilding of Edinburgh's Royal Hospital for Sick Children, universally known as the Sick Kids. As it happened, I had a distant cousin who was a nursing sister there and when I visited the existing building, I was struck both by the miraculous work being done, often on the tiniest of new-born babies, by doctors and nurses of great sensitivity and skill, and by the appallingly cramped and dilapidated conditions in which they worked.

I was determined to help and, when an appeal was launched in the autumn of 1991 for £10 million to build a new hospital, I was able to contribute £1 million through Lothian Health Board's budget. It still wasn't enough. A European Court of Justice ruling meant that VAT had to be paid on hospital buildings and that took the cost up to £11 million. Despite a well-supported public appeal they were still £2 million short. As the financial year-end approached we began a 'candle-ends' search for additional funds – after all, I reasoned, the VAT would come back to the Treasury and if I could help the appeal to bridge the gap, the leverage of taxpayers' funds would have enabled a valuable new asset for the health service to be created. At last, in February 1992, we managed to find the money and the new Sick Kids went ahead.

A bizarre postscript to that episode arose a year or so later. Health officials in the Scottish Office suggested I should visit the construction work then under way, to inspect progress. I replied that if it would not disrupt work and if there was a worthwhile stage to mark, such as a topping out ceremony, I would be happy to go. Would I be willing to go to unveil a plaque? Yes, if there was an event there worthy of a plaque I would be glad to unveil it. A gap was found in my diary, and late one winter afternoon I duly arrived at the building site. I clambered up ladders and along uneven passages still open to the elements, amid the all-pervading smell of wet concrete. We arrived in a dim assembly area of some kind where, despite the absence of electric light, I could make out some shadowy figures waiting patiently behind a rope. They were, it transpired, the Friends of the Sick Kids, amongst whom was Edith Rifkind, Malcolm's wife.

I wanted to greet them but was asked first to unveil the plaque to mark the still unknown event that had brought me here. I duly pulled the cord and there, set into the wet plaster on the wall behind me, was a neatly engraved plaque bearing the legend: 'This plaque marks the visit of the Secretary of State for Scotland' and the date. I was still trying to work out the surreal nature of this situation as I was led stumbling on a tour of the dark, empty shell. I never did get a chance to talk to the Friends. They were probably as bemused as I was.

A hospital of a different nature brought me no end of trouble a year or two later. It was the private Health Care International Hospital at Clydebank.

This was originally an inward investment project that had seized the imagination of the Scottish Development Agency and Locate in Scotland in the early 1980s. Two Boston surgeons wanted to build a brand new state-of-the-art hospital on derelict ground on the banks of the Clyde at Clydebank, at the time one of the most deprived areas in Scotland. There they would assemble a team of top-notch surgeons, specialist doctors and nurses who would apply frontier surgery and medical treatment to a stream of several thousand patients a year, flown in from countries in the Middle East and south-eastern Europe. When I first heard of the scheme in 1986 I thought it was completely dotty.

However, they were serious. They had had a variety of accountants pronounce on aspects of their business plan, including Coopers & Lybrand and Ernst & Whinney. Locate in Scotland were in deadly earnest to attract them, and in 1985 had given them sufficient comfort to decide in principle in favour of Scotland over Ireland. I was still sceptical and at a breakfast meeting in Boston with the two surgeons, Dr Eraklis and Dr Levey, I drove Locate in Scotland's man, Howard Moody, close to despair by my detached approach to their dream project.

For a year or two nothing much happened. Then suddenly the project came alive. It was to be a 260-bed hospital, with a hotel next door for the relations of patients; an estimated 1,800 jobs would be created and the total cost would be £150 million. The bulk of the funds would come from a syndicate of banks led by the Royal Bank of Scotland, the Midland Bank and Credit Lyonnais; but they were all looking to the Government to close the funding gap. The SDA, led by its chief executive George Mathewson, who was about to leave to join the Royal Bank of Scotland, had decided to commit its maximum delegated limit of £5 million and wanted to do more. Their view was that this was a project that would revitalise Clydebank, on a site they were already keen to clean up environmentally, polluted as it was by methane gas and asbestos. Moreover, it was in a targeted growth sector of the economy, with sixteen other healthcare projects under consideration. HCI should have a catalytic effect upon them.

Before agreeing to let the project go into the appraisal process in the Scottish Office, Malcolm Rifkind convened a three-way telephone conference call with me as industry minister and Michael Forsyth as health minister, plus our respective officials. There was concern about blood supplies and the possible poaching of nurses from the NHS, and we were all still a bit sceptical about the viability of such a strange project.

My own predominant view, though, was that here was an opportunity to enable a potentially exciting new project in the private health sector to be won for Scotland. It might help to break down the doctrinal prejudice against private healthcare and introduce possibilities of partnership with the NHS. Malcolm and Michael took the same view.

Regional Selective Assistance, the main instrument for attracting jobs to deprived areas throughout the UK, was not decided by ministers: the misguided intervention by Tony Benn in the 1970s to overrule officials over two notorious cases had afforded a cautionary tale. Officials in the Scottish Office, the Treasury and the SDA carried out their appraisal of HCI's application in the usual way and made a recommendation to the Scottish Industrial Development Advisory Board. That august body, manned by distinguished and successful Scottish businessmen, recommended that an offer of £12 million of grant be made, and in 1990 officials duly made that offer, which amounted to about 8 per cent of the total value of the project.

What changed after that to raise the total public sector commitment was that the European Court of Justice made a ruling, as in the case of the Sick Kids, that required the imposition of VAT on new hospital building. This threatened the whole scheme but, acting on the logical basis that the VAT, which would total £10 million, would return to the pockets of the Treasury after construction was complete, Malcolm persuaded the Treasury exceptionally to increase the offer to HCI to £22 million. Add to that the environmental work to remove pollution from the site, which would have been undertaken anyway, at a cost of £10 million, plus the SDA's commitment to the project from its delegated budget, and the potential total exposure could be well over £30 million.

As fate would have it, it was just when such an exceptional combination of circumstances had come together to create unusual exposure to an unusual venture that things went wrong. Fate had also decreed that by that stage I would have succeeded Malcolm as Secretary of State and would therefore be to blame for it all.

One member of the investment consortium had withdrawn because of its environmental concerns. The SDA asked me to let them take an even bigger stake, to fill the gap. I was still sceptical, but to save the deal from collapse before it had begun, I allowed them to take £5.5 million worth of shares, on condition that they found another investor to buy them on, in short order. This they duly did. In June 1994, when the spanking new hospital was ready, I was invited to perform the opening ceremony. By now I was uneasy. I had heard that the marketing programme for patients had barely got off the ground and there were said to be few in the hospital. Begged by my officials and by the SDA to do the honours in support of the Government's financial aid, I duly relented and agreed.

When I toured the empty echoing corridors my worst fears were confirmed. So it was no surprise when I heard five months later that HCI was in crisis. The Opposition, who hated private medicine anyway, went into overdrive and of course the media played and replayed their newsreel shots of the opening ceremony.

By and large I escaped serious personal criticism on most issues, both as Secretary of State and throughout my political career. I sometimes used to feel like the traditional white-faced clown in the circus – the one who, in pointed hat and sequined tunic, bossed all the other clowns around and, alone amongst them, never got egg on his face. But on this occasion it was different. The abuse was vicious, vindictive and very personal. Even then the HCI company could have survived, as all the investors were willing to stand their corner for the new funding package that was needed and a saving deal with the Abu Dhabi government was imminent. But Credit Lyonnais suddenly had to pull out because of unrelated problems in France, and so the whole venture collapsed.

The roof fell in. Tony Blair, on his first official visit to Scotland as leader, pronounced it all a 'monumental waste' and, of course, it was all my fault. It mattered not that the key decisions had been taken in the time of my predecessor, and mainly by his officials rather than by him. It mattered not that government funds went not to sustain a company but to create jobs – and six hundred construction jobs had been created over the three-year building period. It mattered not that Scotland now had a shiny new hospital and hotel on a site recovered from dereliction. In the musical chairs of politics the incumbent gets the blame – and if government funds are 'lost' there is plenty of blame. The hysteria and abuse ran on for weeks.

By the time I went before the Select Committee on Scottish Affairs to receive what the media anticipated would be a drubbing, I had been able to gather all the facts together and some of the hysteria had subsided. Indeed, after I had given evidence and answered all their questions in detail, they decided that really there was no case for me to answer. Far from issuing a damning report, they issued no report at all, confining themselves simply to publishing the transcript of our session together. Meanwhile, the hospital survived and continued in business.

It was a tale full of ironies. I, who had thought the project unviable and who had taken none of the key decisions other than to instruct the SDA to divest themselves of part of their commitment, had to take on the chin the abuse of an outraged Scotland. It was ironic that the court that was to deliver the *coup de grâce* in Parliament could not bring itself even to reach a verdict. It was ironic that the hospital that was so censured as a white elephant, a 'monumental waste', should have been rescued at the end of 1994 by one of its original investors, the Abu Dhabi Investment Company, who have continued to run it ever since, not at the level originally envisaged but providing top quality medical care, a high-grade hotel and 400 jobs in a regenerated Clydebank.

It is ironic, too, that all that taxpayers' money 'lost' in a doomed project should by now have been more than repaid to the Treasury through taxes. But perhaps the biggest irony of all is that our opponents sneered at a venture that aimed to bring patients from the Middle East, Greece and Turkey and that would 'compete' with the National Health Service. In 2002 the newspapers have carried stories of complaints about Scottish NHS patients being deprived of places at the HCI private hospital because of the flood of patients referred there from England and Wales, and of British NHS patients being sent abroad to such countries as Greece, Turkey and Tunisia for medical treatment.

I had thought my tenure at the Scottish Office would continue until the 1997 general election. There were, after all, barely enough Scottish Conservatives at Westminster to crew the Scottish ship of state. I had had to choose as my parliamentary private secretary an Englishman, Simon Coombs, who was the MP for Swindon, but he put up stoically with the interminable demands upon me – and therefore upon him – of Scottish politics. There was, however, one talented potential successor waiting in the wings, at the Home Office, in the person of Michael Forsyth. John Major's successful leadership election in July 1995 gave both of us a chance for a change.

I had found my five years at the Scottish Office testing and exhilarating. I do believe it was one of the best jobs in government. But I was more than ready to move on.

EIGHT

Saving the Union

'The fact cannot longer be concealed that Scotland is becoming dissatis-fied, impatient, even disaffected, in consequence of the treatment which her affairs have received and are receiving at the hands of the Government which she did so much to put into power. There have been mutterings of discontent in many quarters for some time, but now the suppressed mutterings have given place to outspoken and emphatic remon-strances.'

The Times, *24 May 1881*

Devolution was a hovering presence throughout my time in Scottish politics. Often muted, occasionally dominant, but always there casting its shadow over every passing political issue, it was like the bass drone of the bagpipes.

Ultimately, for me it became an issue of irreducible principle. I knew that lots of people wanted it. I knew opposing it had cost us support in elections. I knew it was one of the reasons why the media hated us. I could see the arguments, of heart and head, in favour of it. I sensed that sooner or later it would happen in some form, probably under a Labour government. But after I had thought about it long and hard, I could not bring myself to do anything other than stand firm over an issue that I could not believe to be in the best interests either of Scotland or of the United Kingdom. So I opposed it because I could do no other.

It was never an easy issue. The history of home rule generally had been a troubled one for British governments and it had presented problems over the years for all parties. At different times, each party in turn has been supportive of it, and I often wished that the issue had been dealt with earlier in quieter times, before the rise of nationalism, when it might have taken root as just one more anomaly in a nation state that is full of them. Asquith's policy of 'Home Rule all round' could well have done the trick, but for the intervention of the First World War. Federalism has few friends in the European context and I am not one of them, but as a constitutional mechanism for governing a disparate nation state it has both pedigree and integrity. It could have been made to work in the United Kingdom, despite England's preponderance – and still could. But perhaps the moment passed in 1914, just as other moments were to pass over the decades of the turbulent twentieth century. Whatever the reason, over the years substantial constitutional change never happened.

Administrative devolution got going in the 1880s, when a Conservative government established a Scottish Office and a Scottish Secretary. Later Conservative administrations gave the Secretary Cabinet status and created him Secretary of State, and in 1936 set up a Scottish Office in Edinburgh.

But that did not meet the aspirations of those who wanted elective and legislative home rule. The Labour Party paid lip-service to home rule in the 1920s and 1930s, and Tom Johnston, the wartime Labour Secretary of State in Churchill's National Government, was said to favour it. But after the landslide of 1945, Labour were too busy building the new Jerusalem throughout the United Kingdom and staunch unionists took over in that

Party. In the same way the Conservative Party, reacting against Labour centralisation, began once more to seek further administrative devolution, only to abandon it after one or two cosmetic measures in the 1950s.

When I first became politically active in the 1960s, the Labour Party was strongly and credibly opposed to devolution. Willie Ross, the dominant Labour Secretary of State of the time, would have no truck with it, nor would the trade unions nor the large cohort of Old Labour Scottish MPs. After all, Scotland was part of Labour's powerhouse, and the party of centralisation, nationalisation and the man in Whitehall had a visceral resistance to anything that might jeopardise that. Conservatives, by contrast, believed instinctively in decentralisation, diversity and the little platoons. Conversely, we also felt a seminal obligation to maintain the integrity of the nation state.

Winifred Ewing changed all that. When she took Hamilton for the SNP in a sensational by-election victory in 1967, Tories started thinking hard and the Labour Government started to panic at the sudden threat to its heartlands in Central Scotland. It was we who, under Ted Heath, made the first substantive move. Without any consultation that I could discern, he suddenly announced at our Perth annual conference, in what he called his Declaration of Perth, a commitment to the establishment of a Scottish Assembly, with legislative, deliberative and inquisitorial powers. I was on the platform for that speech, as one of the party's candidates, and I was bemused by it. On the one hand, all my instincts were against it, but on the other I wanted to be loyal to my leader – another basic trait of Conservatism (in those days).

Sir Alec Douglas-Home – he who had been asked nearly twenty years earlier by Churchill, as 'Home, sweet Home', to become Minister of State at the Scottish Office in order to 'go and quell those turbulent Scots' – was asked by Heath to work out the details. I wonder if Sir Alec had been consulted.

I decided to take up the open invitation to submit ideas to Sir Alec's Committee. In my submission, I accepted that we had to respond to the widespread perception that Westminster could not adequately handle the interests of Scotland, even though it was unjustified. I went on:

> *The aims and functions set out by Mr Heath in his Perth speech are absolutely right. His proposed solution is not. I am instinctively unhappy with the creation, from nothing, of an entirely new body in our constitutional make-up. It is an alien and unsettling intrusion into a pattern that has always been evolutionary.*
>
> *There is a danger that, unless such a body is formed to fill a truly overwhelming need, it will create the more serious problem of being otiose. Constitution-making is fun, especially for historians and lawyers. We must not fall into the trap of indulging in it for its own sake. For these and a number of more specific reasons, I believe a new, elected body to be both unnecessary and undesirable.*

I went on to talk of over-government, the danger of a 'talking shop', the potential for conflict with Westminster and the threat of dominance by Scotland's central belt. It would, I said, 'be a halfway house, and one built at the top of a slippery slope'. But I also recognised the need for action of some kind. My proposed solution was three-fold. Firstly, I suggested that the planned reform of local government to create a two-tier structure should take account of the devolution debate, with its powers strengthened accordingly. Secondly, administrative changes in the Scottish Office and its ministerial team should make it more open and accessible to the people of Scotland, to demonstrate the huge extent to which Scotland was already self-governing.

Thirdly, I called for all Scottish MPs, supplemented by enough Scottish life peers to maintain the political balance of Westminster, to meet regularly in Edinburgh, there to conduct Scottish business. It would be a modified version of the Scottish Grand Committee, with added powers to initiate legislation, hold a regular Question Time and summon ministers, including English ministers, to participate and be held to account. This would respond to the aspirations of the day, avoid weakening the Union and Scotland's participation at Westminster, and mean that what would come to be known as the West Lothian Question need never be asked.

Tam Dalyell's question took various forms, but in essence it was: 'Why can Scottish MPs vote on (for example) education in England, when English MPs cannot vote on education in Scotland?' A Scottish devolved parliament would take the latter to Edinburgh. It was a good question and one that has never been answered. It can only be answered by further constitutional change at Westminster – for example, to limit the voting powers there of Scottish MPs. But that would, in turn, create further anomalies and two tiers of MP. Some argue that the problem can be ignored, citing Northern Ireland, but Ulster MPs, proportionately much fewer in number, are not members of the political parties that can form the United Kingdom's government.

Sir Alec's Committee cheerfully ignored my proposals, in favour of a directly elected Assembly, to be known as the Scottish Convention. It was to have very limited powers, which found favour with no one and was taken no further. My own ideas were to form the basis sixteen years later of my *Taking Stock* White Paper.

Having U-turned to make his Declaration of Perth, Ted Heath U-turned again as Prime Minister and did nothing to implement his plans during his four-year tenure, the excuse being that Harold Wilson had set up a Royal Commission before losing the 1970 election and it would be wise to await its findings. I suppose Heath had discovered how little support they had in the party. Nationalism had not gone away, however, and in the two general elections of 1974 the SNP won six new seats and then four more, taking three from Labour and seven from Conservatives.

Harold Wilson leapt into action. Lord Kilbrandon's Royal Commission had published its report and Wilson embraced its recommendations. Willie Ross at first acquiesced and then in 1976 retired; and in 1977, after an abortive attempt to enact a combined Scotland and Wales Bill, which had almost no friends, John Smith, the up-and-coming MP for Lanarkshire North, was given the job of taking the Scotland Bill through a Parliament in which Labour had a majority of just three. This Bill to set up a Scottish Assembly was not a popular measure either, even within the Labour Party, and it was Labour rebels, rather than the Conservative Opposition, who succeeded in inserting the requirement that there should be a referendum on its proposals, in which at least 40 per cent of the Scottish electorate must support them, before they could be implemented.

By then, James Callaghan had replaced Harold Wilson as Prime Minister, Margaret Thatcher had replaced Ted Heath as Leader of the Opposition and after a long period of reflection had reversed our stance on devolution; and I had been adopted as prospective Conservative candidate for Galloway.

It had been a difficult time for Scottish Tories. I remember sitting uneasily at the back of the conference hall in Perth in the early 1970s and watching only the elderly Lord Strathclyde and his son, Tam Galbraith MP, oppose a motion in favour of devolution. Most of the MPs on the platform abstained, as I did; many had absented themselves altogether. I remember Margaret Thatcher addressing her first Scottish Conference as Leader in the Caird Hall in Dundee in 1975, and unequivocally renewing the party's commitment to devolution; and I remember a year later the same Margaret Thatcher abandoning this policy, to the apparent relief of the great majority of the party, including myself.

The referendum campaign of March 1979 was a godsend for me. It gave me a high local profile, campaigning against an issue on which those who lived in southern Scotland held strong views. With the active support of such Labour luminaries as Tam Dalyell and Robin Cook, Dumfries & Galloway voted 'No' resoundingly, as did half the regions of

Scotland. Across the country as a whole the devolutionaries, by telling the electorate that an abstention counted as a 'No' vote, won a very small majority of those who voted, but came nowhere near the 40 per cent hurdle. The Government's policy was in ruins. Margaret Thatcher tabled and won a motion of 'no confidence' and the Government fell. They were already deeply unpopular on account of their catastrophic mismanagement of the economy and the 'winter of discontent', but it was their devolution policy that brought them down.

By chance, I travelled to London by sleeper on the night before the 'no confidence' debate and met the SNP's George Reid MP in the restaurant at Euston. We breakfasted together and I had to bite my lip to stop myself telling him how crazy the SNP were in their plan to abandon their pact with the Government in the vote that was to come that night. I think it was Callaghan who described them as 'turkeys voting for an early Christmas'. He was right. In the general election that followed the SNP were reduced to two seats, with the Conservatives, including myself, winning back seven from them.

I made my maiden speech in Parliament that summer in support of the repeal of the Scotland Act, in which I described it as 'spawned on the stony ground of expediency: conceived in panic, by opportunism out of appeasement.' I criticised it as a way of creating second-class Scottish MPs at Westminster, who would be able 'to fight, and vote, for better housing, better hospitals and better schools for England but not for Scotland'. I then agreed that we Conservatives as 'the natural party of devolution and the diffusion of power away from the centre' should continue to seek ways of improving the government of Scotland, urging the Government to set up a Select Committee on Scottish Affairs – something that happened soon afterwards. I concluded: 'I stress that the clearing away of the debris of the Scotland Act 1978 is not an end of the matter but is an essential prerequisite to seeking a real lasting improvement in the quality and nature of Scotland's government, within the framework of a strengthened and reinvigorated United Kingdom ... Our task now is to ensure that that United Kingdom goes forward economically, socially and constitutionally as one nation.'

Devolution as an issue went quiet again for several years after the 1979 watershed. Labour had other problems to address and the nationalists' threat appeared to be receding. More significantly, it was clear that there was no strong or sustainable support for devolution within Scotland. Certainly, if asked whether they would like a closer involvement in their own government, some 70 per cent tended to answer in the affirmative – just as they would have done if asked if they favoured sunshine, or prosperity. But as a political issue, devolution was only regarded as important by a small minority – at one stage, in 1987, only 2 per cent. Other matters such as jobs, inflation, health or education took precedence in every opinion poll, with devolution rated well below them. That was to remain the position, despite Labour's sporadic attempts to fan the flames, for most of the next decade.

When they planned a great Festival for Democracy for an anticipated 50,000 people on Glasgow Green in the late 1980s, only 5,000 people turned up. It was the rebellions over the payment of the poll tax that were to reignite devolution on the political agenda.

I never believed that many Labour MPs, few of whom later stood for election to the new Parliament in Edinburgh, were sincere believers in devolution. Certainly, few of them ever bothered to carry the debate further than the mere mouthing of slogans. For most, it was at first an easy vehicle by which to engender a sense of grievance in their fellow Scots and a facile response to their fears of nationalism. Over time, so often had they mouthed their slogans, many of them did develop an almost irreversible commitment to the concept, but in all the years of debate the real arguments were rarely addressed.

The main exception to this was Donald Dewar. I think he was a true believer and an unwavering one. But even he, despite his fertile mind and his eloquent debating skills, preferred to circumvent the arguments against devolution rather than answer them. To him devolution seemed to be an end in itself, with little thought as to what it would actually achieve once in place.

He should have known better than to echo his colleagues' whines about Scotland's democratic deficit and the lack of accountability of the Government in Scotland. In reality Scotland had a democratic surplus, whether measured by the number of its MPs, the various vehicles in Parliament by which they could debate and legislate, both on Scottish and British issues, or the British resources devoted to Scotland. Scottish Office ministers could also be held to account in more ways than their English counterparts. The truth was that Labour, happy to rule England from time to time with a parliamentary majority derived from Scotland and Wales, did not like it when the situation was reversed.

As the 1980s advanced, the opposition parties decided to try to bid up the stakes. They changed the name of their proposed Assembly to that of a Parliament and they decided to give it tax-raising powers. In this, I think they overplayed their hand. A National Assembly, distinct from Parliament, could have had a natural status and dignity. Calling it a Parliament, however, underlined the ambiguity of its relationship with Westminster and the potential for conflict between two bodies, each implicitly claiming sovereign powers, with the devolved body being ultimately inferior. There was more than a grain of truth in the description of it by the Scottish comedian Billy Connolly as 'a wee pretendy parliament'.

At that stage, Malcolm Rifkind, his special adviser Graeme Carter and I had a discussion about how to react. We discussed the idea of campaigning against the tax proposals, describing them as the 'tartan tax' and the 'Taffy tax'. In the event of course, Labour decided against tax-raising powers for its Welsh Assembly, and we did not pursue the tartan tax idea, partly because we feared it could sound a little patronising with its 'Brigadoon' connotations and thus be counterproductive, and partly because John Smith's broader tax-raising plans for the whole country provided a meatier target. I kept the idea in mind, however, and some years later decided that I would campaign on the 'tartan tax' in the (anticipated) 1996 general election. In early 1995, I field-tested the idea in one or two speeches and in a live televised debate in Aberdeen, where it went down well. However, I thought it important to get the timing of a full-blooded campaign right, which meant keeping it until the run-in to an election, so that Labour would find it difficult to modify its plans. In the event, I was promoted to the Department of Trade and Industry in July 1995 and Michael Forsyth, who succeeded me, made effective use of the 'tartan tax' label against an Opposition that did indeed become rattled by it and was clearly seen not to have thought through the implications of its own policy.

Another attempt by our opponents to give life to devolution came in the form of the self-styled 'Constitutional Convention'. This pretentious posturing, based on the claim that sovereignty rested with the Scottish people rather than the Crown in Parliament, involved some of Scotland's opposition MPs, plus a few hangers-on, strutting through Edinburgh to hold meetings from time to time at which they drafted a document entitled *The Claim of Right for Scotland* – as though Scotland were some kind of subject nation, denied its basic human rights. The *Scotsman* loved it all, but the rest of Scotland ignored it. I thought it demeaning and dishonest. Apart from its constitutional bombast, it was permeated with socialism, calling as it did for economic planning powers, power to initiate public ownership or control of and responsibility for the protection of Scottish industry. In other words: interventionism at home and protectionism from the world outside. However, over time it did come to form part of that congealing consensus that presaged constitutional change and eventually formed part of the foundation of such change. Indeed, it was just as well that it did do some of the basic planning for devolution, given the speed with which the Labour Government of 1997 were to rush through their proposals in Parliament.

As the 1992 election approached – it had to be held by the spring of that year – I began to consider how, as Secretary of State by then, I would run our campaign in Scotland. Since succeeding Malcolm Rifkind in November 1990, I had been reviewing our policies across the spectrum. In some areas I had planned or implemented new initiatives. I chewed over devolution for many weeks. Whilst I felt unable to concede on the central issue of a separate Parliament, which I was utterly convinced could only be to Scotland's long-term detriment, I did feel the need to be constructive rather than wholly negative. Constitutions should evolve, as ours had done in the past. Federalism could work, even though England was so dominant, and it would lack the instability and potential for conflict of what our opponents were demanding. But there was no mood in England to contemplate it.

On 7 November 1991 we were holding the by-election in Kincardine & Deeside, following the recent death of Alick Buchanan-Smith, an utterly dedicated constituency MP and one of the few Conservative pro-devolutionists. After Cabinet the previous day, in the near certain knowledge that one of our ten Conservative seats was about to be lost, given the party's great unpopularity in Scotland as throughout the UK, John Major had suddenly asked four of us – James Mackay, Douglas Hurd, Malcolm Rifkind and myself – to stay behind for a few minutes. He wanted to discuss Scotland.

There were, he thought, three possible Scottish outcomes to the impending general election: one, we would lose power overall, in which case Scotland's future would be for Labour to determine; two, we would win well, both in England and Scotland, in which case we could if we wanted continue as before; three, we would retain power on the basis of English seats, but be further reduced or even wiped out in Scotland (as the opinion polls predicted), in which case something would have to change in Scotland. So there was a two-to-one probability of constitutional change after the election and it seemed sensible to consider our position ahead of that.

He particularly wanted our views on what we should do in the third eventuality. It was not the moment to point out to him that there could be a fourth outcome: that we would do well in Scotland but not in England. I said instead that I had been pondering this throughout the autumn and had just about concluded that at this stage there were no credible options for change open to us. If devolution had to happen, as sooner or later it probably did, it could not credibly come from us: better to stand on principle and conviction and, if necessary, lose. The others agreed broadly, but we all felt that there were things we could do to try to improve our image in Scotland over devolution. The Prime Minister then asked James, Malcolm and myself to form a small *ad hoc* committee to consider the matter further and report back to him on what proposals, if any, we should contemplate for our manifesto.

I was about to head off for Japan again on an inward investment mission, but we did not need to deliberate for long. Malcolm immediately favoured a commitment to hold a referendum after the election. I was not wildly enthusiastic about that idea. It would undermine our stand of principle and make the general election a referendum on devolution; and I did not see how I could subsequently remain in office to implement devolution if still Secretary of State at that time. I did not anyway, in a parliamentary democracy such as ours, favour the use of referenda as a way out of tricky situations. But, *faute de mieux*, I agreed that if the Prime Minister was insisting on a new policy option, this was one to consider and we jointly minuted him to suggest it. As it turned out, Margaret Thatcher unwittingly put paid to this proposal when, as I saw on the BBC television news in my bedroom at the Tokyo Embassy, she stood up in Parliament to call for a referendum on the Single Currency. The Prime Minister rebuffed her, though he was later to change his mind, and in so doing put all referenda in baulk.

I now knew exactly what I wanted to do and was free to get on with it. I understood too, that feeling of calm certainty after the agonies of indecision that so many others have described in the past, in wrestling with great issues of principle. I would reverse the policy of recent years, of playing down or ignoring the devolution debate in the hope that it would go away – as it had done for long periods. I would challenge the devolutionists head-on. Not only that, I resolved to make devolution the centrepiece of my election campaign. Although our record was good on health, education and the economy, we would gain no ground on such issues. I would rise above all that. I at once got down to making detailed plans with my indefatigable special adviser, Alan Young.

Labour's dominance in Scotland and our minority status had been exaggerated over the years by the vicissitudes of the first-past-the-post system in a country with Scotland's demographic extremes. For example, in the 1983 general election, although Labour had won almost twice as many Scottish seats as we did, we had still gained four votes for every five Labour ones. Our support was spread across the country, however, and had to contend with pockets of liberalism and nationalism in the remoter areas as well as concentrated Labour support in the central belt. The 1987 collapse in our support gave Labour almost twice as many votes as us – and five times as many seats. But it was the seats that mattered and there was no disguising the fact that we were now in dire straits.

The Scottish Conservatives' morale was in poor shape at the end of 1991: low in the polls, defeated in the by-election and wondering anxiously what the general election would bring. It was hardly surprising. The loss of the Kincardine & Deeside by-election had reduced our Scottish parliamentary seats to nine: single figures. We were now the third political party in Scotland, in seats if not in votes, behind the Liberals. Wipe out was widely predicted by opinion polls and pundits, and the whole question of our legitimacy to govern Scotland, so sedulously nurtured since the 1987 débâcle, first by Malcolm Rifkind and then by myself, had been reopened.

Devolution had hardly featured as an issue during the by-election – indeed, the north-east had always been robustly sceptical of it. The setting up of a health trust to run Aberdeen's hospitals was the big issue. But it was there, underlying everything as our defeat (which was in line with other by-election defeats throughout the UK) cast its shadow across our standing in Scotland. Devolution was poisoning the well. It had to be tackled. I knew that the vast majority of our party supporters shared my opposition to it, as did my two most stalwart junior ministers, Michael Forsyth and Allan Stewart. I also knew that my strategy on the subject, which would be ridiculed as suicidal by our opponents, was not without a certain low cunning. In most opinion polls, around a quarter of those questioned opposed devolution: more than the 19 per cent then planning to vote Conservative. So there was a constituency out there that needed to be represented. In two speeches, to Hillhead Conservatives and in West Renfrewshire, I nailed my colours to the mast. The robustly pro-Union message was very well received and I began to sense we were on the right track. We had to seize the initiative in this way in order to maintain our authority.

The last thing my opponents expected was that I would seek to raise the profile of devolution at this time. As it dawned on him that this was what I did want, the Shadow Secretary of State Donald Dewar greeted the development with a mixture of mockery and salivating disbelief. The Glasgow *Herald* accused me of writing 'what looks like a political suicide note'. I at once publicly challenged the opposition parties to agree that we hold four debates in the Scottish Grand Committee over the ensuing weeks on four different aspects of devolution. After some clearing of throats this was agreed, though I was amused at the moderation of Labour's enthusiasm to debate the matters on which they claimed such dominance. One or two of the debates were to be broadcast live by BBC Radio Scotland; and we held one of them, of double the normal length, in Edinburgh, to underline the flexibility of the Westminster Parliament to handle Scottish business in a way accessible to Scots.

Magnus Linklater, the editor of the *Scotsman*, had been trying to fire up the public's interest by seeking to hold a Great Debate on Devolution in Edinburgh. He needed all four party leaders' agreement, so the odds would be the usual three to one against me. I had held out against accepting his invitation, which was preventing it from happening, but as we walked together into the Patrons' Dinner at the National Gallery of Scotland in late November, I told him I would do it. He was surprised but delighted. So was I, because it fitted perfectly with my plans. As I had expected, the Scottish media decided this debate was a perfect curtain-raiser for the now imminent election. Kirsty Wark was to chair the proceedings, now to take place in the Usher Hall, the largest available venue. It was to be broadcast live and saturation coverage was guaranteed, not only in the *Scotsman* but in the rest of the press as well.

Participating was, of course, an ordeal. The announcement of the closure of Ravenscraig was less than two weeks old. The odds of three to one against were replicated in the allocation of tickets to the audience; and of course Conservatives tend to be quieter and politer than supporters of Labour or the SNP, especially when the latter are stirred up by thier populist leader Alex Salmond. In the run-up to the debate I asked Alan Young what I should say. 'Say you've got 'flu', was his helpful reply. I noticed that Donald Dewar found the proceedings uncomfortable too, even facing a slow handclap at one stage. For the man who could talk in torrents in the Chamber or committee rooms of the House of Commons, a television studio or a public platform brought out the habitual 'ers' and 'ums' in his answers to questions and he clearly shared my distaste for Salmond's thuggish tendency. After all, to the SNP Labour's heartland was the real target. We Tories were already beyond the pale.

A lively audience of 2,500 was crammed into the hall. Sweltering under the television lights, they booed, heckled, cheered and jeered almost every statement throughout the two and a half hours of debate. Often drowned out in the hall, I concentrated on the much larger outside audience listening to the broadcast and tried to put my case across to them in terms as calm and lucid as I could manage. I pointed to the organic nature of our constitution and my willingness to contemplate continuing change, but not in a way that would put our place within the United Kingdom at risk. Breaching that integrity, as a devolved parliament would do, put at risk not just our rights and representation at Westminster and our financial security, but could also lead on, through disputes with Westminster, 'against a background of rancour and disunity, into the abyss of complete separation.' I urged the audience not to take that risk. Alex Salmond described Labour's proposals as a 'Plasticine parliament' and between us he and I gradually polarised the debate, leaving Dewar and the Liberals' Malcolm Bruce having to face both ways. Rows between Labour and the SNP were just what I wanted; they were to continue until polling-day and beyond.

Press coverage during the following days was extensive, the consensus being that Alex Salmond had been the winner of the evening, that I had been beleaguered and humiliated and that Donald Dewar had been given an equally uncomfortable time. Tactically, I was content with that appraisal, which raised the constitutional stakes. But three years later in a valedictory article in the *Scotsman*, our erstwhile sponsor Magnus Linklater, describing the Great Debate as 'one of the most electrifying political events I have ever attended', wryly concluded that, 'In retrospect, though many would have said that it was Alex Salmond's evening ... the winner was probably the dogged and stalwart Ian Lang, whose solid defence of the Union perhaps struck more of a chord than many of us realised.'

By now the whole issue of Scotland's constitutional future had really taken off. Andrew Marr, in his thoughtful book *The Battle for Scotland*, describes how 'London-based journalists found their pulses racing at the rare spectacle of a lively and crowded hustings'. I knew I was riding a tiger, but my own party had been uplifted by it and were now raring to get their teeth into the election campaign. At No. 10, a few days after the Great Debate, the Prime Minister and senior colleagues endorsed the line I was taking, though there was a flavour of Rorke's Drift about it all. This was not the time for grand schemes and new departures, though. I was trying to win a general election. A meeting with our prospective candidates revealed unanimous support and only a tiny handful elsewhere in the party resisted my stance – and were lionised by our opponents in other parties and the press. The media, sensing a dramatic dénouement, set up televised studio debates and interviews and I found myself addressing audiences in such countries as Canada, Germany and New Zealand as well as those at home. By the beginning of March, opinion polls were beginning to move on the issue, showing an 8 per cent rise in support for the status quo compared with two months earlier.

In one televised discussion, again with Kirsty Wark, I put the Shadow Health Secretary Robin Cook on the spot by flourishing a quotation of his from years earlier when he had been an opponent of devolution. This led him to announce that if a Scottish Parliament handling health matters were established in Edinburgh, he could no longer hold office as the Minister for Health in a Westminster government. This restatement in a new form of Tam Dalyell's West Lothian Question helped to carry the debate to the rest of the United Kingdom. I immediately wrote an open letter to Neil Kinnock, himself a known opponent of devolution, asking if this doctrine applied to all the Scots in his Shadow Cabinet. The Prime Minister and other colleagues took up the charge and started to put other Labour shadow ministers on the spot.

In fact, the West Lothian Question has never been answered. It has been ignored, perhaps in the hope that time and custom will erode its significance. The test will come, though, when a government of the United Kingdom with a small parliamentary majority is forced to rely on the votes of its Scottish MPs in order to pass laws affecting only England and Wales.

Magnus Linklater helped me unwittingly a second time when, soon after the Great Debate, he published the results of an opinion poll jointly commissioned by the *Scotsman* and ITN News, which could, with a bit of spin, be finessed to show that half the population of Scotland supported independence. Both he and ITN duly drew this conclusion. The SNP, with their slogan 'Scotland Free by '93', were suitably euphoric and my campaign was correspondingly galvanised. Opinion polls also showed the Scottish business community to be robustly supportive of our stance and I sent out 50,000 letters to businesses throughout the length of Scotland to bolster that support. I asked them to speak out but few did, with the distinguished exceptions of Viscount Weir and Sir Alick Rankin, until the election was over.

John Major's growing commitment to a firm stand on devolution was another advantage for our Scottish campaign. He had already taken a close interest in Scotland. I briefed him regularly on Scottish issues and at the outset of his premiership I had asked him to try to change the tone of prime ministerial visits to Scotland from that akin to an official foreign visit to something more routine and informal; and to include Scotland more in United Kingdom events. He responded handsomely. The Service of Thanksgiving for victory in the Gulf War was held in Glasgow Cathedral and the 1992 European Heads of Government meeting was fixed for Edinburgh; and he established a good personal rapport with the people of Scotland on many and varied visits. When, during his first visit to a Scottish Conservative Party Conference as Prime Minister, he announced his decision about the Heads of Government meeting, he received a standing ovation in the middle of his speech.

I had laid plans to keep the devolution profile high right up to polling day, and to that end one of my proposals was to ask him to come up to Scotland before he called the general election to address a meeting not, as party leaders usually do, on the whole range of political issues of the day, but solely on Scotland, the constitution and the threats posed by devolution. He readily agreed and the tactic worked. His speech was a storming success with the party, whilst extensive media coverage carried the arguments to a wider audience. 'I believe with passion and conviction', he said, 'this party should stand for unity – not division. We are a Unionist Party. We should fight for the Union ... Not because it's always been good for us, but because it's always seemed right to us.' But he added two further points that I had also been emphasising in speeches, trying to change the nature of the debate: 'No nation can be held irrevocably in a union against its will. We can do it. We can break up the United Kingdom', and 'But that is not a choice that will affect Scotland alone. A solitary Scotland means a solitary England, alongside Wales and Northern Ireland ... In place of Great Britain, a little Scotland and a lesser Union.' These comments underlined both the responsibility voters must accept in voting for change and the potentially stark consequences of such change; and they broadened the debate to stress that there could be implications for the rest of the nation too.

One of the interviews we had set up for him during his visit was with that doyen of Scottish interviewers, the late and now much missed Kenny McIntyre. Kenny's skill and energy in seeking and securing the interview that made news was legendary. He was scrupulously honest and impartial, and over the years he and I used to have regular, off-the-record informal chats over a Scottish Office sandwich lunch, from which we both benefited. As I drove into Glasgow with the Prime Minister on the morning of the speech I warned him that one of the questions he would probably be asked was what he would do about Scotland and devolution if, improbably, the Conservatives won the forthcoming election. I told him that in a similar interview with the BBC's James Naughtie a few days earlier I had simply said that we would take stock. I suggested he should say the same.

He agreed and said so when the question duly came up. So now we had two major strands of our campaign in place: firm opposition, on points of principle, to the establishment of a devolved parliament, but a willingness to take a broad, positive look at how aspirations for better Scottish government could be addressed without putting the Union in peril. We could no longer be portrayed as stubbornly blocking change of any kind. What form that change might take remained a moot point. My own view was that, if the worst befell, a Committee of Inquiry into Scotland's constitutional relationship with England might be the next step, rather than a protracted Royal Commission, though I was careful not to rule out the possibility of a referendum.

My next initiative was to publish a Scottish Public Expenditure Paper, which would set out in authoritative detail the revenue raised and the revenue spent in Scotland by central government. This, I felt, would undermine the casual and wildly inaccurate claims being made by the SNP – and by many irresponsible Labour MPs, who so fecklessly sang to the separatist tune – that Scotland wasn't getting a fair share of the UK cake, or was even subsidising England. I had timed this to be published just after the Prime Minister's speech, and officials in the Scottish Office and the Treasury worked hard to produce the necessary figures. Unfortunately the Chancellor Norman Lamont put a spoke in the wheel by objecting to the publication of such information by my department. He feared it would create resentment and demands for higher expenditure in other parts of the country. This was rather to miss the point, and I was able to persuade the Prime Minister to overrule him, but my timing had been upset by the delay and we were not able to make as much of the figures as we had planned.

During the subsequent election campaign, somebody in one department or the other leaked the correspondence I had had with the Prime Minister and Chancellor about this, and our opponents sought to make hay over it, showing me as a supplicant and the Treasury as secretive. Of course, it rebounded against them. I was able to deploy the figures again to good effect, as well as showing that I had won an argument with the Chancellor.

What the details that our departmental officials had gathered together actually showed was that Scotland, with 8.9 per cent of the United

Kingdom's population, contributed just over 8 per cent of tax revenues and received 10 per cent of identifiable expenditure. Government spending per head in Scotland was 24 per cent higher than in England, making Scotland a net beneficiary from the United Kingdom to the tune of perhaps £3 billion. The contribution to the Exchequer of the whole of the North Sea at this time was only around £1.2 billion, so it could not provide the salvation the SNP claimed for it even if it were all to come to Scotland. Naturally there were qualifications to the calculations: some spending, such as that of the Foreign Office and the Ministry of Defence, could not easily be disaggregated on country-by-country lines; and social security payments seemed to pose problems of identification. Also, the apportionment of corporate taxation of the profits of English or foreign companies with Scottish branches created problems. But even after making allowances for all this, the picture that emerged was compelling and I believe it had a significant impact on the campaign.

Having pushed devolution high up the list of topical issues in Scotland, I now sought to keep it there as we moved seamlessly into the election campaign itself. Leaving my ministerial team of Michael Forsyth, Allan Stewart, James Douglas-Hamilton and Lord Strathclyde to make what running they could on the issues for which they had detailed responsibility, I concentrated almost exclusively on the constitution. A Secretary of State for Scotland used to have the same saturation coverage in the Scottish media as a Prime Minister has on the broader United Kingdom stage, so I had a distinct advantage. Labour's election manifesto, when it came, raised the stakes by its clearly nationalistic tone. In a clear lurch from devolution towards separation, it spoke of a Scottish parliament whose powers it would be 'unacceptable to alter ... without the consent of that parliament.' The Campaign for a Scottish Assembly spoke of civil disobedience if we won the election.

The next milestone was the Prime Minister's election visit to Scotland. During the day we took him to some marginal constituencies. I vividly remember the town centre of Cupar, in Fife, being brought to a stand-still by the huge crowds who came to cheer him there. The election had truly come alive and John Major's immense skill at establishing a rapport with an open-air crowd – he was soon to revive his soap-box stump that became such a feature of the campaign – showed again why the opinion polls always rated his popularity well above that of his party. Indeed, soon after he had become leader, he had had the highest opinion poll rating of any leader in the history of the party.

In the late afternoon we arrived at Bute House in Edinburgh and settled down to work on the vital speech he was to make at a rally that evening. The scene in the drawing room as the Prime Minister, Norman Fowler (then acting as his special adviser) and I crawled around the floor amongst some thirty sheets of foolscap, scattered across the carpet, had an element of farce about it. But unfortunately John, a stickler for perfec-tion, laboured too long on refinements, and as a result the speech was late in being released to the media. Consequently it received less national coverage than it deserved. But what really mattered was that he had now become fully engaged in the constitutional issue and saw its potential impact on the wider national campaign. I had already urged all senior government colleagues to talk about devolution during the campaign and Douglas Hurd had made some distinguished contributions on the subject. But when the Prime Minister decided that day that he would speak up in England on devolution and call on Britain to wake up to the threats it posed, our campaign in Scotland gained another great boost.

Throughout the campaign and during the difficult months before it, I was greatly helped by the strength of the support I had from the Chairman of the party in Scotland, Lord Sanderson of Bowden. Russell Sanderson had willingly stepped aside in 1990 from his burgeoning government career as Minister of State at the Scottish Office when Margaret Thatcher asked him to take over as Chairman, to restore a party that had become fractious and unsettled. Calmly and steadily, Russell rebuilt order at the centre and morale amongst the constituency associa-tions. I could not have had more staunch or wise support than he gave me. We had already become good friends as fellow ministers of state, and I felt a bond of complete trust in him when I became Secretary of State. That enabled us to share freely our anxieties and discuss all our plans together. He stayed calm as the opinion polls stayed gloomy: in my own constituency massive defeat was predicted for me, by a margin of 7 per cent. 'It's no Lang noo', claimed the SNP posters.

In addition, our Scottish Conservative Central Office team was led by the redoubtable James Goodsman, whose authoritative efficiency delivered a good fighting machine. Russell and James commissioned excellent publicity material on the devolution theme. Our final election broadcast featured a drystone dyker building a wall in the hills of the Scottish Borders. As he laboured away, the camera panned slowly back to reveal that, far from being built straight and strong to keep people out, the wall was built in a circle and the dyker had trapped himself inside it. With a telling 'voice-over' commentary, it delivered a powerful message. Our final poster featured the injunction to 'Vote Conservative', with the 'X' voting symbol provided by a billowing Saltire, Scotland's flag – that same Saltire that I had accused the separatists of wanting to tear out of the Union Flag. We were determined to show ourselves as proud Scots, who far from being defensive over Scotland's place in the United Kingdom had the self-confidence to take pride in both our nation and our nation state. The images projected were effective in the mood of the times.

As the campaign drew to a close, I was sure we were winning despite the gloom of the polls and the derision of the media, who saw only wipeout – and, of course, wanted it: devolution would create a whole new media circus for them in Edinburgh. After a rally speech in support of Phil Gallie, our candidate in Ayr, one member of the press had asked me mockingly how it felt to have made my last major speech as an MP and

Cabinet Minister. (It is, incidentally, ironic that since the Scottish Parliament has come into being, circulation of the Scottish broadsheets has fallen sharply.)

When the Prime Minister rang me a week before polling day, he too felt that we were going to win. Michael Heseltine came to my constituency three days before the vote. He was convinced that the polls were wrong: they were lagging by several days and had missed a firming up of our vote. In my final speech of the campaign I called for a ringing vote of confidence in the Union and the rejection of 'the downward path of devolution – separation by stealth'.

I arrived at my count on 9 April in a mood of exhausted calm. I had done my best and I still believed my strategy had been right. I had my elder daughter Venetia with me for moral support, as my wife had been unwell for some time with ME and had to harbour her energy. The press were assembled for the kill. The count began badly as the ballot boxes from our weakest areas were opened first. Then a strange, quiet bewilderment crossed the faces of my SNP opponents. They could see their own votes piling up ahead of mine – and my agent, Ian Mackie, had given me the blunt message: 'We're leathered.' Yet, whilst the news from England was unpromising, with many seats falling, from around Scotland came through the magical news, not of wipeout but of seats being held and even seats being won – something that was happening nowhere else throughout the United Kingdom. For a while it looked as though I was about to fall in battle at the very moment of victory, but at the last minute my own vote surged and it was clear that I too would be part of it.

Numerically, the election outcome in Scotland was only a gain of two seats, from nine to eleven, but we Conservatives had gained 6 per cent in support since the polls of the previous autumn and 2 per cent since the 1987 election, compared with a swing against the party of 2 per cent in England and Wales. The SNP won only 3 seats. Our critics and opponents were dumbfounded; our success seemed all the greater as their built-up expectations rebounded on them. Had we been wiped out, as the official script had decreed, John Major would have been barely able to form a government. There were probably other factors that influenced it besides the constitutional debate: John Major was more acceptable to Scots than Margaret Thatcher and Scotland's economy had strengthened considerably (though that could also lead to the confidence to vote for change). My own view is that devolution was the added ingredient in Scotland which contributed most to a result that diverged so markedly, and so much against the long-term trend, from that in the rest of the country. It certainly felt like a triumph of the kind that every politician should have a chance to savour once in his career, so long as he does not forget that other great impostor waiting in the wings.

'Congratulations,' said Alan Young as we left the count. 'You've saved the Union.'

'Yes,' I replied, 'until the next time.'

NINE

Breaking the Back of Britain

Scotland's status within the United Kingdom must change.

The Times, *20 January 1992*

Constitutional reform is a favourite bête noire *of the English pragmatist. 'For forms of government let fools contest,' wrote Pope. 'Whate'er is best administered is best.'*

Pope was right. The only changes to the constitution that count are those that improve the quality of government. What is needed in 1993 is not a utopian blueprint but a clear acknowledgment that these questions about the state and its institutions are no longer the refuge of the defeated or the opportunistic.

The Times, *1 January 1993*

When the Queen opened the first session of the new Scottish Parliament in July 1999 one of many hyperbolic claims that were made by its progenitors was that Scotland's

Parliament, suspended in 1707, had been restored to it. Thus were the deprivation, the exploitation and the oppression of three centuries at one fell swoop in the deep bosom of the ocean buried. Nationhood, self-respect and democracy were restored and all would be well again. This pretentious nonsense was fraudulent on several levels.

Firstly, the Parliaments of both England and Scotland were abolished in 1707, both of them having voted for the Act of Union; and a new Parliament of Great Britain was established.

Secondly, Scotland's place in that Parliament was – and remains – disproportionately large, with special protection given to her traditions, her institutions, her law and her Church.

Thirdly, by almost any yardstick of measurement, Scotland has benefited enormously from – and contributed greatly to – the United Kingdom. The eighteenth century saw Scotland flourish and prosper as never before; and at the time the new Scottish Parliament was established in 1999, Scottish living standards were higher than ever, both in absolute terms and in relation to the rest of the United Kingdom – and Scottish politicians were more dominant than ever before in the United Kingdom's government.

Fourthly, in exchange for the perception of greater control over her own affairs created by her new Parliament, Scotland will pay a price over the longer term for the consequent reduction in her representation and power at Westminster. The present high preponderance of Scots in important positions in the United Kingdom's government cannot long be sustained. Today's is the last generation. No more can the too-high number of Scottish MPs at Westminster be justified. Both these points, denied vehemently before devolution, are now generally accepted. Already Scotland's backbench MPs at Westminster look detached and unsure of themselves, as they sink to second-class status, with not enough to do.

But the most fraudulent of the pretences made for the new Parliament in Edinburgh is that it is a revival of the old, sovereign body that voted for the Union of 1707 and thus its own abolition. Though that may follow, it has not happened yet. The new Parliament is a devolved body of the Westminster Parliament, whose powers to make laws for Scotland remain intact. Its powers are not sovereign, but delegated and limited. It has the power to spend money without the responsibility of raising it. True, it has very limited taxation powers, but if used, these could be nullified by the UK Treasury. Thus has the Scotland Act conceded the principle of taxation powers without allowing the substance, creating a supplicant and dependent Parliament – a sure recipe for the politics of grievance and the fostering of a dependency culture.

The First Minister and his twenty-one ministers, performing some but not all of the tasks once performed by a Secretary of State and four junior ministers, is not even a big fish in a small pond; he is a smaller fish in a small pond. Thus is his power to achieve diminished, something that is readily apparent, even when he is of the same political complexion as the government at Westminster. Within the United Kingdom, Scotland has been sidelined; and though Scottish politicians prefer to ignore the fact, the United Kingdom does still matter to Scotland.

Against that background, Tony Blair's hand-written legend on the late Donald Dewar's copy of the Scotland Act – 'Scotland and England together on equal terms' – is almost as bizarre as his earlier comparison of the Scottish Parliament with an English parish council. He has never seemed sure-footed on constitutional issues, and his body language has always revealed his unease. The casual and partisan manner in which his government has imposed a series of unrelated but fundamental changes to the British constitution underlines the need for new arrangements in this field to guard against the further erosion of our constitutional base. Constitutional change, once enacted, is hard to reverse.

Former Secretaries of State were often asked, as though it were a clever, trick question: 'Are you Scotland's man in the Cabinet or the Cabinet's man in Scotland'? The answer wanted was the former, though in fact the only sensible answer was 'Both.' But the new First Minister is neither;

and that is a measure of his diminution. He is simply Scotland's man in Scotland. As Secretary of State I always fought Scotland's battles hard when the cause was a just one and sometimes succeeded. But I was also a unionist. I saw myself as a team player and I recognised that what mattered in the end was the unity and cohesion of the government as a whole, without which public support would be forfeit.

Now the dynamic has changed irretrievably. No longer has the First Minister of Scotland power to influence British Cabinet decisions on foreign policy, defence or the major fiscal and economic issues of the day. The last vestiges of that power still reside with the dwindling post of Secretary of State for Scotland – a Cabinet minister who no longer has a country to run or a department to run it. It is well known that Cabinet ministers without departments are ignored in Cabinet, unless they are the Prime Minister. Indeed the post, like *Alice in Wonderland*'s Cheshire Cat, will soon disappear altogether. Even now there is not much left but the grin.

Apart from saying 'No' when the Scottish Parliament seeks to encroach on Westminster's reserved powers, there is little else for him or her to do. No longer can the Secretary of State credibly fulfil the important role of arguing Scotland's funding case in Cabinet, because Scotland's needs and priorities are now a matter for the Edinburgh government. Nor can Scotland's First Minister make the case, for he is not in the British government. Substance has been traded for semblance.

Every past Secretary of State for Scotland, probably without exception, successfully secured extra spending for Scotland from time to time and successfully defended the distribution formula that governed Scotland's share of the UK cake from the regular attacks that English colleagues mounted against it. I only had to threaten resignation once, in 1994, to stop an attempted bully-boy raid on the Scottish block, overriding the Barnett formula. This is the well established formula that controls the annual changes to government spending levels in Scotland (and Wales) by reference to such changes in England. In fact if, instead of such banditry, they had asked me to agree to an impartial reassessment of Scotland's relative needs, I would have felt obliged to agree to it and to abide by its outcome. But that would have taken a year to carry out and the Treasury always lived for today. The point is, however, that the dynamics of the system enabled me, as a Cabinet minister with a territorial department, like my predecessors, to keep the Treasury at bay.

In fact, it was not the arithmetic but the principle and the politics that dictated such a stance. The real scope for protecting Scottish interests lay in the side deals and the special *ad hoc* negotiations that stood outside the corral of the 'block and formula'. I calculated after two years as Secretary of State that the Barnett formula had reduced the Scottish Office budget by £17 million, whilst separate deals with the Treasury had increased it by £340 million. The very existence of the Barnett formula, far from inhibiting me, enabled me to concentrate on special deals to augment our resources.

It is extraordinary how much wrong-headed nonsense has been spoken and written about the Barnett formula over the years and continues to this day. What protects the Scottish budget is not the formula, which applies only to annual increases, but the underlying level of the Scottish spending block, which is much higher than in England. The Barnett formula was introduced in 1978, unannounced at the time, not to protect Scottish spending in relation to English levels but to reduce it. After all, Joel Barnett, its eponymous begetter, was Chief Secretary to the Treasury, not Scotland's fairy godmother. Though it had never been admitted until recently, his formula, negotiated with the then Scottish Secretary Bruce Millan, must have been designed specifically to bring about the gradual convergence of *per capita* spending in the two countries. Certainly that is its inescapable effect, which Treasury officials must have realised; and that is what, slowly but surely, it has been achieving.

The formula makes no attempt to define need. Based on the conclusion that Scotland was clearly overfunded when it was negotiated in 1978, it set out to bring spending there gradually into line. In those fraught times, as since, the Treasury preferred what seemed a quick fix to a fundamental appraisal. Gradualism is, though, the key to Barnett: it operates slowly and at the margin, and its impact reduces as convergence gets nearer. It also provides stability and avoids more protracted and regular haggling between Scotland and the Treasury. Of course, as it bites deeper, the Barnett formula may not remain a force for stability, but become instead the focus of bitter dispute.

The concept of using population shares as a means of dividing expenditure between the different countries of the United Kingdom had originally been devised by George Goschen, the then Chancellor of the Exchequer, in the 1880s. His was a simple formula to distribute the same increase per head in annual expenditure in both countries, for certain comparable programmes. Over the years, however, as government spending became more extensive, Scotland's special problems were recognised and the Scottish Secretary of the day sought and won additional funding to deal with them. Thus, the Scottish spending block swelled, so that the same percentage figure for the annual British increase came to produce differing results between the two countries. For example, if existing spending levels stood at £100 per head in England and £125 per head in Scotland, a 5 per cent increase would deliver an extra £5 per head in England and £6.25 per head in Scotland.

Barnett's formula remains population-based – and when the 1991 census revealed a falling Scottish population and a rising English one I readily volunteered to Michael Portillo, then Chief Secretary to the Treasury, that the formula should be adjusted accordingly, thus incidentally heading off any further assault on my budget for that year and also getting a Treasury minister to put on record for the first time in many a year that Scotland's spending needs per head were appreciably higher than England's, and that the Barnett formula would not be allowed to reduce Scotland's share of spending below a level justified by need.

The Barnett formula had changed things by expressing the annual increase in Scotland from 1978 onwards not as a percentage figure to be applied to existing spending levels there but as a cash figure, equal to whatever cash the English percentage increase *per capita* had delivered. So, in the example quoted above, a 5 per cent increase per head in England would raise spending there by £5 per head; and a consequent £5 per head increase to the Scottish block would deliver an increase there of only 4 per cent. That may not seem much of a variation, but if inflation at the time were 3 per cent, the increased purchasing power thus achieved would be 2 per cent in England and only 1 per cent in Scotland.

Inexorably but gradually, convergence of spending levels between the two countries is being achieved – faster at present, ironically, with the Chancellor's large public expenditure increases – without the pain that a direct assault on the Scottish block would inflict. I spent long hours as Secretary of State explaining this to individual members of the media and to the opposition parties. I was always met with deaf and blind disbelief. I think they know now.

The accumulated mass of the Scottish 'block', which forms the spending base to which each year's increases are added, remains essentially intact under Barnett. The formula affects only the annual increase, not the underlying base, and ensures only that public spending will increase at a lower rate in Scotland than in England. It has been less effective than was expected in achieving that modest objective for a number of reasons. Firstly, before devolution Scotland regularly secured additional spending deals outside the scope of the formula, which were then absorbed into the 'block' baseline for subsequent years. Secondly, Scotland's population has fallen relative to England's in every year since the formula was introduced, but the formula has not been regularly adjusted to take account of that. Then there have been those increases in spending to which the formula does not automatically apply, such as special calls on the reserve, or adjustments made in mid-year rather than at the annual spending review.

Now such factors will increasingly cease to operate. Annual population changes are being factored in, with Scotland's population expected to fall further over the next few years; and the devolution settlement has tidied up those loose ends of Scottish public expenditure that used to enable Scottish Secretaries of State to exploit them to Scotland's advantage.

This means that the Barnett formula will now work more efficiently, to Scotland's detriment. Scots can hardly complain, however. The spending gap is still in Scotland's favour by around 20 per cent, which is substantially more even than the 16 per cent advantage identified as being needed in the 1970s to cater for her greater poverty, unemployment, housing needs, climate problems, rural sparsity of population, etc. Since then such conditions in Scotland have improved dramatically in many respects, both in absolute terms and in relation to the rest of the United Kingdom – though not the sparsity aspect, nor the relative health and morbidity statistics.

Only a major new appraisal of relative need could enable further change to be contemplated to the present distribution arrangements. It would almost certainly demonstrate that Scotland is overfunded by several billion pounds, but it would be hard for the Treasury to impose such a major cut to a rolling expenditure programme which could only lead to the closing of schools and hospitals on a large scale, even if spread over several years. It would also be hard, anyway, to achieve agreement on the terms of reference for such an appraisal now that devolution has happened. After all, the evaluation of needs in Scotland and the policies announced to address them – care for the elderly, for example – already diverges from comparable evaluations in England. Besides, the Government made it clear in passing the Scotland Act that the Barnett formula would remain the basis of the annual distribution of Treasury funds to Scotland. To depart from that now would be difficult. But it was unwise of the architects of the constitutional settlement to leave decisions on UK funding in the hands of the Westminster government alone.

It may be that, far from strengthening the convergence power of the Barnett formula, the Government may find over time that the only way to hold Scotland within the United Kingdom is by bribing it with public funds. That is a demeaning prospect for both sides, but it does not disguise the present reality which is that the Treasury holds the purse strings, the Scottish Executive has no power to negotiate with them and the Secretary of State for Scotland no longer has the locus or the strength to fight Scotland's corner in Whitehall or Westminster. So a Scottish government that is already by its very existence consuming funds from Scotland's block, that is facing the tightening vice of the Barnett formula and that has raised expectations with its expensive promises to the Scottish people, may one day soon find itself stuck between a rock and a hard place.

Of course, it must be acknowledged, there is more to devolution than pounds and pence, and more still to separation. 'You cannot answer a poem with a balance sheet', said Bob Kernohan many years ago, as Director of the Scottish Conservative Central Office. And it was always difficult to score with our real but often prosaic arguments against the nationalistic fervour that from time to time surged into the Scottish political arena and then subsided.

Devolution sought to displace nationalism but actually reinforced its place on the political agenda. It was less dominant in the 1997 election than it had been in 1992, though the lower electoral swing against the Conservatives in Scotland than in England may be accounted for by our continuing resistance to it. Because our slender Conservative majorities in Scotland led to the loss of all our seats it has wrongly been assumed that there were specifically Scottish reasons for that. In fact, the opposite was the case. Devolution was there certainly, as a drumbeat, an analogue for all the other grievances, but somehow beyond debate – 'a mere habit of words,' as the poet Sydney Goodsir Smith had put it thirty years earlier, 'signifying naething'. Devolution brought down the Labour government in 1979, and opposition to it strengthened the Conservative vote then and in 1992.

Devolution won in 1997 almost by default. It won because Labour won the general election. They won the election for reasons that ran nation-wide and have been well rehearsed: an electable leader on an electable policy platform; time for a change; even the determination upon revenge of the media who had got it so wrong in 1992. Above all Labour won because we were a disunited party, tainted by sleaze and obsessed with Europe. Tactical voting, within the vagaries of Scotland's four-party system, could and did also have a potent effect in a first-past-the-post election.

Whatever the reason, the fact remains that all our Scottish seats, with their small majorities, were lost in that watershed election, and in the mood for change that swept Scotland, culminating in the Devolution Referendum that autumn – rushed through while the new Government was riding high – it became impossible to disprove the claim that it was, to use Enoch Powell's phrase, 'the preponderant and settled will' of the Scottish people that they should have a devolved Parliament. Despite this, I feel it was wrong of my party so readily to abandon its principled oppo-sition and fail to oppose the Scotland Bill. Nothing better illustrates the insidious nature of the pre-legislative referendum, reinforced by the ques-tionable doctrine of the manifesto mandate. The time to abandon that stance was after the Bill had been enacted, not before.

Ironically, it may in part have been the previous Conservative Government's very success in establishing strong economic growth and rising prosperity in Scotland as the 1990s advanced that gave so many Scots the growing confidence to risk change, both in the colour of their government and in their constitutional status. Anyway, by 1997 devolu-tion had become a catalyst for all political opposition, a mantra that precluded rational discussion, its eventual enactment inevitable. However, the charge from our political opponents that always rankled with me over the years leading up to 1997 and again as the Bill passed through Parliament, was that in arguing against devolution, we were somehow being anti-Scottish, that we did not love or care for Scotland and its historic destiny. That was a low blow that I always found hurtful.

I defer to no man in my love of Scotland. I have walked its rivers and glens in sun and in rain. I have sailed its western waters, where the shining islands beckon, ridden the Atlantic swell that crashes blue-green across the bow and whips the spray in one's face. I have seen the evening light fall on drystone dykes that pattern the grass-green hills of Galloway. I have thrilled to the turn of an antler on a Highland hillside, where the mountains sweep the sky. I have heard the grouse-croak; seen the first, wet glint of the silver grilse. I have watched autumn's browning bracken and the fattening berry on the rowan tree. I have taken the salute from the Royal Box at the Edinburgh Tattoo. I have seen great ships slide down the slipways of the Clyde, the cheers of the workers drowning out the grind and crackle of the restraining chains. I have smelt the grease and metal and sweat amid the steam and noise of engine workshops; and I have smelt the honeyed air of the moors, thick with the drowse of bees in heather. I have sat alone at the still of dusk, in a drifting boat on the black, glassy waters of Loch Duich, where the only sound was the drip of water from the blade of the resting oar, watching the pink fade from wisps of cloud above the Five Sisters of Kintail, as the western sky turned pale beyond the dark mass of the Cuillins. I have breathed deep that wild air, so free and sweet and almost palpable that all life's cares were carried away on the ripples of the wind. I defer to no man in my love of Scotland – my own, my native land. But there is more to it than that.

It was the elevation of the condition of the people that Disraeli identified as the mainspring of Conservatism. Although we would express it differently today, helping people to attain for themselves a better life remains a surer lodestar than romantic, constitutional posturing. Alexander Pope was indeed right when he said that whatever was best

Arriving at 10 Downing Street for my first Cabinet meeting, November 1990.

'Mr Lang's delighted Prime Minister – he's tank testing the new frigates now!'

Cartoonist Bill Caldwell's view of the news that Jarrow's shipyard had won a contract from the Ministry of Defence.

Repealing the poll tax, December 1990.

Entertaining HRH the Crown Prince of Japan, with my wife Sandy.

Speaking in the 'Great Debate' in the Usher Hall, Edinburgh, January 1992.

After the count on election night 1992 with my daughter Venetia.

With Chancellor Helmut Kohl at Edinburgh Castle (above) and Mikhail Gorbachev (below) at Bute House, my official residence in Edinburgh. Note the hands.

Opening trade links with China's premier Li Peng, 1996.

With the Prime Minister John Major in Edinburgh.

Celebrating victory after John Major's leadership campaign, July 1995, in the gardens of 13 Cowley Street (above), and 10 Downing Street (below), with the Prime Minister and Brian Mawhinney (party Chairman).

Briefing the press during the return flight from a mission to India and Pakistan, January 1997.

Kersland, our home in Ayrshire for the past thirty years.

administered was best. That was what I now sought to achieve: to counter emotive slogans with practical improvements. I could not contemplate changing tack on such an issue of principle and proposing the kind of devolution others sought. However, having laid the trail in the preceding two years, I was able to embark after the 1992 general election on a more positive approach to how Scotland should be governed and to her place within the United Kingdom. We had won a reprieve in 1992, we had promised to take stock if we won that election, and now we must find ways of bringing the Union alive. That was what I set out to do.

One of my predecessors, Tom Johnston, had said many years earlier: 'All parties, classes and groupings sense the innate folly of administration 400 miles away,' and since then further administrative devolution had taken place. Scotland's government was administered not from Whitehall but from St Andrew's House in Edinburgh, but that was not perceived to be the case. I had proposed an initiative a few years before, which Malcolm Rifkind had readily accepted, to raise the profile of the Scottish Office within Scotland and to promote its activities in a host of ways – even the simple expedient of putting up Scottish Office signs alongside new road improvements helped to register the existence of this huge but largely unknown monolith in the minds of the Scots it served. But more needed to be done. I was also keen to find new ways of making ministers and MPs more visibly accountable to their electorate within Scotland.

After the election, I had called for a new tone in Scotland on constitutional issues and a mood of reconciliation. It soon became clear that the Labour Party contained internal splits over its continuing focus on a Scottish Parliament. Gordon Brown MP was quoted in the press as having said, 'I think we are making a mistake if we just assume somehow there is huge enthusiasm for home rule in Scotland,' whilst his more nationalistic colleague, John McAllion MP, was soon to call for 'mass extra-parliamentary action by the Scottish people back in Scotland'. But I did not hold high hopes of gaining much cooperation from our political opponents. It was clear that I must be proactive in setting the constitutional agenda and, in a speech at the Party Conference in Brighton that autumn I set out some preliminary ideas I had for breathing life into the Union.

I spoke of it being not inert but organic, and of the need to make it relevant for both Scotland and England. Whilst Scottish government and policy-making should continue to be distinctively Scottish – union did not mean uniformity – the Scottish dimension should feature more in the governmental process throughout the United Kingdom. I was determined to get away from the kind of thinking within the Treasury that had referred to Scotland, Wales and Northern Ireland as 'the territories', as though they were some form of sub-colonial pond life. Scotland remained a nation – and a distinctive one – within the United Kingdom and there needed to be a much more sensitive recognition of that fact. The patronising insensitivity towards Scotland that one sometimes encountered from English colleagues, usually based on ignorance rather than prejudice, grated just as much on me as it did on my fellow Scots.

I also wanted there to be more 'home-grown' policy in Scotland. I wanted to emphasise too, that whilst a Scottish Parliament would have been a centralising force within Scotland, from the extremities to the central belt, our approach was one not of institutional devolution – from government in London to government in Edinburgh – but of devolution from government to people. Tax reductions, council house sales, school boards, health trusts, denationalisation and wider share ownership – all these things had led to the diffusion of power from the government to the people of Scotland, as to the rest of the United Kingdom. I wanted to see if the same concept could be introduced to our constitutional thinking without jeopardising the Union.

Since the summer I had been putting together a raft of proposals to include in a Government White Paper that would deliver our 'take stock' promise. In doing this I had the help of Alan Young and of Peter Fraser, our Minister of State in the House of Lords whom I had asked to take on responsibility for constitutional matters. In September the Prime Minister and I held a seminar at Bute House in Edinburgh with a cross-section of Scots, distinguished in various walks of life, which yielded a number of interesting views. I also visited the ageing Lord Home at his home Castlemains, to learn what I could from his long experience of Scotland's politics. There was much interest in 'taking stock', which was by then the only show in town for those interested in constitutional matters, and I detected a more sympathetic tone in the Scottish media for what they acknowledged to be a positive and proactive approach. Eventually, after clearance of most of my proposals by the Cabinet, I was able in March 1993 to publish the White Paper *Scotland in the Union – A Partnership for Good*.

We knew that, in a field that had been ploughed over countless times during the past century, we could not produce a new 'big idea' in this document, but we did hope that by bringing together a large number of specific proposals to improve both Scotland's standing within the United Kingdom and the mechanisms of Scottish government we could offer a substantial and worthwhile package of measures that might help to soften the demands for a breakaway Scottish Parliament. I also hoped it would be a useful vehicle for educating the Scottish electorate on the extensive degree to which Scotland was already self-governing, but within a unitary framework. Most of all, because I realised that there was a limit to the number of practical and administrative improvements we could bring about – changes that could in themselves lead to more, not less, concomitant demand for local accountability – I sought to achieve a more sensitive recognition of Scotland's status as an historic nation within the United Kingdom, whilst avoiding tartan tokenism.

My specific proposals were focused on the procedures for passing Scottish legislation. Not many people realised that an average of six specifically Scottish Acts of Parliament were passed into law, often after extensive consideration, each year at Westminster – and that was in addition to all the UK-wide measures, which often contained Scottish provisions. The main vehicle for the changes I now proposed was the Scottish Grand Committee, the Commons committee to which all Scottish MPs belonged and which met at Westminster – and occasionally in Edinburgh – to debate Scottish issues.

I proposed that in future it should not only meet more often, for longer and in the other main cities and towns of Scotland, but that it should also undergo a progressive widening of the range of business it handled. In particular, it should be able to hold Second Reading debates of Scottish Bills so that, for the first time, the most important stage of such legislation could be debated in Scotland. In addition, I was keen to expand the use of the Special Standing Committee procedure, whereby after the Second Reading of a Bill such a committee could meet, in Scotland instead of at Westminster, to take oral evidence from specialist outside interest groups before the Bill underwent its detailed clause-by-clause consideration by MPs. These procedures would be particularly suitable for Law Reform Bills, of which there was a steady stream from the Scottish Law Society, to keep the law of Scotland up to date.

I also proposed that the Scottish Grand Committee should hold a regular Scottish Question Time in addition to the standard Westminster session, including for the first time participation by Scottish ministers from the House of Lords, and that it could be used for ministerial statements on Scottish issues and for adjournment debates, in which Scottish backbenchers could raise issues of specialist or constituency interest. Thus would the opportunities for Scottish MPs to secure more parliamentary time be greatly enhanced, ministers be held more extensively to account and government be brought closer to the people of Scotland.

The second main strand of the White Paper proposed the devolving to the Scottish Office of various governmental responsibilities in Scotland that were still handled by the United Kingdom departments. The Scottish

Arts Council, for example, was still the responsibility of the National Heritage Department and various industrial support schemes for Scotland still rested with the DTI. Training programmes were still the responsibility of the Department of Employment. These and others would now be transferred to the Scottish Office. A range of other plans was designed to strengthen Scotland's role in the institutions of the European Community and, in a host of ways, to improve the links between Scots and their government department, the Scottish Office. I was already committed to reform local government in Scotland, reducing the two-tier system to one. This change was one I undertook on its own merits, but it also formed part of the package of constitutional change I was now considering. As an aside, I was well aware that if and when devolution were ever to happen, my reformed local government structure would not be incompatible with it. In addition to all these changes, various commitments were given to develop new ways of acknowledging and enhancing within the institutions of the United Kingdom the distinctive identities of its constituent parts.

The opposition parties dismissed these proposals on the day we announced them, but they later took up almost all the new opportunities they afforded as they were progressively introduced over the next year or so. I had stressed that this was the first step in a continuing process and we continued to deliver incremental measures during the rest of the Parliament. The press too were disappointed that we had not broken our election pledge to resist the establishment of a Scottish Parliament. But the *Scotsman* concluded that the White Paper 'has made more difficult the Opposition's task of persuading the Scottish people that they need to withdraw some of the sovereignty from the Westminster Parliament.'

All the procedural changes I had proposed were eventually agreed by the other parties, and in a speech eighteen months after the event I was able not only to report that we had delivered on all our constitutional pledges, but also to list the components of our distinctively Scottish policy agenda and to demonstrate the initiatives we had taken to enhance Scotland's standing. The reformed Scottish Grand Committee could do virtually everything that Labour's devolved parliament would be able to do, except raise taxes. Yet the power and status of Scottish MPs at Westminster remained undiminished.

But by then, in truth, it was really all too late. It was a package which if implemented thirty or forty years earlier might have done the trick. Now, though – ironically, as transport and communication links between Scotland and London were quicker and easier than they had ever been – the perception of a distant Westminster was stronger than ever. The mounting problems the Government faced in other fields were dominating the headlines, and as our standing in the polls declined, the leaden determination of the other parties re-emerged, minds closed to all argument, to deliver their devolution proposals should they win the next election, and so feed the demand they had created. Inexorably, such an outcome came to be taken for granted.

In October 1994 a motion on the constitution was chosen by ballot for debate at our Party Conference in Bournemouth, and I was asked at short notice to reply to it. I seized the chance to carry further the debate about Scotland, and it was clear from the warmth of the audience's ovation that maintaining the integrity of the United Kingdom was indeed a visceral issue. 'Scotland is no less Scottish now', I said, 'for being part of the United Kingdom, and nor is England any less English'; and I finished with a frankly jingoistic peroration about our great nation, bonded in war and our obligation to 'honour our historic inheritance and hand it down intact to future generations.'

The Prime Minister echoed my speech in his own at the end of the conference and I hoped that once more we might raise the profile of the issue as the general election, still almost three years away, approached. Sadly though, devolution was overwhelmed by other events, the election was to be lost and Scotland was to get its Parliament, by then *nemine contradicente*.

Since then, there has grown a sense of a Scotland slipping away from Britain. When the Treaty of Union was signed in 1707, Queen Anne expressed the hope that all her subjects, of both nations, would henceforth act with 'all possible respect and kindness to one another, that so it may appear to all the world they have hearts disposed to become one people.' At many times over the centuries, especially when Britain went to war, that almost seemed to happen. Not any more. Since the devolved Parliament was established, the subjects of both nations seem to have drifted further apart. In Scotland, stories of Anglophobic violence have not diminished. In England, Scotland is certainly no more loved. Elgar's music is becoming unperformable in the Usher Hall; and 'Flower of Scotland' is unlikely to feature in the Albert Hall. The Labour Party often appears to be engaged in a civil war, fought between its MPs at Westminster and its MSPs in Edinburgh. How much worse would that battle become if the government at one or other parliament were to be of a different complexion, as one day it will be?

When the Second Reading of the Scotland Bill was debated in the House of Lords in 1998 I admitted in my speech to a real sense of foreboding, because 'I cannot remember a Bill being laid before Parliament that brought with it so much potential for division and damage to the fabric of our nation.' Labour, I pointed out, had been telling us for years of the need for a Scottish Parliament to put right – as they claimed – the democratic deficit and to make up for the lack of accountability. 'Thus are all the special privileges Scotland enjoys in this place [the Westminster Parliament] dismissed in those two empty, glib phrases. I refer to the higher share of MPs; the Scottish Grand Committee; the Scottish Select Committee; the Scottish Standing Committee; the territorial department of state; the Cabinet Minister and his four junior ministers; the higher spending levels; the special Scottish legislation ... That is not a democratic deficit. Indeed, there are many English who might consider that that is closer to being a democratic surplus.' I warned that 'Scotland's voice may be loud in Edinburgh, but at Westminster and Whitehall it will be reduced to a whimper', and I criticised the lack of a revising chamber in the new Parliament – a democratic deficit if ever there was one, and perhaps the most serious single shortcoming of the entire project, as the poor quality of legislation will over time reveal.

One should not judge too harshly, in its formative stages, the early performance of the new body now established in Edinburgh. It is the hobbled child of a troubled marriage, but it began its life with widespread good will which I share fully. Now that it is there, Scotland's future wellbeing depends in part upon its success. If that early good will and the optimism of July 1999 have been partly vitiated by the many early stumbles, that was only to be expected. the *Scotsman*, a newspaper long wedded to home rule, was withering in its scorn soon after the new body was opened: 'It is clear that the calibre of some MSPs is embarrassingly bad.' In time they will surely get better. My concern is with the underlying structural faults.

When the original estimate of the cost of the new Parliament building was given as £30 million in 1995, I was ridiculed for suggesting that £40 million would be nearer the mark. My successor Michael Forsyth was viciously attacked for scaremongering with an estimate of £50 million. As the cost now heads towards £300 million – all of which must come out of the Scottish spending block – it is no wonder that our fellow Scots have begun to look askance at what they have been led into.

At least one should concede that the decision to go for proportional representation was a sensible one. It deliberately and sensibly differed from the Westminster system, and it recognised the existence of four-party politics in Scotland. It also conformed to the more naïve expectations its supporters had of a less abrasive kind of politics in Scotland – not yet delivered. More importantly, it was a different system from Westminster's, underlining the different nature and role of the body. I welcome too the increased emphasis on pre-legislative scrutiny and study of draft Bills, which I had myself espoused in the past. More troubling is the extent to which the Parliament's latent defects are already beginning to show – and the introspection, the policy drift, the squabbles with London and the dullness and paucity of the early legislative record are hardly the harbingers of a great new democratic dawn.

In *The Battle for Scotland* Andrew Marr concludes: 'A Scotland genuinely at ease with itself would be an argumentative, grown-up Scotland with a lively parliament ... And when it does speak, its voice will be sharp and fresh. And its views will perhaps surprise us.' Perhaps it is too soon to judge, but I fear his idyll is not yet discernible. Indeed, the devolution measures in the Scotland Act, vaunted by Donald Dewar in 1999 as Scotland's new constitutional settlement, look rather unsettled already. His Welsh counterpart Ron Davies was more perceptive when he described devolution as 'a process, not an event'.

In debates in the House of Commons, Donald used to enjoy provoking the Hansard writers, not just by speaking very quickly, but also by using Scots words that they did not recognise, such as 'thirled' or 'glaikit' or 'girn'. 'Thrawn' was one of his favourites, and, despite his high aspirations, I fear that a 'thrawn' Scotland is what we now see – and one whose Parliament is dominated, as we warned it would be, by the interests and attitudes of the central belt.

Devolution is certainly here to stay. It cannot be reversed: the smoke will not go back in the bottle. The more important questions are: will it remain stable; will it lead on to something akin to complete separation; or can it be made to work? The fault lines run deep. The risks it runs are now becoming more apparent. If England were to contemplate some kind of quasi-federalism in the longer term, of which an English Grand Committee at Westminster could form an embryo, perhaps some kind of constitutional stability might ultimately be salvaged. At present, though, I have to say that my hopes for Scotland are not backed by my expectations.

With increasing calls for more powers to be devolved from Westminster, the concept of Britishness is rapidly evaporating from the

Scottish psyche. It is now confined to a few international sports events, the armed services, the BBC and the monarchy. But support for the Crown in Scotland often seems, sadly, to be faltering and spasmodic, despite the utterly dedicated service to Scotland of the Queen and other members of the Royal Family. Though Her Majesty has many loyal and devoted subjects in Scotland, the contrast in the coverage of the heart-warming Golden Jubilee celebrations, north and south of the border, was very marked. For the rest, the focus is all on Scottish broadcasting opt-outs, Scottish regiments and Scottish athletes. All of this suggests that Scotland is already sliding fast down the proverbial slippery slope.

One stabilising force thus far has been the permanent civil service. There are two reasons for this. Firstly, the Scottish Civil Service remains part of the United Kingdom Civil Service. Secondly, because so much of Scotland's government was already separately administered by the Scottish Office, the administrative disruption caused by devolution has been much reduced. But there are dangers here too. No longer needing to plug in at all levels to their counterparts in Whitehall and pursuing increasingly divergent policies, the Scottish arm of the civil service will become increasingly isolated. English departments will in turn become increasingly Anglocentric. So, despite the paraphernalia of concordats, committees and conventions that have been stuck on to the devolution settlement to try to make it stable, civil service links to the centre will become increasingly tenuous.

It could all have been avoided. The upsurge of nationalism in the 1960s and 1970s could have been just one more of those emotional spasms that have gripped Scotland from time to time over the centuries, if the Labour government of the day had not set out to appease it. Certainly, valid grievances should always be met by government; and there is always room to improve the mechanisms of government and of democratic accountability. What Scotland now has, however, is an unstable hybrid that lacks either the resources or the powers to be what its begetters pretend it to be, or the people who voted for it want it to be. That product of delusion and self-delusion will in time be seen for what it is.

I fear the *Scotsman* was wrong in 1999 when it said: 'The dire perform-ance of Scotland's parliament to date has killed independence stone dead.' So was George Robertson MP, then Labour's Shadow Secretary of State for Scotland, when he said before the 1997 election that devolution would bury nationalism. When he said it the SNP had no platform in Scotland and only three MPs at Westminster. Now they have five Westminster MPs and thirty-five members of the Scottish Parliament, where they constitute the official opposition. They are temperamentally suited to opposition, but they have not forgotten their sense of destiny; and the rancour towards Westminster that they will continue to engender will eventually become endemic. It will come to replace devolution as that bass note on the bagpipes. With the devolution settlement and Brussels both conspiring to strengthen the links between the European Union and its regions and with what Lord Denning once described as the 'incoming tide' of the Treaty of Rome, one can but speculate as to how long the term 'United Kingdom' will continue to have real meaning. Already it is being drained of substance.

There can never be certainty as to where it will all end. My criticism through the years has always been that devolution would bring risk and uncertainty, with the probability that a devolved Parliament would be the beginning, not the end, of the process. That is why I believe it was wrong to impose that risk upon us. It may end with complete independence or it may end with some kind of compromise whereby only defence and foreign affairs remain under a United Kingdom banner. Or, indeed, it may settle in the Slough of Despond that is now emerging, with trench warfare wringing occasional further concessions. Whatever happens, more has been lost than has been gained.

In my Second Reading speech in the House of Lords, I concluded that 'as it stands, this is a Bill that will break the back of Britain.' I believe that

that is what is now happening. Disguised at present by two decades of sustained economic growth, by the abundance of public expenditure and by the commonality of the governing party at Westminster and in Scotland, the irretrievable fracture has nevertheless already occurred. I hope I am wrong and I want to be proved wrong, but in a few short decades I fear that it will become clear by how much we have all been diminished.

TEN

'*Put Up or Shut Up*'

At 8.30 a.m. on Thursday 22 June 1995 I was scanning the morning papers at my Scottish Office desk, overlooking Horseguards Parade, when I had a telephone call from No. 10. It was Howell James, the Prime Minister's political secretary. Would I come round to see the Prime Minister? 'What, now? Ahead of Cabinet?' 'Yes, now.'

It was a fresh summer's day and, having no sensitive Cabinet papers to carry, I walked the short distance from the Scottish Office to a peaceful and deserted Downing Street. I was directed to the little waiting room near the Cabinet room and after a few minutes, Howell joined me there. He came straight to the point. 'He's going to tell you that he's resigning the leadership of the Party and standing for re-election. He wants you to play a leading role in his campaign team, handling the whole media side of it.'

It took a moment or two to digest this. I shouldn't have been surprised though, because morale in the party was very low, with endless speculation in the press about splits and leadership challenges. The Prime Minister himself had been visibly low in spirits. So depressed had he seemed when I saw the television clip of his return a few days earlier from a G7 meeting in Halifax, Nova Scotia, that I had taken the unusual step for me of telephoning his PPS John Ward to suggest that I and others should perhaps see him soon to cheer him up and stiffen him. My fear then had been that he might simply throw in the towel and resign.

When I went into the Cabinet Room a few minutes later however, I found the Prime Minister calm and businesslike. He repeated what Howell had just told me, added that Robert Cranborne would be leading his campaign team and asked me to join him and to act as the campaign spokesman. I at once accepted. I added that although I had not thought of what he now proposed, my immediate reaction to it was that it was the right thing to do and I was sure he would win. It should clear the air and might bring the party dissidents to their senses.

Of course, a leadership campaign by a serving Prime Minister would be quite different from the 1990 fixture. Some would argue that it was wrong to throw caution to the winds in this way and that it would split the Conservative Party down the middle. But the truth is that it was not the Prime Minister who had put his leadership on the agenda. The ideological right wing were already determined that there should be a contest that autumn and cared nothing about splitting the party to advance their policies. All John Major was to do was to bring the date forward, thus wrong-footing his critics and, it was hoped, sparing us all several months of uncertainty and in-fighting.

At this stage only a small handful of senior colleagues knew of the plan and at his request I went through the connecting doors to No. 11 and thence to the Chief Whip's Office at 12 Downing Street, where I joined Robert and Tony Newton to start roughing out our plans for the campaign. Tony was much preoccupied with his burdens as Leader of the House and the various procedural committees that he was busy chairing at that time. For that reason he was not to play a prominent role in the team, his place being taken by Alastair Goodlad, but Tony continued to provide invaluable advice and help in the background.

I found time to ring my curious and mystified private office at the Scottish Office to ask them to send round my Cabinet papers and to switch to Thomas Strathclyde, the Fisheries Minister, a meeting I had planned for later in the day with a delegation of Scottish fishermen.

Cabinet convened in a spirit of outward calm, with those in the know showing no sign of the convulsions to come. We were preoccupied with the start of the Public Expenditure Survey, so nobody seemed to notice that the Leader of the House of Lords was absent, although when the Chief Whip and the Chairman of the Party slipped out halfway through, David Hunt did whisper to me across the Cabinet table: 'What's going on?' I had to shrug and try to look perplexed.

Because Cabinet leaked like a sieve, it was vital to keep the Prime Minister's intentions secret at this stage. He planned to make an announcement at five o'clock, and surprise was important to enable his campaign to get off to a good start. If the story broke before Prime Minister's Questions the result would be a chaotic launch. By chance I had been at a Press Gallery Reception in the House the night before and there had been no inkling there of the news that Thursday would bring.

Back in No. 12 after Cabinet, those of us who had met earlier resumed our urgent planning. John Ward was there, with Graham Bright – current and former PPS – and we identified others we would recruit. Campaign headquarters had already been identified in Cowley Street and telephone lines were being installed. We considered the statement the Prime Minister would make that afternoon, then returned to the Cabinet Room for a short meeting with him to discuss that and his proposed visit to an EC Heads of Government meeting at Cannes that weekend. Notwithstanding the disastrous impact of Margaret Thatcher's absence in Paris during her leadership duel with Michael Heseltine in 1990, it was our firm advice that the Prime Minister should go to Cannes. There were runs to be made there: he was the incumbent who must be seen still to be in charge of events and, besides, there was still no challenger and there might be none. He took the same view. We also agreed which Cabinet colleagues still in the dark would be told of the plan and by whom. I was to reach Malcolm Rifkind, William Waldegrave, Stephen Dorrell and John Gummer, and also a senior backbench colleague, Norman Fowler.

As we broke up, agreeing that the campaign team would meet at Cowley Street at seven o'clock that evening, I returned to the Scottish Office and we all set about giving the appearance of business as usual. No doubt the Civil Service antennae were already quivering and the telephones humming in several departments around Whitehall.

As I struggled to tackle the urgent papers in my red box and scanned my forward diary to see what could be cancelled and what could not, I resolved to keep precise diary notes of the days ahead. It promised to be a challenging but fascinating time and I would experience it from the inside. What follows derives from those notes. It is not intended to be a comprehensive story of the campaign, but tells it in detail from my perspective, with a few additional comments.

Thursday 22 June

2.45 p.m.

I reached Stephen Dorrell by telephone from my room at the House. He was watching cricket at Lord's. I told him what was afoot. Then William Waldegrave came to see me to hear the news. He was about to make a Health statement in the Chamber at 3.30 p.m. Norman Fowler called in. A good friend of the Prime Minister, who was at his side almost throughout the 1992 general election, he would be a staunch ally again.

After he had left I reached Malcolm Rifkind, who was by now in Scotland on Department of Transport business, but I failed to track down John Gummer, who was already *en route* to New York.

4.30 p.m.

Back to No 10. to meet Howell James. We discussed the terms of the statement the Prime Minister was about to make. I didn't much like the line, 'It's time to put up or shut up.' It seemed petulant and unstatesmanlike, but when he joined us with Norma, JM was adamant. It was a line that had been used recently in an editorial in the *Sunday Times*, but one he had already included before that in an earlier draft. It echoed Bernard Ingham's retort in 1990, which had helped to flush out Michael Heseltine's challenge to Margaret Thatcher.

It was a lovely summer afternoon and through the open Cabinet Room windows we could hear the hubbub of the press corps assembling around the neat rows of gold, cane-backed chairs on the lawn. Inside, the air was electric with the tension of the moment. JM had already broken the news to the officers of the 1922 Committee, whom he described as 'dumbfounded'.

Brian Mawhinney [then Secretary of State for Transport] had arrived at No. 10 and JM asked him to join the campaign team. He also told us that Michael Howard had pressed to be included, so of course he had agreed.

No questions were to be allowed at this press conference, just the statement bombshell, but we discussed one or two lines to take on issues likely to be raised in the next day or two. In response to one topic, as he headed for the verandah door, JM retorted, 'If they think I'm going to change my policies, they can think again.'

With Ian McColl, his PPS in the Lords, standing behind him, he read his prepared statement from a lectern, whilst Norma watched with Brian Mawhinney and myself from the verandah. As he turned and walked back in, bedlam broke out amongst the hacks. We had achieved our surprise.

I set off for my first couple of media interviews. Between them I visited 13 Cowley Street, a fine old terraced house in a quiet backwater very close to Parliament. It had a solid door, installed to withstand the Gordon riots.

I don't think Sir Neil Thorne, a former colleague in Parliament, can have realised what he was in for when he generously agreed to its use as our campaign headquarters.

Friday 23 June

Another glorious day.

8.00 a.m.
To Millbank for the *Today* programme.

Afterwards, recorded five or six more interviews, both at Millbank and on the Green. Then to a meeting at Robert Cranborne's room at the House of Lords. Also present: Alastair Goodlad, Archie Hamilton, Tony Newton, Brian Mawhinney, Howell James and George Bridges from No. 10. Portillo said to be very upset, though he has pledged support.

I went on to our Cowley Street headquarters, where the beginnings of an organisation were becoming established. As the campaign's General in the Field, as Robert dubbed me, I had overall command here, but as I had to continue doing my Scottish Office job, as well as other campaign tasks, I was fortunate in the quality of the team. From No. 10 Howell James was available whenever the Prime Minister could spare him, Damian Green came to coordinate broadcasting and Tim Collins to liaise with the lobby. Jonathan Hill, Howell's predecessor, took leave from his PR employers to come and help and Gregor Mackay, my special adviser, resigned from his job (as civil service rules required) to give invaluable support. So did Michael McManus, who was David Hunt's special adviser.

From day one, we managed to give the outside world a perception of calm control of events. Inside, the truth was of a lot of bright and energetic supporters gradually hammering order and system out of chaos. In this we were greatly helped by Sophie McEwen, Robert's personal assistant in the House of Lords. Over the days, as others came and went she, along with Gregor Mackay, was an ever present dedicated worker, who set up an Incident Board and a method for receiving, processing and responding to the tidal wave of bids from the media that would soon engulf us, requiring another dozen telephone lines. Two other tireless workers were Debbie de Satgé and Barbara Kyriakou.

Unknown to each other in many cases at the outset, these individuals formed the core of a team that was soon handling efficiently the demands of the world's press, as well as helping us monitor the media, prepare press releases and newspaper articles, respond to scares and alarms, plan and implement our own initiatives and generally hold our campaign together. I was to be the public face of the campaign, but I made sure other colleagues were involved as much as possible. Indeed, given the huge demands that quickly developed, that became inevitable.

We occupied a tiny ground-floor sitting room overlooking the garden at Cowley Street and had the use of the basement also. Occasionally we overflowed into the garden itself: indeed, the garden gate became a convenient exit and entrance route, which we were able to use throughout the campaign when we wanted to come and go discreetly without running the gauntlet of the press army camped outside the front door. Amazingly, they never spotted it.

The dining room was taken over by our head-counters and intelligence gatherers, concerned with the thinking of the 329 colleagues in the parliamentary Conservative Party who constituted our electorate. The cast list in the dining room varied as the campaign progressed, but once it became clear that they had in place an efficient, secure system I decided to leave them to their own devices. Their intelligence was passed to Alastair Goodlad who became our Chief Intelligence Officer – an appropriate post, as he was soon to become the Government Chief Whip.

12.30 p.m.
More interviews for the lunchtime news programmes, just after Douglas

Hurd's retirement had been announced. This an unwelcome development, open to mischievous misinterpretation; and of course the need to fill the post later could create further opportunities for unhappiness in the party.

3.00 p.m.
My first press lobby in the large Ministerial Conference Room beneath the Commons Chamber, briefed and rehearsed by Tim Collins. The reptiles behaved quite well, more interested in getting a feel for it all than in their usual agenda.

Back to Cowley Street. Rumour that Redwood is quietly distancing himself from the Government.

At five o'clock, still in baking heat, I managed some quick shopping since I am to be stranded in London over the weekend, before returning to my flat to tackle my box. Then at 8.30 to Millbank to record an ITN interview and from there to No. 10, where I chaired the campaign meeting

Saturday 24 June

7.45 a.m.
To Cowley Street to scan the newspapers.

8.30 a.m.
To No. 12 – Campaign meeting. No news of any challenge. Norman Lamont expected. What's Redwood up to?

Personally, I think there's a good chance that no one will challenge. That might make the whole exercise look a bit fatuous. A Lamont challenge could be a threat, but I doubt it.

His disloyalty and the sourness of his resignation statement still rankles. Our preference, if there is to be a challenge, is that it should come from John Redwood. We want a credible challenger, rather than a backbench stalking horse and, of the potential candidates, Redwood would be the easiest to beat. He has been a complete flop in Wales, plays little part in Cabinet or committees and is a nightmare to deal with as a ministerial colleague.

10.15 a.m.
To the House of Commons to meet Michael Forsyth.

The House was shut up for the weekend and my room in the Cabinet corridor was locked. All the lights were off, so we stumbled down darkened staircases until we reached Michael's room beneath the Chamber. There we discussed the campaign and he pledged his support to the Prime Minister. He also undertook to try to contact John Redwood, who had gone to ground. Michael sees, as I do, that if I am promoted after this is over, he will get the Scottish Office. I doubt if I will be, but if it happens Michael will do the job well, so long as he has the sense to become a charmer. I told him this.

Just before lunch JM came to visit the Cowley Street HQ, after addressing a meeting of constituency chairmen in Central Office, which went very well. Photo-call.

Lunch: Alastair Goodlad and Tristan Garel-Jones at Alastair's house in Lord North Street.

I spent the afternoon at Cowley Street as we worked to get our systems in order, then to Lord North Street for dinner.

Sunday 25 June

Up at 6.15. Just after 7.00 a car came to take me to London Weekend Television HQ for live interview on GMTV with Alistair Stewart. Twelve minutes. It went well, especially on Major-the-man and on housing. Alan Clark, David Mellor and Bernard Ingham were also there. All felt we had made a good start. I had the feeling that they all had pangs at being out of it now.

Back to Cowley Street. Radio interview in a van for London Radio News. The line was lost two or three times. Quick meeting with Alastair Goodlad. Lamont still considered to be the threat. JM's *On the Record* interview will be the main event of the day. Discussed the briefing for it. Cowley Street office better organised – beginning to settle down.

9.30 a.m.
Going to be another glorious, sunny day.

Walked with Brian Mawhinney to No. 10 to watch the recording of *On the Record* in the large meeting room in the Whips' Office, next door in No. 12. Did a couple of short interviews myself while we waited. Afterwards, watched the video with JM in his sitting room. He was very good – robust and relaxed, though a bit defensive on the Single Currency. Then back to Cowley Street with Tim Collins and George Bridges.

Spent most of the afternoon at Cowley Street, much of it on the telephone, then home to Vincent Square, where I sat on the grass and watched the cricket, flicking through the papers from my red box.

9.30 p.m.
Round-up meeting at Lord North Street. We have taken to using Alastair's house in Lord North Street, just thirty yards away from our Cowley Street headquarters, for all serious campaign meetings.

Monday 26 June

Up at 6.30. Walked round to Cowley Street. Filmed arriving and – what every politician dreads – knocking on a door that no one comes to open.

8.00 a.m.
Meeting, Lord North Street. The news is that Redwood is now certain to stand. Can he have any support of substance amongst colleagues?

Announcement timing not known. Lilley being elusive. We divided the lunchtime media programmes between myself, Michael Howard and Brian Mawhinney. Line to take on Redwood: 'This is a strange decision. He recently declared his support for John Major and of course has sat around his Cabinet table for two years.' Of course, he could cause there to be a second round, when he would disappear.

Divided the morning between Cowley Street and the Scottish Office. Agreed statement for Robert Cranborne to make, and lines to take. Lunch at the House. Tearoom quiet.

2.00 p.m.

Redwood duly announced. Sounded manic. Looked spooky. Good at questions. Surrounded by a bizarre ragbag of party rejects. He was probably going to be dropped in the imminent reshuffle, anyway.

3.00 p.m.

Robert made statement on steps of Cowley Street, where a crowd had gathered, as well as the press phalanx. A bit declamatory. When he finished with a flourish by saying 'and the winner will be …' a wag shouted 'Tony Blair!', which took the edge off it. I called Stewart Steven, editor of the *Evening Standard*, to put our line. Tried to reach Portillo – uncontactable.

4.00 p.m.

To Dover House. A little work, then to the House for a division. In the division lobby lots of support, advice, comment, info, etc. Then in Central Lobby a chat with Robin Oakley [BBC Political Editor] and with Jeffrey Archer, followed by a meeting in Robert's room in the Lords and then off to do two television interviews and radio.

6.30 p.m.

Back in Cowley Street. Trouble fixing up Heseltine and Portillo to do interviews on tomorrow's *Today* programme. Neither keen. Later, worked at the House. Drink on the terrace with John Mackay and Gerry Malone. After dinner, meeting in Michael Howard's room.

11.00 p.m.

Lord North Street with Robert and Alastair. And so to bed.

Tuesday 27 June

My birthday.

7.25 a.m.

Virginia B. [Virginia Bottomley, secretary of State for Health] rang, offering health figures and general discussion and support. She's keen to help, but not sure how best to fit in. To Cowley Street. Press scan then Lord North Street for an hour and a half then to Scottish Office.

11.30 a.m.

When I was trying to catch up on Scottish business a panic call came through from an undermanned Cowley Street. Redwood was said to have put out his manifesto. The press were screaming for a reaction. I rushed round and slipped in through the back garden just ahead of Robert, Alastair and Michael Howard. Robert was planning to react robustly to a manifesto of which we had only the sketchiest details. I said no, don't upgrade the issue. I suggested that Michael step outside at noon and say a few brief dismissive words: nothing really new, some policies we are already pursuing, some we are considering, etc.

It went well. We were credited by the media with a swift response, but it was touch and go. Only afterwards did any of us actually see any detail of what Redwood's manifesto contained. My view of him is that his campaign will flare and fade; we should let it do so. The image of the

BBC footage of Redwood pretending to know the words of the Welsh National Anthem lingers on, happily.

1.00 p.m.

To the House to call various colleagues to fix up speakers for various programmes. Their producers were being tricky about whom and what they wanted. So were some colleagues. Some programmes only fixed up an hour before transmission.

4.00 p.m.

Another hour at the Scottish Office, then back to Cowley Street. Door-stepped by BBC for the six o'clock news. Quick dash to the House for an anticipated division – chance for more lobbying and sounding. Slightly calmer than yesterday, but rumours abounding. Robin Oakley had said on the six o'clock news that Redwood's campaign had stalled. Rumour therefore that Hezza and Portillo releasing their people to abstain, instead of supporting JM.

8.00 p.m.

ITN interview outside Cowley Street for ten o'clock news. Then dinner at the House. Tim Renton trying to steady the pro-Euro group. Michael Spicer had been doing the same with the antis. Meeting in Michael Howard's room. Agreed morale better but lots of nuts and bolts to be dealt with. Nuts and dolts, too. I took over the chair when Robert went off to brief JM, who was just back from Cannes. Ken Clarke's over-the-top interviews from there were very harmful. Just when we are trying to bridge the divides within the party, he tosses in a grenade. Deliberate or thoughtless? You never know with Ken.

10.15

Division. Then I rushed round to Millbank to do *Newsnight* live. Challenged on Portillo's plans, I said: ignore the rumours, he has pledged support. Bed at midnight. Happy birthday.

Wednesday 28 June

Another day that started grey and cool, but became hot and humid as the sun burned through.

7.45 a.m.

To Cowley Street for press scan. Agreed most likely issues today would be the economy (Redwood) and Europe (Cannes). Then to the usual Lord North Street meeting round Alastair's dining room table. The press still seem not to have noticed and continue to camp outside Cowley Street. Mood generally: Redwood's campaign has not taken off. PM's return gave us the initiative. Need for him now to be seen around, meet MPs, individually and in groups. After the meeting I had a post-Cannes chat with Howell. I am beginning to wilt. I have simply been carrying too much of the burden and have to delegate some of my roles. Caught Robert, who agreed David Maclean should be asked to be my deputy, especially at Cowley Street. My first suggestion was David Davis, but David M. will do it very well.

After this I went to Dover House, to find all my (Scottish Office) ministerial colleagues sitting around the table in my room waiting for me. My private office had failed to cancel the meeting we normally have at this time. So I gave them a resumé of the campaign. They were all supportive. We also discussed Monklands – Labour sleaze: jobs for the boys in Scottish local government.

Rang Ken Clarke to suggest tactfully that he be a bit more statesman-like in his interviews. He took it well. Asked Virginia to do some health stuff on Redwood who has been majoring on cottage hospitals, of all things.

12.15 p.m.

An hour in the Cabinet Room with JM, Robert, Michael, Brian and officials, working on the text of his Cannes statement. JM relaxed and robust. He said that when Redwood rang him on Monday to resign he sounded so embarrassed and uncomfortable that JM had rather warmed to him! Lunch at House. Mood placid, for the moment.

2.30 p.m.

Scottish Questions. I had had almost no time to brief myself. However, I announced the establishment of an inquiry into Labour scandals in Monklands, under Section 211 of the 1973 Act. Afterwards sat next to JM for his Statement on the Cannes Summit. He got a great cheer on his arrival in the Chamber – and even applause from the Public Gallery (strictly forbidden). Everyone forgets how much more popular he is in the country than the party is.

Statement went v. well. Lovely stroke-play and good phrases.

Afterwards, I did a reflective ITV interview on the campaign so far, sitting on a garden seat on the lawn with Westminster Abbey behind, followed by meeting with Robert and Howell to discuss the PM's programme.

6.15 p.m.

Meeting with Hezza on the privatisation of the nuclear electricity industry. He was relaxed and cheerful, enjoying the buzz of a leadership campaign, and watching for his opportunity, like an old jungle lion.

Later, Howell and Peter Gummer to discuss press plans, and after dinner a round-up meeting in Michael's room at House. Bed, midnight.

Thursday 29 June

We've been going a week. It feels like three months.

7.15 a.m.

First caller Jeffrey Archer, doing an article for *Mail on Sunday*. I suggested 'grassroots opinion' as his theme. I wanted to mobilise the force of the almost wholly loyal constituency associations on MP opinion, when they are in their constituencies over the weekend.

Quick visit to Cowley Street to scan press and check all well.

On to Lord North Street. Tim Collins told us JM wanted quips on topical issues to spice up PM's Questions. Various offered. My contribution, on why extra telephone lines are being installed in another house in Lord North Street (rumoured to be for a Portillo challenge), was: it just shows how quick, easy and cheap it is now to get a telephone, post-privatisation. JM later used this to good effect.

Back to Cowley Street. David Maclean taking charge. David Davis, who has also been working hard there, keen to do more. As David M. is not too well, David D. might take over – he has great drive.

Then to Scottish Office. A little departmental work and prepared for Cabinet. Rang Stewart Steven at *Evening Standard*. Signed 150 thank you letters to MPs who have offered help.

10.30 a.m.

Walked to No. 10 for Cabinet. Meeting brisk and cheerful. His last? I think not. William Hague welcomed as Redwood's replacement – can only be an improvement. Stayed behind afterwards to discuss JM's programme with him, Tony Newton, Brian and Michael, but left before they finished to be at Cowley Street when nominations close at noon.

Arrived there to find panic. The BBC had told David Davis that as Marcus Fox, who had signed JM's nomination papers (along with most of the 1922 Committee) though he had not proposed or seconded him, was also to be the Returning Officer for the election in his capacity as Chairman of the 1922, they might be invalid.

I rang No. 10 to warn them and also tried to reach Marcus. No. 10 rushed fresh nomination papers round to the Commons, had them signed by two Cabinet colleagues and tried to lodge them, just in case. Too late – nominations had closed! Marcus coolly announced, however, that the original papers were valid anyway. This drama has not leaked.

I, equally coolly, did a doorstep interview: clear-cut choice, time to reinforce the PM's authority.

1.00 p.m.
Lunch at Lord North Street with Robert and Howell. Cecilia Goodlad is being a saint allowing her house to be treated as a restaurant. Agreed on press contact list to be followed up. Discussed points of detail with Howell. Then over to the House for briefing with Scottish press in my room at the House, followed by calls to [*Times* journalists] Peter Riddell, Simon Jenkins *et al.* Scottish Office and constituency paperwork. Weather very hot and sticky.

5.45 p.m.
Cowley Street. Radio interview with Kenny McIntyre of BBC Scotland, followed by a television interview with David Rose for ITN in a moving taxi. At least it was cool.

Worked in room at House then gave Howell dinner in the Strangers' Dining Room. Afterwards we were both summoned to the PM's room overlooking New Palace Yard. Robert was there. JM very tired, but we could look back on a triumphant day: good meetings with party groups on terrace, etc., and his best Question Time ever. Warm support even from Labour (and not just because they thought it suited them). This despite the panache with which he threw back at Labour their own words on NHS reorganisation, swiped at their 'charade' of ditching Clause 4, used my crack on new telephone lines and, as usual, beat Blair comprehensively. Blair: Redwood resigned 'because he disagreed with the direction of the Government'. PM: No, he resigned 'because he was devastated that I had resigned as leader of the Conservative Party', adding for good measure that 40 per cent of the Labour Party had voted against

Blair's election as leader. It may not translate so well to the written page, but it did well in the Chamber. At one point Madam Speaker had to intervene with: 'Order. This is great fun.' A watershed.

Later
Round-up meetings in Michael's room and at Cowley Street. Then home.

Friday 30 June

Brief call at Cowley Street – in good order now. David Davis well in charge. Fewer speaker requests and the pattern more predictable.

Meeting Lord North Street. We listened to JM's interview on BBC's *Today*, which started badly but got into gear once the issues were engaged. It finished strongly. Stewart Steven at the *Standard* told me later that he and his team at his news conference thought it 'brilliant'.

I introduced a discussion on the overall campaign so far and the endgame strategy, plus lines to develop. Widely agreed – Robert asked me to put it all on paper as general marching orders.

In essence our strategy had been to 'hit the ground running' on the first day of the campaign, capitalising on the element of surprise and seeking early momentum to carry us through the period of the Prime Minister's absence at Cannes, which was also likely to coincide with the entry of any challenger. We had hoped for a boost on the Prime Minister's return, which he delivered, with several fine performances at the despatch box and in interviews, in contrast to the poor campaign of John Redwood. Now, with MPs going home for the weekend, we hoped to benefit from the loyalty of the constituency associations, on which we had been working.

Our themes for the final run-in were to concentrate on a positive message: we were going to win and only John Major could provide unity, so let's make it decisive and use the contest to give him renewed authority as we approach the general election. The alternative, of an extended campaign and damaging division, would seriously undermine our prospects. Allied to this message, there was a need for a massive, coordinated campaign to ensure that, after the result, our views on it dominated the airwaves.

Redwood expected to go on law and order today, so I spoke to Michael, also David Maclean and Michael Forsyth. Short discussion with Howell and Tim Collins about the Lobby Briefing I am doing later. Back to Cowley Street and then to the House at 9.45 and do some letters.

11.30 a.m.

Did a Lobby briefing in the subterranean gloom of the Ministerial Conference Room. It went well. Press have got their bearings on the campaign now.

Various media bids on the Green and door-stepped in Cowley Street. Rang colleagues who are doing articles for the weekend press, to ensure harmonisation of themes and coverage of the points that matter. With a huge sigh of relief, at 1.30 I headed off to the airport to fly to Edinburgh.

5.00 p.m.

Bute House. Two hours' peace before my dinner in Edinburgh Castle for the Scottish newspaper editors. All five ministerial colleagues present at dinner – briefed them first – resumé of lobby briefing. Editors friendly – felt at the centre of things.

After dinner, a late-night journey, seventy-five miles, home to Kersland – first time since the campaign began.

Saturday 1 July

What bliss to be at home, if only for a morning! A glorious summer's day. The lawns are as hard as concrete and in the fortnight since I was last here the garden has moved on dramatically. Rhododendrons almost over; roses out and well on everywhere, many looking bleached and blown. Albertine almost over already – it never lasts long; icebergs looking healthy. Shrubbery and big beds full of colour, weeds rocketing.

Listened to Redwood doing a frightful *Today* interview by telephone. Otherwise, the mood generally favourable to us.

Rang Gillian Shephard for a good and useful chat – I had heard she was a bit miffed at being out of things. Also rang Richard Ryder. Took a few press calls. Checked all well at Cowley Street. Spoke to Robert and arranged to meet him and Alastair for dinner at 19 Lord North Street.

A couple of hours' dealing with domestic matters and packing for the week ahead, including morning coat and dinner jacket for next Thursday's Holyrood Garden Party and Royal Week duties. Fortunately I have been excused royal duties until the campaign is over.

[Royal Week, when the Queen is in residence at the Palace of Holyrood, was normally a busy, though mainly ceremonial, time for the Secretary of State, who accompanied her on many of her engagements. I always enjoyed it, but on this occasion, although I would never have asked, I was relieved to be excused by a monarch sensitive to my dilemma.]

2.30 p.m.
Off to Glasgow Airport. Michael Howard tracked me down there in an excited state: who was meant to deal with the *Mail on Sunday*? I told him Robert and Howell would have dealt with that. They had.

6.00 p.m.
Got to Cowley Street where all were looking more rested and cheerful. David Davis in control. JM had just left after a good relaxed visit. Rumours abounding about what to expect in tomorrow's press – discussed our possible reaction. Good speakers lined up for all tomorrow's programmes. I am doing *On the Record*, pre-recording as live.

Dinner – Lord North Street, with Robert C and all the Goodlads. Then a quick chat with Robert upstairs – plans all falling well into place – before we went down to the round-up meeting. The mood there was less tense than before; all systems now running smoothly. I feel we are going to win. I've always felt that. But it has been stressful, because this time he is a serving Prime Minister, not just an outsider candidate.

11.00 p.m.
Home. Quick call to Malcolm Rifkind to thank and congratulate on his Friday *Newsnight* appearance, which I had not been able to watch, but which Cowley Street had said was terrific.

Sunday 2 July

Usual pattern – Cowley Street briefly, then Lord North Street. Watched Redwood, then JM on *Frost*. Redwood was better than he has been, but JM was better still – v. good, in fact.

Briefed for my *On the Record* interview, checked the media situation was under control, then off to BBC at Shepherds Bush to the tender mercies of John Humphrys. Eleven minutes. It went well, though Humphrys v. cunning – he tried to trap me several times. My message: strong support from constituencies; springboard for next election victory. JM reasserts his authority, etc.

Humphrys is a good interviewer. I liked him, although most colleagues didn't. He is quick and foxy, but he listens and responds to an answer and he does normally give you a chance to put your case forcefully. My most difficult interview with him was once in Edinburgh for *On the Record*, not because of his hostility or interruptions, but because half the scenery fell over with a very loud bang in the middle of the programme and I had to go on speaking as though nothing had happened.

From the BBC to my flat – lunch and telephoned some twenty

colleagues to thank for help, take soundings, etc. Watched myself and other lunchtime media.

3.00 p.m.

Meeting with Robert and Alastair in the upstairs study at Lord North Street. The grey, humid weather gave us all a sense of lassitude, enhanced by a feeling that the hard grind was behind us, our campaign was going smoothly and our plans were shaping up well. The media were champing at the bit for a news item. We decided, when Howell and Tim joined us, to rest on the *Frost* interview and the mood of MPs returning from the weekend with the supportive comments of their constituents.

Still trying to influence the press for tomorrow. *Evening Standard* may publish constituency association opinion poll figures, which we think will be v. supportive. Robert to speak to Basil Feldman of the National Union. We talked through next Tuesday – decided to discuss it at the evening meeting.

4.30 p.m.

Back, via Cowley Street, to flat in Vincent Square to ring around, do box, read newspapers and crash out for an hour. Got Willie Whitelaw at home; he agreed to write to JM as a precautionary step, urging him to cling on regardless for the sake of the party. We have discerned a determination in JM to go if he does not win decisively.

Dinner at Lord North Street, followed by the evening meeting. Long discussions on the '92' meeting to be held tomorrow night and on plans for Tuesday; both referred to sub-committees for tomorrow. Home 11 o'clock.

Monday 3 July

Eve of poll. Quick call first thing at Cowley Street – all under control. Press has some good articles (M. Parris and P. Riddell in *The Times*; JM in the *Telegraph*). But bad editorials – both papers against.

The Times says: 'If Mr Major wins tomorrow he will be even less amenable to the sceptics than he has been ... If MPs want change they must vote for Mr Redwood whether they like him or not.' The *Telegraph* harrumphs: 'It is time for Mr Major to go.' How little these press ayatollahs understand what our problems are really all about.

8.00 a.m.

Usual Lord North Street meeting. Started to map out Operation Overrule, my plan to sweep JM back regardless, swamping the media with our line on the outcome. We will man all media points from five o'clock – saturation by loyal colleagues.

Later, a session with Alastair, Graham Bright and Archie Hamilton, to look at the figures condensed from the past ten days of intensive polling and canvassing. They were just about as I had expected: 70+ for JR; 220+ for JM and 24+ abstentions. We know of course that at least 10 per cent of colleagues have lied to us.

To Scottish Office, to deal with immediate business and plan contingency for any reshuffle. Officials more confident of this than I am; I have always assumed I am here for the duration of this Parliament. But then, I got it wrong five years ago.

12.30 p.m.

Back to Cowley Street before media interviews on the Green. We are on the home straight and I am more relaxed about the fear of dropping a brick, also more confident about the outcome. Lunch in the House – fairly quiet, but the mood of MPs returning from their constituencies is, as I had anticipated, good. My line in the media interviews was: 'Our supporters in the country would not forgive us for failing to reinforce JM.' 'Abyss' features in headlines for PM's article, another of our key words. Back to the Scottish Office. Diary session and more work.

3.00 p.m.

Meeting (or was it this morning? – only hours ago and I can't remember!) with Robert, Howell and Tim in Lord North Street to discuss the details of Operation Overrule.

Operation Overrule was aimed at three targets: the opponent, John Redwood; the media, whose interpretation of the vote result might be hostile regardless of the figures; and the candidate himself, who might not accept that he had won and should continue. The first of these was addressed by the continuing campaign, which would go on right up to the close of poll on Tuesday.

For the second, I prepared briefing documents for the press and for the senior colleagues whom we would ask to spread all over the House and surrounding media points to convey the same clear message. The press document was factual. It listed the relevant statistics of all previous Conservative leadership contests (excluding the Anthony Meyer 'stalking donkey' contest of 1989), from which a number of useful facts could be drawn: no winning candidate had ever had a majority above 146; no winner had received more than 55 per cent of the vote; no winner had ever received more than 204 votes and no loser less than 128. In the recent Labour leadership election, Tony Blair had won only 60.5 per cent of Labour MPs and MEPs. We were confident (rightly) that John Major would beat all these records and we wanted the media to know it.

The briefing for our media interviewees gave them a factual interpretation of a range of outcomes, from 165 votes ('a clear win'), through 220 ('two thirds of the vote: a two to one majority'), to 240 ('off the top of the chart') and an appropriate comment, ranging from 'a good result' to 'a great victory'. Each of them was given a specific destination to seek out the media, so that our clear message would reach as many outlets as possible within the first twenty minutes of the result.

As for overruling the candidate himself, this would be difficult, but between us we contacted various senior influential figures in the party whose opinion we knew he would value. We also made sure that he, too, was aware of the quality of his victory, at whatever figure might emerge. In fact, he knew we were running an operation on this, because some of those who wrote to stiffen him copied their letters to Robert Cranborne. He has insisted since that no amount of stiffening would have persuaded him to continue if his vote had been below 215.

5.00 p.m.

To the House: some work, some mingling.

Division at 7.00, then Alastair came to my room to discuss mathematics and implications. We went together to Robert's room in the Lords for an eight o'clock meeting with Howell and Tim.

9.00 p.m.

Watched the news then to the 9.30 meeting in Michael H's room, at which Marcus Fox joined us later to discuss the arrangements for the count. Telephone lines are to be installed in the Committee Room so that the candidates can be told directly, without anyone having to fight their way through the press in the corridor outside.

Quick check on Cowley Street, then home. I was told earlier that word has come down that David Hunt is to be squeezed out of the 5.30 slot on BBC tomorrow. Too tired to wonder why.

Tuesday 4 July – Polling Day

Day of tension and triumph.

The morning meeting was put back half an hour so that Michael Howard and I could do media bids. He did the *Today* programme and I did BBC breakfast-time TV, live from the Green, and Radio Scotland from Millbank.

Before that I had looked in at Cowley Street, where the press was all over the place. *The Times*: 'Tories fear hollow victory' – a useful headline. *Daily*

Mail viciously hostile. I had a quick and useful telephone chat with Stewart Steven of the *Evening Standard*, whose first edition will be important.

At the meeting we covered all the remaining details for the day, in particular Operation Overrule, the main concern being the degree of enthusiasm on the part of the candidate to seize victory if the result is in the grey area.

By 11.30 I had completed, at the Scottish Office, the preparation of two briefs: a fact sheet of earlier leadership election figures and a Bullet Points brief. The problem was that the press had set targets that were hopelessly high and they now claimed that 220–230 was the beginning of the safe area for John. I had also prepared a short press release for immediate issue, designed to put a good spin on whatever result emerged and, if necessary, try to force his hand.

By noon, with almost all the day's formal media bids allocated, I had a rather unsettling meeting in the Lords with Robert, who had just seen the PM and found him in wobbly shape, determined to go if he judges his vote to be too low. Rumours about the way the vote was going were not good: concern about the Heseltine lot, none of whom had voted. We discussed steps to steady him, especially wheeling in Douglas Hurd, but also Clarke, Rifkind, Mayhew *et al*. Robert told me that John wanted him, me, Brian and Alastair at No. 10 for the result.

12.40 p.m.
Back to Cowley Street to do ITN and BBC street interviews, also Sky and one or two radio slots. Sandwich lunch inside, then over to the House.

Earlier this morning, after the Lord North Street meeting, I had done some rapid ringing around Cabinet colleagues, fixing up some of them to go to Michael Howard's room at the House at 3.30 for briefing and ten others to come to mine, in two groups, at 3.30 and 4.00. Before all that, however, I tried to snatch twenty minutes' sleep in my room at the

House. No such luck; after ten minutes the telephone rang. It was a friend in the Lords saying he had done some asking around and, should the worst befall, I should not rule myself out for future rounds. I thanked him politely and demurred, but was unable to doze off again. So I worked on my box for a while then at 2.45 went to discuss with Michael how we would brief colleagues later. I left batches of the two briefs with him; the fact sheet was already being issued to key media figures and would soon be distributed to the army of ministers and senior backbenchers we had lined up to invade the Green and commandeer all the media interview slots just as the result came through.

The idea that I should stand for the leadership if John Major fell was the kind of distraction I did not want in circulation at that time, just as we approached the climax of our campaign to keep him in post. It was true I had done my own reputation no harm during that campaign – and the campaigning team might in large measure have come in behind me. However, if John Major had fallen I would only have contemplated running if I could have been persuaded that that was the only way to prevent the party from splitting between the Heseltine wing and the authoritarian right. I would not have been easily persuaded – either then or later, in early 1997, when the bookies' odds on me started to narrow sharply. Happily, John Major's success saved me from having to reach a decision in 1995, just as the general election result was to take the issue out of my hands in 1997.

At 3.15, in the Chamber for PM's Questions. He performed well, but below his best. Labour childishly flourished Redwood leaflets. I had Matthew Parris's article from yesterday's *Times* in my pocket, in case it should become necessary later to make JM read it, to strengthen his resolve.

3.30 p.m.
The first batch of Cabinet colleagues trooped into my room: Virginia Bottomley, Stephen Dorrell, Jeremy Hanley, Gillian Shephard, John

Gummer and David Hunt. We went through the briefs and discussed lines to take and who would go where and when. They all seemed happy with the plan and keen to help.

4.00 p.m.
Repeated the exercise with Jonathan Aitken, Paddy Mayhew and William Waldegrave. Paddy told me he was going to see John to try to bolster him.

Soon afterwards there was a division. In the division lobby a senior backbench colleague asked for a word. We went to my room. Would I, if necessary, be willing to stand in the next round? Again I demurred. Would I at least consider it? The machinery was in place, I was in charge of it and it would probably remain intact and willing to work for me. I said I was not willing to think beyond today. He said he wasn't just speaking for himself, but reflecting a growing view.

I then went by car to Dover House and walked down Whitehall to the Cabinet Office entrance, hoping to reach No. 10 discreetly by this internal route, rather than by the heavily media-manned Downing Street. But I was filmed anyway by a TV crew in Whitehall.

As I made my way through to No. 10, Robert and Alastair appeared and we all converged on Howell James' office next to the Cabinet Room. Brian and Paddy were there already. The mood was subdued and anxious, news of the PM's state better. At 5.00, as the poll closed, we were summoned up to the sitting room: as well as John and Norma we found there Douglas Hurd and John Ward, his PPS and the No. 10 team of Alex Allan, Tim Collins, Howell James, Jonathan Hill and George Bridges.

I suppose this was one of the most tense but exciting political moments I have ever experienced. There was no false jollity, but a rather brittle calm. John, pale but placid, stood in front of the fireplace with a large glass of brandy. The rest of us arranged ourselves around the room, I on a chintz-covered window seat in the corner. White wine or water was offered around. On television, commentators burbled their nonsense as they, like us, waited for hard news.

At about 5.20 Howell, sitting next to me, thought he heard a telephone ring in the bedroom next door where John Ward had gone to await the call. He went to check and a minute later came back behind John Ward, who was clutching a large white notepad. His face gave nothing away as he handed the pad without a word to JM. From where I was sitting I could just see the number 218 in large writing at the top. The candidate gazed impassively at the result for what seemed an age before slowly reading out all the figures.

The relief that swept around the room was almost palpable. We all gave a suppressed but warm cheer and congratulated him on a famous victory. It was indeed. Redwood got 89; there were twenty abstentions and spoiled papers and two non-voters. John had won two thirds of the vote and that was higher in votes, in share of the vote and in majority than any previous leader had achieved. Nothing less would have done.

Indeed, the real question at this moment was: would it do? There was no clear mathematical dividing line between defeat and victory. He had had to beat comfortably the minimum requirement of 50 per cent of the poll and a 15 per cent majority, to retain any kind of credibility, and he had done that. Rather, it was a matter of whether or not the candidate who had called the contest, to ask for a vote of confidence in his leadership, felt that he had achieved it. We felt that he had, but our cheers and congratulations were, in part, intended to will the end. He was a tired and depressed man, who had felt betrayed by many in his party and undervalued and misrepresented by the media. All of us in that room shared those feelings. It was still possible that he would say the result wasn't good enough to go on. We waited for his verdict.

As I looked across at him, I thought he looked flat and unconvinced of his achievement, but after a pause he eventually said that he had set a minimum acceptable figure in his mind and this was only just above it.

That was good enough for me. I rang Debbie de Satgé, one of the hard-working secretaries in the campaign, who was waiting downstairs for the signal. She then rang Cowley Street and the roll-out of press releases and briefing began.

In the upstairs sitting room we listened to the broadcast of Marcus Fox announcing the result to a loudly cheering 1922 Committee. A further round of congratulations to the deflated-looking Prime Minister, who quietly thanked us all, before he and Norma went to tidy themselves up before facing the media.

I went downstairs with Howell to his room, to check that the roll-out media plan of our College Green army was going smoothly. Almost at once we saw evidence that it was. Robin Oakley on the BBC conceded a good victory and every later report and interview carried the same news, in the words we had prepared. John Redwood was seen making a courteous short statement conceding defeat.

Soon after six o'clock John and Norma came downstairs to be greeted by a warm round of applause from all the No. 10 staff, who had gathered in the hall. Just as the doorkeeper was about to throw open the front door the PM asked him to pause and he stood absolutely still, as though in prayer, for well over a minute in that dim and silent hall, considering precisely what he was going to say

Then he signalled he was ready, the door opened and he and Norma strode out to the biggest barrage of cameras, clicking and flashing that I can remember. We all lined up on the pavement behind him and listened to a good, fluent speech before trooping back in again.

Champagne appeared in the Cabinet Room and after a quick drink we agreed on a visit to Cowley Street now and a full party event to be held in No. 10 on Thursday evening. We began to disperse. I slipped out through Horse Guards and went round to Cowley Street to get there ahead of John and Norma. Again, a huge media crowd. The staff all came out on to the pavement as they arrived and gave him a great cheer. Then forty or fifty of us, including some we had barely seen during the campaign, all crammed ourselves into the little house and its garden. Champagne, three cheers repeatedly, another eloquent speech and the tension dissolved in jokes and laughter in a warm summer's evening.

7.00 p.m.

Got to the House in time for the vote. Mood very good. Rebels coming back on board. One had the sense of a cathartic experience, like winning a general election. Whilst I was sitting in the empty Aye lobby, just ahead of the division, discussing the events with Raymond Robertson, Michael Heseltine suddenly strode past at high speed, his eyes fixed firmly to the front, electricity sparking off him. His role and motives in the campaign had always been something of an enigma, but certainly now he had something very much on his mind. Whether it was a ploy that had failed or one that was about to succeed we could not tell.

After the division, more drinks in Michael Howard's room with the inner team, then a quick call to Stewart Steven to keep a promise for an article he is planning in the *Evening Standard*. John Major, I said, is now more powerful than he has been or will be again until he wins a general election. The party must unite behind him. The press must stop letting their proprietors and editors set the agenda and start reporting the facts. One lives in hope.

A relaxing dinner party in the House with Michael Ancram, Robert Atkins and Raymond Robertson. Then to No. 10 for yet another party, jolly but weary. Another division in the House at 11.00, during which many colleagues said nice things to me. Nicest of all was the Chief Whip, who told me to go home and go to bed.

The next morning, the mood at the Scottish Office was one of certainty that I would be promoted in the reshuffle now anticipated. Because of the small number of Scottish MPs I remained doubtful, but at least I was ready for it on this occasion when the summons came at ten o'clock. The press outside No. 10 seemed unsurprised to see me. I was taken in almost at once to the Cabinet Room where the Prime Minister was sitting in his usual chair at the table.

He gestured to the place on his right. He thanked me warmly for all I had done in the campaign, then: would he be right in thinking that I might not welcome an offer of the chairmanship of the party? He would. (I did not feel that I could cope with that job, which would require me to be in London, or elsewhere in England, almost every weekend. My own constituency was vulnerable and I doubted my stamina for so demanding a job, pure and exciting politics though it would be.) Would I welcome, then, an offer of the Presidency of the Board of Trade? I would. I seemed disappointed? No, I was just a bit stunned. What about Michael? He was going to do a new job and become Deputy Prime Minister. So, offer made and accepted. Did he think I should keep the title of President? He did and was glad to be able to offer me a big job on the UK stage. We discussed the other DTI Ministers and also the Scottish Office ones. Then I returned to the Scottish Office to say immediate farewells and clear my desk. Power transfers instantly. My job there was already over. I would return only to throw a farewell party. I held the record, at nine years (excluding my five years as Scottish Whip), as the longest continuously serving minister in the 110-year history of the Scottish Office. I was ready for a change – and I expect they were, too.

I could not go at once to DTI, so I based myself in my room at the House. From here I went to Jermyn Street for lunch with Michael Heseltine at Wiltons. He gave me several useful pointers for my new job, though our lunch was disturbed several times by telephone calls to him. Afterwards I took the chance to buy some shirts and ties in the summer sales before returning to the House, where Peter Gregson, the DTI Permanent Secretary, came to brief me.

Then it was time to go to my new Department, to meet my new private office staff and pick up my first box of papers. I did a few quick media interviews there before heading to Admiralty House for my first official duty, to present an honorary CBE to a leading American oil executive. Peter Morrison, a former energy minister, was there, deep in an armchair, looking overweight, florid and sweating profusely in the continuing heatwave. He wished me well and said he had already written to me. By the time his letter reached me two days later, he had died. It was a sad end to a life and a career that had once held so much promise.

The campaign of July 1995 was an experience of such intensity, so demanding physically and mentally, as to form a vivid milestone in the memories of my political career. It was for me personally supremely testing and correspondingly rewarding. The next day *The Times*, doing less than justice to Robert Cranborne's admirable leadership, hailed me as the 'campaign mastermind', who had been rewarded with one of the top prizes.

In reality, whilst I had controlled the operational side of the campaign and played a high-profile media role, Robert was indeed the leader of the team. With all the silken charm and finesse of the Cecils he had exercised brilliant overall control. Whilst keeping in touch with the hard work that was going on at Cowley Street and Lord North Street, he also maintained close links to opinion-formers at Westminster and in the media. Most importantly, he was the reassuring link between the candidate and his campaign, influencing both to good effect. It was a pity that, after victory was secured, Robert took against the victorious Prime Minister's reshuffled Cabinet.

In particular, I think he objected to Michael Heseltine's appointment as First Secretary of State and Deputy Prime Minister (or, as it rapidly came to appear on all his departmental papers, Deputy Prime Minister and First Secretary of State). That did not constitute a 'lurch to the left', though, or in any other direction. Michael was already *de facto* the Prime Minister's deputy following Douglas Hurd's retirement, and while he and Kenneth Clarke were two committed Europhiles in strong Cabinet positions, the balance of the Cabinet remained pronouncedly sceptical over the European Single Currency, though most of us understood the need for restraint in our public profiles on that issue. Such changes as John Major made to his Cabinet following the departure of Douglas Hurd, David Hunt, Jonathan Aitken and John Redwood had little overall effect on that balance. The leadership election had not, after all, been called as a battle of right versus left or Eurosceptic versus Europhile, but of loyalty versus disloyalty.

But what did that strangely surreal episode, fought out in a few hot, tense summer days within the confines of Westminster, actually achieve? It could have cleared the air. It could have purged the tired and riven Conservative Party of its divisions. In a party that still had any spark of moral fibre or team spirit, it should have done. But the ideological virus, so alien to Conservatism, had all but destroyed the traditional pillars of loyalty, unity and common sense. To the leader, who had placed his career at their disposal, his parliamentary party returned it grudgingly and without the willingness to be led. He had saved their bacon in 1992 and he believed that if he could overcome the infighting and reassert his leadership, as his victory should have allowed, a reunited party could still win again on the rapidly rising tide of economic success, or at any rate lose by a recoverable margin. If they rejected him, then there would be the chance to rally round another.

He offered them that chance, but you cannot save a party that no longer wants to be saved. Apart from John Redwood, the malcontents didn't put up and they didn't shut up. Had he known how the destructive minority within the party would continue to behave after July 1995, and the débâcle that would follow, John Major might well have stood down and let others fight for his job that autumn. As it was, his re-election as leader brought him only a short respite; and his party brought upon itself the later electoral cataclysm.

ELEVEN

In Trade

Another department, another desk. The office I inherited from Michael Heseltine as President of the Board of Trade (I kept the title as a courtesy to my predecessor) was much smaller than the chandeliered state room I had had at the Scottish Office. Low sofas lined the walls and his chair was wound so high that I couldn't get my knees under the desk.

This story leaked out to the diary columns of the press, which I regretted because, although in some of the events described in this book Michael was cast in the role of adversary and I disagreed with several of his policy stances, I never enjoyed less than friendship and support from him. Except on the EU where, to be fair, he was provoked intensely by the Europhobes, he was a party stalwart who always understood the importance of party discipline. I thought his judgement was haywire on some issues, such as the handling of the coal mines or of Post Office privatisation, but he was self-deprecating, with a good sense of humour, and he worked a lot harder in support of the Prime Minister and the Government than many of his critics in the party.

When Michael left DTI to become Deputy Prime Minister he took with him responsibility for deregulation and competitiveness. These were two core responsibilities of the department which I considered vitally important, so I resolved to keep them at the centre of the department's mission. Without them it lacked its central purpose. He also kept responsibility, at my request, for Lloyd's of London, then moving painfully towards reconstruction after years of heavy losses for its Names. Although I had resigned as a Name on joining the Cabinet I still had potentially enormous outstanding liabilities. This was a nagging worry that hung over me throughout my years in the Cabinet, so it was important that I should see no government papers and be involved in no decisions relating to Lloyd's.

While I strongly endorsed Michael's commitment to deregulation and competitiveness, I was less enamoured of some of the other initiatives he had launched, bequeathing them to me with often rather hazy forward funding arrangements. 'Business Links', for example, a scheme to develop 200 local, privately led enterprise support units – or 'one-stop shops' – around England, was similar to the local enterprise companies we had set up in Scotland a decade earlier, when economic conditions had been quite different. Michael had announced this flagship programme only days before the reshuffle, so I could hardly cancel it – the party would not be well served by a Cabinet Minister resiling ostentatiously from the commitments of his predecessors – but I no longer considered such schemes really necessary in the strongly improving economy we by now enjoyed. I decided to set up a review of all the business support schemes then being operated by DTI and subsequently reduced the total from 140 to 30, introducing a private sector input to their design and operation. Michael and I were to cross swords again when he wanted to reduce the rights of employees in small businesses and I wanted to keep them, and again when I wanted to encourage the use of the Arbitration and Conciliation Advisory Service (ACAS) in disputes, in order to reduce the number of cases going to industrial tribunals. No. 10 found in my favour on both points.

I was also less enthusiastic than Michael on backing 'national champions', which to me seemed incompatible with a belief in free markets and competition. But again I had to move away from Michael's stance gradually; and of course, where only one major British company was in contention for a large foreign contract I would give it my strong support.

Initially, most of the press accused me of maintaining the Heseltine agenda, but gradually I began to develop and spell out my own priorities, so then I was accused of abandoning it. I made it clear at an early press conference that I was not an interventionist and had no plans to intervene before breakfast, lunch, tea or dinner – as Michael had famously resolved to do at the party conference in 1992 – but that I did believe in the department giving help to industry, particularly to compete with heavily subsidised foreign industry. This, according to the *Financial Times*, made me neither an interventionist nor a believer in *laissez faire* but a pragmatist. Did I have an industrial strategy – that bane of the ideologues? Yes, to help industry and commerce to prosper and gain market share by exploiting every economic opportunity open to them.

Although many of the decisions required of me needed a pragmatic approach, one of the things I did want to do was to set DTI on a more rigorous philosophical course, based on a principled commitment, which I expressed in my Swinton Lecture at Bournemouth in 1996 as being 'to promote and achieve free trade, free enterprise and free competition'.

The first issue I had to deal with, on my first day in office, was to take a decision on which new attack helicopter to support for a major contract the Ministry of Defence was keen to place – an intriguing echo of the Westland crisis that had caused my predecessor such grief when at the Ministry of Defence a decade earlier. I asked Michael Portillo, the new Defence Secretary, to come round to discuss it. He favoured the American

Apache bid and, once he had agreed to press the Americans for a much higher percentage of British components in the final package, so did I. He also agreed to my request that in negotiations in future my officials specialising in Britain's defence equipment manufacturing capacity would be brought into the loop earlier by the MoD, to ensure that where we could match or better foreign manufacturers' componentry we would press our case sooner, securing a higher content of such contracts for our own companies. It was an encouragingly positive start after the divisions of the leadership contest, which was reflected briefly between other departments around Whitehall. Soon, though, the old internecine strife between departments, otherwise known as creative tension, reasserted itself around Whitehall.

Where the Scottish Office had had a taut hierarchical structure that brought the decision-making process efficiently to the top, DTI had a more modular and linear structure. It was full of separate unrelated pockets of expertise and with seven junior ministers it was more dispersed than I liked. In other times I would have wanted to take it apart, re-examine and challenge every function and put it together again with a clearer and more coordinated sense of its purpose. But with the next general election imminent and the Government brought constantly to the brink of collapse by its ideological rebels, this was not the time for departmental navel-gazing.

I was not in the camp of those purists who said we did not need the department at all. After all, Adam Smith had pointed out the need to police the market. And our trading achievements over the two centuries of the Board of Trade's existence had been remarkable. I did think, however, that it needed a thorough review of every function, leading to a clearer focus based on first principles. It contained much expertise but it tried to do too many things. It should be smaller and more efficient, and it needed to be given a more precise sense of purpose.

At the same time as losing official ministerial responsibility across government for deregulation and competitiveness, I inherited at DTI responsibility for science and technology from the Cabinet Office and for pay, industrial relations and the unemployment statistics from the abolished Department of Employment. In addition, the department had absorbed the old Department of Energy in 1992. Tim Eggar was already an experienced industry minister, with a special understanding of energy matters, and Peter Fraser, who had come across with me from the Scottish Office as our House of Lords Minister of State, took over the energy portfolio with skill when Tim retired. Anthony Nelson became minister for trade, spending most of his time abroad on trade missions. Jonathan Evans, Richard Page and Phillip Oppenheim each presided over his own bit of the department and brought to our twice-weekly meetings a stimulating range of Conservative views. Later on, John Taylor and Greg Knight joined us. Completing the team, Ian Taylor was a fluent and accomplished science and technology minister, who clearly understood what he was talking about. This was just as well, as it was a period of dramatic global advance in that field and, following the liberalisation of our telecommunications industry a few years earlier, Britain was at the forefront.

We launched a campaign called the Information Society Initiative to involve small businesses in the use of new technology, in the hope that more of our frontier innovations could be successfully translated into commercial ventures. We launched another to help new companies in the field of biotechnology. I went to the United States, where I found a ready listener at the White House in Laura Tyson, President Clinton's economics adviser, on the benefits of telecommunications liberalisation.

I took my responsibilities for science and technology seriously and had the valued support of the Government's chief scientific adviser Sir Robert May and of Sir John Cadogan, Director General of Research Councils. As I had no scientific background myself, it was with some trepidation that I found myself hosting a weekend conference soon after my appointment of the science ministers of all the G7 nations. But all went well; the basic issues were political, not scientific.

I valued the quality of our blue skies research in Britain, but I also wanted to encourage greater interaction between the science base and industry. In this context one of the initiatives I strongly supported was the Technology Foresight exercise, to improve relations between academe and industry, and in a speech to the Social Market Foundation a year after taking office I gave what the science publication *Research Fortnight* described as 'a closely reasoned justification for continued government funding of basic research.' They were also kind enough to credit me with 'setting out the most coherent theoretical basis for government funding of research by a Cabinet minister for years.'

The most difficult and contentious area of operations for a Secretary of State for Trade & Industry was in the field of acquisitions and mergers. I was a supporter of the tripartite system that then operated, whereby the Office of Fair Trading, the Monopolies and Mergers Commission and the Secretary of State, operating personally in a judicial capacity, each contributed from their own standpoint to a considered and informed judgement. Of course, personal discretion can lead to a wrong, a biased or a politically motivated decision. Restraint and propriety is needed, as well as judgement and conscientious scrutiny. But the whole premise of good government rests on those qualities, and, however inadequately, I always tried to exercise them. In the public utilities, their regulators had a role as well. But my ambition was to see the regulators work their way towards a much reduced role as competitive markets developed. Meantime, there would soon be scope for merging some of them.

I am not sure if the ever-present threat of judicial review acted as a constraint in my consideration of mergers, but it certainly made it difficult to explain as fully as one wished how a particular decision had been reached. In anticipation of this, when I announced my first three decisions on takeover bids in the electricity industry, I took the opportunity to enunciate the principles that would guide me in future decisions. Electricity was a complex industry, newly developed in the private sector, so it was a particularly sensitive area.

Despite that precaution, I was to be accused at first of inconsistency. Critics did not seem to realise that the same principles, consistently applied, will not necessarily deliver the same outcome if the circumstances to which they are applied are different. Nor was there a formal blueprint or game plan to achieve a particular overall picture. Each case had to be considered in detail on its own merits.

I made it clear that the regional electricity companies, the still young, private sector companies that had been nurtured to help create a competitive market in electricity, should be subject to the normal disciplines and opportunities of the market place. In considering mergers involving the regional suppliers I would take into account the need for the Director General of Electricity Supply to discharge his regulatory duties for the benefit of the customer and the possible adverse impact that the loss of one or more independent comparators could have on that. I also said that the extent to which an enhanced degree of vertical integration – for example, the combination of a generating company with a distributing company – might jeopardise transparency or competition would be taken into account, though vertical integration was not inherently unacceptable. I stressed above all, that competition would be the underlying determinant of all decisions.

With the support of the Director of Fair Trading, I cleared the first three bids to cross my desk. This was controversial because one bidder was an American company and another, Scottish Power plc, was a vertically integrated one. But the last thing competition should exclude was foreign competition, if a free market was really to develop. There was no jeopardy to the comparator considerations; and Scottish Power, though vertically integrated in Scotland – I had helped to set it up – had only a limited share of the generation market in England, where its target, Manweb, operated. The basic structure of the emerging market would be unaffected.

Three months after this, the two great generating companies, National Power plc and Powergen plc, launched bids for the regional companies Southern Electric plc and Midlands Electricity plc respectively. They seemed blithely to assume that, having cleared three quite different bids already, I would now clear theirs. But these bids were quite different, in magnitude and in structural terms. I had no doubt at all that they could substantially inhibit the developing competitive market, which was not expected to be fully formed until 1998. With the support of both the Regulator and the Director General of Fair Trading, I referred them both to the MMC. Bedlam ensued. I was traduced by the generating companies and their City supporters. Their share prices, talked up in previous weeks, came down to earth.

The *Independent* came out in my support. So did *The Times*, pointing out that I had said that 'at this stage, more than two years ahead of the arrival of full competition in the supply of electricity to private homes, someone must say how far the wholesale dismemberment of the sector should go.' Others were less charitable, referring to 'shock waves', 'chaos', and 'turmoil' being thrown into the industry and blasting me for inconsistency. I held my peace, as I had to do.

In due course the MMC delivered its findings. They found the merger to be against the public interest, due to the extent of vertical integration it would create on either side of the sensitive and complex electricity pool. They drew attention to the large market shares that the two companies would have in the generation and supply markets and their possible access to privileged information as a regional supply company about other generators' future plans. By a majority they recommended, in spite of these problems, that the bids could be allowed, subject to various undertakings as to future conduct.

I was not convinced, so I blocked both bids. The degradable nature of the undertakings sought and given did not give me confidence that they would suffice, but the reasons identified by the MMC as to why the bids would operate against the public interest and be detrimental to competition in the current state of the market's development were, anyway, too fundamental to ignore.

A billion pounds was wiped off the value of the electricity companies following my announcement. One newspaper called the decision 'courageous', which in *Yes, Minister* code used to mean foolhardy to the point of madness. But once the disappointed bidders and their backers had let off steam I was relieved to see a change of tone in press comments. The *Independent* identified a 'Lang doctrine' of competition emerging, returning to the free market principles of Margaret Thatcher's government after the more corporatist approach of Michael Heseltine. It approved my 'rejection of national champions in favour of competition'. It was my clear view that if national champions were to emerge, able to compete globally, they should be forged in a highly competitive home market, not nurtured into domestic monopolies. The *Financial Times* said my instincts were right and gradually the underlying consistency of my approach came to be acknowledged.

In the airline industry, British Airways sought my help in its bid to form a partnership with American Airlines. That would have put it in a very strong position on the transatlantic route. Was BA a national champion? Virgin Atlantic and British Midland would not think so. BA were in a league of their own, however, and there was a huge potential gain if an open skies policy resulted, something that had always proved elusive. I reasoned that the price for the deal should be landing slot surrenders, rather than simply blocking it, and was pleased when John Bridgeman, the Director General of Fair Trading, accepted the view that 168 slot surrenders would be a fair penalty. We both knew that the EU would seek a higher price and so indeed it proved. But the real test would be the United States Transport Department. It was sad, for BA and for hopes of an open skies breakthrough, to see the protracted negotiations that then ensued, with years of dogged persistence before the two airlines finally had to admit defeat.

My attitude to the vexed issue of monetary union and the future development of the EU was straightforward. Like most people I had welcomed the growth of the Common Market as the economic bulwark against future war on the continent and as a liberalising measure of value to Britain's trade. I did not see the need, still less the desirability, of closer political union, or the monetary union which would inescapably bring it about. Free trade areas do not need political or monetary union; I made a widely ignored speech to make that point.

So I had greatly welcomed the central thrust of the Single European Act of 1985 which had led to a free trading area across the member countries, though not yet perfectly implemented. Unfortunately Margaret Thatcher conceded too much in order to secure the single market prize, not least in the field of qualified majority voting. This Act led inexorably to the Treaty of Maastricht and all the problems the Conservative Party was subsequently to face.

John Major pulled off a great coup in drawing the teeth of Maastricht, not just in the opt-outs from monetary union and the social chapter but also in the adoption of the principle of subsidiarity, better budgetary controls and substantive progress towards the implementation of the single market. He won against the odds through a mixture of stamina, determination, diplomacy and a mastery of detail. Rightly, he was hailed as a conquering hero on his return – reminiscent of Disraeli's return from the Congress of Berlin.

Multiple negotiations were always one of John Major's strengths. His analytical powers and the tenacity of his grip, both on the facts and on the different nuances and strands of argument, enabled him to weave an agreed solution out of opinions that had often diverged widely at the outset. I saw this often in Cabinet and I recall another occasion when his capacity for handling the variable geometry of EU negotiations served us well. It was at the European Community Summit in Edinburgh in 1992, not long after our election victory. The Queen was hosting a reception on the royal yacht *Britannia* for the Heads of Government, to which I, as Secretary of State for Scotland, was also bidden.

As I was talking to Chancellor Kohl, whom I had entertained in Edinburgh earlier in the year, the Prime Minister came up and conversation turned to the deadlocked issue of national budgetary contributions to the Community budget. Spain was holding out for more; we and the Germans, as contributors, were resistant. Other leaders were talking in groups. Our Chancellor, Norman Lamont, was deep in discussion with the Moderator of the General Assembly of the Church of Scotland. Soon, however, our group expanded as Felipe Gonzalez, other leaders and even the Queen herself were drawn in. With a mixture of joshing and hard arithmetic, the Prime Minister spelt out a possible solution, and while disclaiming that this friendly chat constituted a negotiation – it was neither the time nor the place – laid the ground for the deal that was hammered out later that night.

After his return from the negotiating success at Maastricht, the Prime Minister won a ringing endorsement from the party in Parliament, that same party that was to return victorious on his coat-tails in the 1992 general election and then to resile from what they had so enthusiastically endorsed. The indiscipline and disloyalty of the 1992 Parliament was a black period in Conservative history. Those who indulged in it brought about, on their own, the disaster of 1997 and all that has followed.

My own task was to defend the social chapter opt-out the Prime Minister had won at Maastricht against the European Commission, who wanted to undermine it, and the Labour Party, who wanted to surrender it.

The social chapter opt-out was one of the factors in an economic performance that put us head and shoulders above the rest of Europe. Yet our European partners resented that success and instead of emulating it sought to reduce the improved competitiveness that had won us almost half of all the American and Japanese investment in Europe.

The working time directive was a case in point. The Commission sought to circumvent our opt-out by introducing this measure as a health and safety issue, which could then be imposed on us by qualified majority voting. The European Court of Justice upheld the decision. Our Law Officers advised us to accept the decision, but they did not have to face an angry party in the House. I decided that attack was the best form of defence and made a number of bellicose statements, with the aim of reassuring our backbenchers that we would reverse this breach of good faith at the next intergovernmental conference. We never managed to do so, but the issue was by then defused.

Again, in the autumn of 1996, I decided to go on the offensive in Europe by publishing, in several different languages, a pamphlet on the difference between our approach and that of our European partners on the social chapter. We circulated it round tens of thousands of continental businesses, but I fear it had little impact; and the incoming Labour government was, of course, to surrender our hard-won opt-out the next year, gaining nothing in exchange but diminishing Britain's competitive edge.

Since Margaret Thatcher's achievements in transforming industrial relations in the 1980s, the subject had been an electoral plus for the Conservative Party. This had been helped by steadily falling unemployment, but our opponents were still fomenting the fear of unemployment and in my view we were insufficiently sensitive to the need to sound more understanding and sympathetic on this issue. Speaking at a press briefing after addressing the CBI Conference in Birmingham in November 1995,

I decided to try to strike a less authoritarian and more sympathetic note by acknowledging that there were indeed people who had anxieties about losing their job. It was a state of mind that did exist. Despite falling unemployment, it was understandable and we must try to allay it.

My remarks barely seemed to register with the assembled hacks – it did not suit their cast on us as the cold-hearted party. But one, and just one, journalist whose newspaper inserted the word 'only' ahead of the phrase 'a state of mind' gave my remarks the opposite meaning to what I had actually said. A wholly bogus row ensued, with the Labour Party calling a special press conference to make a huge song and dance about it. I was at a business conference in Berlin with the Prince of Wales when the row broke, which made it difficult to react quickly or clearly. Meantime, some of the more gullible of our backbenchers were lured by the media into criticising what they were told I had said, and the row got worse. 'Mindless fool', leered the *Daily Mirror*.

This episode epitomised the problems the Government faced in those years, with a sometimes venal press, a dishonest opposition and a party only too ready to break ranks. I suppose I was lucky that that was the only occasion in which I gave them an opening to misconstrue my message. After the 1997 election, the reporter in question got a job in No. 10.

Our resistance to a national minimum wage was, I suspect, another issue that cost us political support. I am sure we were right on the substance: a minimum wage introduced at the levels the unions were demanding would certainly have destroyed many thousands of jobs. But we were wrong on tone: again we allowed ourselves to sound heartless as a party. When after the election the new government fulfilled its manifesto commitment by bringing in a minimum wage, though at a cynically low level that would have little impact either on low incomes or the jobs market, I urged my party to drop their opposition to this measure. It was self-defeating to continue to oppose it. I am glad that they took the same view.

Although our strikes record as a nation had improved dramatically, in the summer of 1996 a new phenomenon developed: a surge of strikes in the monopoly public utilities, such as the fire service, the railways, the London Underground and the Post Office. The ruthless use of the public as hostages in these disputes was something many people found distasteful, but our industrial relations officials at DTI had had trouble defining 'essential services' in legal terms, so that industrial action in them might be banned.

I thought they were going about it in the wrong way. I asked them to consider withdrawing the unions' legal immunity from civil lawsuits where the damage and upset caused by their actions was disproportionate or excessive. It seemed to me that if we were to legislate in that way, the resultant uncertainty might inhibit union militancy. Over time, case law would build up, creating a new form of protection for the public.

Somewhat to my surprise, my officials came back and said that we could indeed approach the problem in this way. I then discovered that a similar approach was already used in Belgium and Germany. That might be the kiss of death to my proposals, but I got Cabinet colleagues' approval to publish them in a Green Paper. Seventy per cent of all days lost through strikes were now in the public utilities and we knew it stuck in the craw of most people that those employed in these monopoly industries, supported by their taxes, should hold them all to ransom.

The Green Paper had a good reception and so did my party conference speech at Bournemouth, in which I spelled them out and at the same time tweaked the Labour Party's tail on a subject that embarrassed them deeply. The Green Paper had a number of other proposals, amongst others to double the 'cooling-off' period before a strike could be called; to raise the threshold required for a pre-strike ballot; and to require re-balloting in the event of a significant new offer from the employers.

It was a package of measures that could certainly have helped to fight the scourge of public sector strikes. As it was, of course, the loss of the

1997 election put paid to them, but not before we had seized the initiative in the first week of that election campaign, for almost the only time, by putting the Labour Party on the spot. Meanwhile, the underlying problem has not gone away.

The Post Office, one of the targets of my proposals, had by then already been a hot potato because our own backbenchers rejected Michael Heseltine's proposals to 'privatise' it. In the light of that rejection by our own side, a new approach was needed. A series of one-day strikes had alienated public opinion, and my opposite number Margaret Beckett had further antagonised the public with her reaction: 'I have nothing whatsoever to say.' This led me to accuse the Opposition of taking part in a sponsored silence. It also gave us a chance to revisit the question of the Post Office's future.

Gregor Mackay – who had given me good support as my special adviser, coming across with me from the Scottish Office, via John Major's leadership campaign – had gone to join the private sector by now. To take his place I was lucky to find Greg Clark, an academic with a strong intellectual grip and philosophical drive, who made the most demanding task seem easy. With him I developed a new set of proposals for the Post Office's future.

In essence, I proposed to Cabinet colleagues that we should 'privatise' Parcelforce, which in those days could have a viable future. We should introduce competition into local letter delivery by allowing other companies to bid for the franchise for collection and deliveries in particular regions, at the same time preserving the national identity and livery of the Royal Mail and the universal service obligation. This would be policed and enforced by a Post Office Council; and subsidy would be available in some regions to ensure that the universal service would be upheld in underpopulated areas.

I gained Cabinet agreement to this approach, but we decided not to include them in our election manifesto as they could be so easily misrepresented during an election campaign. I will never know whether, if we had won that election, I might by now have implemented my plans.

The Post Office tackled me, as they have our successors, with bids for what they termed 'commercial freedom'. I steadfastly refused to countenance it. Partly, I disliked the idea of subsidised Post Office competition for other services with the private sector. More substantively, I did not believe they had either the management capacity or the commercial discipline to take on these distractions. Our successors did cave in and the result does not seem to me to have been a glittering success.

One privatisation that we did carry off, rather against expectations, was that of the nuclear electricity generators. A few years earlier it would have been considered impossible, politically if not in economic terms, but early in 1995 Michael Heseltine, Ken Clarke as Chancellor and I met to discuss the prospects. I was still at the Scottish Office then and Scotland had two important nuclear generators out of the eight main ones around the United Kingdom. We had to decide whether to sell them all off in one large public company, or to split them up. Michael and Ken favoured one large company. I knew that a separate company holding just the Scottish plants might not be viable so I agreed, provided the new company was based in Scotland, with all its head office functions there, and had a Chairman with good Scottish credentials. Also there should be a golden share to be held by the Secretary of State for Scotland.

This was brazenly partisan of me, but that is what happens when governments have territorial departments. The Scottish press were already anticipating job losses in Scotland and decision-making going south as Scottish Nuclear Ltd disappeared. Tortuous negotiations ensued, but rather to my surprise I eventually got my way and found myself announcing at the Scottish Conservative Conference in May that Scotland would soon be home to a major new private sector company,

British Energy plc. The Scottish media were so pleased that they forgot to ask themselves whether or not they approved of privatising nuclear power.

The following summer, translated to DTI, I had the trickier task of ensuring a successful flotation. Tim Eggar, then Energy Minister, had undertaken most of the detailed preparatory work, but when it came to pricing the issue I decided to squeeze it up by a penny or two more than had been proposed. When dealings began in July, I visited the Stock Exchange and saw it get off to a good start. It was only then that our City advisers BZW informed me that they had codenamed the project 'Mission Impossible'. Looking back on my involvement in the establishment of a private sector electricity industry over those years, I find I can claim to have acted as co-architect and midwife to what must now constitute three of Scotland's six largest public companies.

As well as wrestling with the day-to-day problems of DTI, I was keen to sharpen policy on trade itself, the core purpose of the department, as it seemed to me that the time was overdue to revitalise our approach and to give it a new cutting edge. In a series of speeches I set out to do that, founding my approach on a strong philosophical commitment to liberalisation.

It was the right time to do this. The Uruguay Round had been concluded two years earlier and the new World Trade Organisation was coming into being, to replace, after fifty years, the General Agreement on Tariffs and Trade. Also, with protectionism still permeating the trade policies of some of our EU partners, there was a need to try to inject a more liberalising approach into their attitudes. The first shot I fired, however, was aimed not at them, but at the United States.

Americans were on the whole strongly committed to free trade, but when specific American interests were at stake, or when congressional or presidential elections loomed, they could be stubborn and persistent opponents.

Our first row was over Cuba. The Americans, in pursuit of their own long-running vendetta against that country, suddenly decided to impose various forms of sanction against the companies from other countries that did business with Cuba. This wholly unjustified unilateral action, pursued under the auspices of the Helms–Burton Act, led to a number of encounters between me and the American Ambassador, the crusty Admiral Bill Crowe, before the row was eventually settled. At one of them he confessed that he had recently been caught smoking a Cuban cigar. When challenged, he had responded: 'Never forget the first rule of warfare – burn your enemy's crops.'

Addressing an economics seminar in Washington late in 1995, I decided to tackle the Americans on their failure to play a full part in the continuing negotiations on the trade in services. They had lodged a limited offer over the opening up of financial services but it did not go far enough to meet the spirit of progressive liberalisation. Shipping was another area where they were dragging their feet. Alone among developed countries they had offered no movement over the removal of barriers.

Of course, the Americans were looking askance at the policies of France and other EU countries who were being slow to come on board, but I was keen to achieve a unity of purpose with them, so that we could make common cause over such matters as public procurement, tighter control of government subsidies, the faster implementation of tariff cuts and better protection of intellectual property rights at the forthcoming EU–US trade talks in Madrid. On these and a host of other specific matters – mutual standards recognition, competition policy, simpler rules of origin, the work of customs authorities – I was trying to build a common longer-term agenda as we looked towards the forthcoming major World Trade Organisation Conference in Singapore at the end of 1996. Even there, though, I was to cross swords with the US Trade Representative Charlene Barshefsky over labour rights, when she sided with those who wanted to involve the WTO in this issue. I believed that minimum labour standards, though important, should be handled through the International Labour Organisation, rather than clouding our trade negotiations with them.

I always considered that a focused, incremental approach to trade liberalisation was more likely to achieve results than the grandstand approach favoured by the Foreign Office of calling for a great EU–US Transatlantic Free Trade Area. Apart from being wholly unrealistic at the time, against a background of deadlock on such vexed issues as agriculture and textiles, it ran counter to the multilateral approach to free trade that was essential in order to bring the developing countries along with us. If they saw the two great trade blocks of the world form one massive trading area from which they were excluded, their suspicions of our motives would be multiplied. The building blocks of the North American Free Trade Area, Mercosur (in South America) and the EU itself were one thing – and on the whole helpful, including as they did poor countries as well as rich – but desirable though transatlantic free trade was, a new trading bloc embracing most of the great economies of the world would be a step too far. Whilst trying to break down the fortress mentality that persisted in some quarters on both sides of the Atlantic, we would have lost the rest of the world.

But as well as a detailed, step-by-step approach on a whole range of specific trade issues, what I felt was needed now was a major new international campaign to maintain the momentum of the Uruguay Round, with a view to starting a new global trade round. Britain was well placed to lead this, as the leading EU free trade nation and with our extensive worldwide trading relationships. It might result in the conclusion of a new trade liberalisation package by, say, 2010. That in turn could lead to a further round that might achieve global free trade by 2020. At any rate, that was the 2020 vision that I launched in a speech to the British American Chamber of Commerce in April 1996. It needed to be followed through, so by the time the WTO met in December I had made a number of further speeches to develop my theme.

In October, I laid out my shopping list for the forthcoming conference. I wanted a substantial work programme to be agreed to put in place the new rules and mechanisms needed to secure the commitments agreed during the Uruguay Round. I also wanted an Information Technology Agreement, real progress on the liberalisation of telecommunications, and a new working party on investment. In November I developed my thoughts on the need for the free flow of investment and finance, as vital to the undeveloped countries of the world as to the richer ones. It was an area in which Britain excelled as a practitioner: not only had we one of the best inward investment records in the world, but we were also second only to the United States as an outward investor, and our financial sector was the envy of the world.

There was no doubt that many of our exporting companies found it easier to open doors in other countries if they took part in a government-sponsored trade mission. Our economic performance at home was running very strongly at the time, with gains in productivity and competitiveness that encouraged them to seek new markets. I took trade delegations to Mexico, India and Russia, and I led the largest trade missions ever to leave our shores, to Japan and China. It was rewarding to see British exports breaking new records. I had a Union Flag installed behind my desk at DTI. I was told this was un-British, but there was a message to send out, to the EU and to the nationalists within the United Kingdom as well as to Britain's markets around the world: British is best.

In the autumn of 1996 I published a White Paper, jointly with the Foreign Office, whose embassies around the world were now so much better geared to the trade agenda. In it the Foreign Secretary Malcolm Rifkind and I joined forces to promote that agenda. At Singapore I made good progress, achieving most of the targets I had set myself. It was a successful and productive conference, but I have to add that interest at home in its outcome was negligible: it was a distraction to the British media, concerned only with the never-ending rows over the European Union.

The storm clouds of the approaching electoral apocalypse were growing darker by the minute. But there was one more interlude of productive trading policy to be pursued before they burst upon us. In January 1997 John Major and I led a trade mission to India and Pakistan, partly to pave the way for the Queen's forthcoming visit to celebrate fifty years of independence. It was an Indian summer for us both. Our Prime Minister, so abused at home by our unique media, enjoyed enormous popularity abroad. All along the route into Calcutta from the airport, the streets were lined with friendly crowds. Banners and flags were waving and as we approached the city centre John Major was cheered by thousands from the densely packed pavements. As I reported to Cabinet on our return, they weren't all just waiting to cross the street.

A similar reception awaited him throughout the tour. Whether being mobbed by the crowds at a cricket ground or cheered by the troops at the Khyber Pass, the welcome was the same. We returned to London feeling buoyed up and relaxed after a highly successful visit. It was just as well, in view of what lay ahead.

TWELVE

Extravagant with the Actualité

The Scott Report

Political crises can spring from a clear blue sky, exploding suddenly like a summer storm and then dissolving, or they can grow slowly from nothing, a tiny cloud on the horizon, until they lower across the political heavens, touching, tainting and overshadowing the entire scene. The 'Arms to Iraq' affair was of the latter type.

I had largely ignored it in its early stages. It was just one more shock-horror story with which the press and Opposition liked to berate the Government. There was probably nothing to it. Preoccupied with my Scottish Office duties and having no involvement in government with either arms or Iraq, I was content to let others worry and to await the report of Sir Richard Scott, the judge chosen by the Lord Chancellor James Mackay whom the Prime Minister had appointed to investigate matters after ever more lurid headlines began to dominate the news.

My arrival at DTI in July 1995 changed all that. On my first day there, my new Private Secretary John Alty said to me: 'Of course you realise,

President, that you have inherited the poisoned chalice?' Which particular one was that? 'You will in due course receive, and will have to present to Parliament, the Scott Report.' Alarm bells at once started ringing. The fate of at least two ministers, possibly several more – indeed of the Government itself – could hang on the outcome of the by now very protracted deliberations of one judge, sitting alone, without the help of assessors or any other kind of balancing mechanisms. Moreover, Sir Richard had been given a free and unhampered brief which he was indulging to the full. When appointed, as an experienced and available judge who was in line to become Vice-Chancellor, his task was expected to take around six months. That was now almost three years ago and it looked as though it might be 1996 before he finished the Report. At least that gave me time to prepare.

The origins of the alleged scandal were diffuse and somewhat obscure, but there seemed to be three strands. Firstly, several firms of dealers in arms and military equipment had been thought to have broken both sanctions and the Government's declared policy in exporting their products to Iran and Iraq after the end of the Iran–Iraq war in 1988. Secondly, government ministers had, it was claimed, both encouraged these exports and secretly changed the guidelines that governed the granting of licences. Thirdly, it was claimed that when HM Customs & Excise had decided to prosecute such companies, ministers had run for cover, leaving the exporters to face the music.

Evidence of all this was at best tenuous – for example, there were no sanctions until the Gulf War after Iraq invaded Kuwait in 1990 – but that was never an impediment to the British press in indignant hue and cry. Fed increasingly outlandish stories by an unscrupulous Opposition, they soon had the public believing that there was a massive conspiracy of corruption, greed and cover-up. The spirit of Titus Oates rode out across the land.

The plunger that was to detonate this particular bomb was held by

Alan Clark, the Trade Minister at DTI when the story started to run and never a safe pair of hands. He had worked tirelessly as a minister to help British exporters of all kinds and was known by colleagues to take a grand imperial view of Johnny Foreigner and of the rules that constrained trade – and why not, up to a point? It was he who proposed to ministerial colleagues in 1988 that the guidelines first agreed and promulgated in 1984 should be revised, to reflect the fact that the Iran–Iraq war to which they referred had ended. Indeed, he had lobbied the Prime Minister on the issue as far back as 1985. But when in February 1991 HM Customs & Excise decided to prosecute Matrix Churchill, a small Midlands company whose lathes had apparently ended up in a munitions factory in Iraq, Clark in his evidence stoutly denied that he had in any way, by word or deed, encouraged or helped them to break either sanctions or guidelines. He repeated these denials to the new Prime Minister and to the Cabinet Secretary, Sir Robin Butler, when confronted with the charge at a meeting in the Cabinet Room in Downing Street in December 1990. He stood by his story in submitting his witness statement in 1991, ahead of the trial; and he reaffirmed it just before the trial began in September 1992.

Four weeks into the trial however, confronted with the minutes of a meeting between himself and the Machine Tool Association several years earlier, Clark, who was no longer a minister or even an MP, seemed finally to realise the enormity of the consequences of his subsequent denials. He changed his evidence to say that yes, he had been 'economical with the *actualité*' (echoing the phrase 'economical with the truth' deployed earlier by the former Cabinet Secretary Sir Robert Armstrong during the notorious *Spycatcher* trial in Australia) and he had indeed given nods and winks to Matrix Churchill. The trial immediately collapsed, on 9 November 1992. Several other cases – Ordtec, Astra, BMARC, BSA – where a number of convictions had already been secured were all thrown into doubt. For the Opposition, the game was afoot. The following day the setting up of the Scott Inquiry was announced.

The Prime Minister had found it necessary on a number of earlier occasions to appoint judicial inquiries in order to deal with alleged scandals. It was not a good tactic in normal times: it gave formality to rumours and innuendo; it extended the life of meretricious news stories; and it took the political agenda out of governments' hands. Perhaps ironically in this case, it effectively gagged ministers, who could not respond to wild opposition charges whilst an inquiry was in progress. But it also reassured the public, took the heat off an issue whilst the inquiry was taking place, and usually ended either with an acquittal or with the dispersal of blame and the need only for a few administrative changes in departmental procedures.

In the febrile atmosphere that pervaded the whole of that fractious 1992 parliament, when the Government was beset on so many fronts by its enemies – the worst front being the one behind it – it was hardly surprising that the Prime Minister sent for Sir Richard Scott and gave him *carte blanche*. *Carte longue*, too: almost three and a half years, during which, far from getting lost in the long grass, the story continued to run with increasing heat and drama.

Labour MPs loved feeling virtuous about opposing arms sales, whilst privately lobbying for companies in their own constituencies. The arms trade was and is a fiercely competitive business, of great value to British industry, but it has always had its shady side. Government licensing arrangements existed to protect Britain's international and diplomatic interests and to inject a fair and predictable discipline into the trade.

After Alan Clark's recantation two things happened almost at once. The prosecution begun in 1991 of the Managing Director of BSA for illegally exporting machine tools to Iraq for use in military manufacture was dropped. Four executives of Ordtec, who in February 1992 had pleaded guilty to a charge of illegal exportation to Iraq of a fuse assembly line, started an appeal process against their sentences. In November 1995 their sentences would be quashed.

In a third case, known as the Dunk case, two executives convicted in November 1985 of the illegal export of arms and ammunition to Iraq via third countries appealed, eventually successfully, against those convictions.

Adding spice to this already heady brew of conspiracy, cover-up and Cabinet ministers was the House of Commons Trade and Industry Select Committee's two-year inquiry into the Supergun case, concerning the seizure at Teesport in April 1990 of lengths of pipe allegedly being exported to Iraq to be made up into a Supergun, capable of delivering its load from Iraq to Israel.

There was also the PII dispute, essentially an argument between lawyers about whether Public Interest Immunity Certificates signed by government ministers at the beginning of various arms export trials were gagging orders or a proper mechanism for drawing to the attention of the trial judge aspects of the case that might impinge on national security. Nobody bothered to contemplate why, if the Government had really been willing to gag anyone, they would have let such cases come to court in the first place.

All these events had unfolded against the shifting background of the raging and, in 1988, the eventual ending of a particularly vicious eight-year war between Iran and Iraq. There were also the Iraqi atrocities against the Kurds; the recall of our *chargé d'affaires* from Iran following the *fatwah* against Salman Rushdie; the withdrawal of our ambassador from Baghdad after the arrest and execution of one Farzad Bazoft as an alleged spy; the Iraqi invasion of Kuwait and, in 1991, the Gulf War.

Events of the kind Sir Richard Scott was asked to investigate can always be given a focus and continuum by a retrospective inquiry that bears no relation to the protracted, sporadic and diffuse environment in which they had actually unfolded. Over the years in question, the many ministers and innumerable officials in the several departments whose responsibilities touched on all these issues were also dealing with a whole range of other events, some dramatic, some routine. The poll tax; the fall of Thatcher; economic problems; the Single Market; the Exchange Rate Mechanism; two general elections and, above all, the problems of Maastricht – all added to the pace and pressure of ministerial lives. That is not to excuse any minister or official who might be found culpable. It is just to put matters in their context. The business of government is often a confused and disorderly one and, despite the legislative role of Parliament, far removed from the measured consideration of precedent and statute to be found in the law courts.

As he settled down to his task Scott appears to have lost sight of that. The detailed procedures were left to him to establish and, once they were in place, the inquiry received tens of thousands of pages of documentation from government files and took evidence from no fewer than 268 witnesses. The Report, when it eventually appeared, was to run to five volumes and 2,000 pages, without a summary of its conclusions. I, a slow reader, would be expected to have mastered every one of those pages, extracted and appraised each conclusion on every issue and be able to offer the Government's preliminary response to each on the day of its publication. It was, perhaps, no wonder that John Alty called it the poisoned chalice.

On 22 November 1995, with still no certainty of when we would receive the Report, I was summoned to a meeting at 10 Downing Street with the Prime Minister, his deputy Michael Heseltine, the Chancellor Ken Clarke, the Foreign Secretary Malcolm Rifkind and the Attorney General Sir Nicholas Lyell. I was asked formally as lead minister to coordinate the Government's response and was offered the support of a Cabinet Office team comprising two very bright officials, Tony Pawson and Philip Colcutt, and the Prime Minister's admirable Press Secretary, Jonathan Haslam. They were a formidable team who greatly eased my task as I began my preparations. Between then and the end of the affair three months later, I was to hold around sixty-five different meetings with ministerial colleagues and officials.

In preparing to receive the Report, part of the problem was that we did not know where Scott would come from, with which – if any – of the Court cases he would find fault, and with which aspects of them. Would he be primarily concerned with export licensing, intelligence handling, openness in government, ministerial accountability, public interest immunity or any one of a host of other aspects of the case? It was a broad and complex range of interacting issues. Certainly the press and the Opposition had maintained their ever more lurid litany of allegations. Because we could find no evidence to sustain them – apart, of course, from Alan Clark's concession which had triggered the inquiry – would Scott similarly find none? Early leaks to the press from the draft of the Report had suggested that damning criticism could be expected, particularly of William Waldegrave, the former Foreign Office minister who now found himself in the eye of the storm.

I had been involved in none of these issues, so I embarked on an intensive reading-in programme, and on a dark December afternoon I set off to the Treasury, where William was now Chief Secretary, to talk things through with him and his advisers, soon to be followed by sessions with another targeted victim, Nick Lyell, and with Ken Clarke, Michael Howard, Peter Lilley and a host of others allegedly involved in the scandal. At a meeting with Michael Heseltine, in his famous 'tennis-court sized' office (which in fact was quite a bit smaller than the one I had occupied for five years at the Scottish Office) he told me it was essential that I must be able to believe totally in what I would say when the Report was published. 'I could not have defended Margaret in the House in 1985 unless I had believed in her innocence.'

I understood his message and had already resolved that if I concluded, in gathering and absorbing all the evidence, that William or Nick (who were both friends of mine and fellow members of the Blue Chips) were guilty in the slightest of the charges levelled at them I would go straight to them and to the Prime Minister and say so. That never became necessary; indeed as my researches continued I became more and more convinced that there was no case for them to answer. Of course there would be criticisms of an administrative nature – there always are: no department is so perfectly run as to be able to withstand a spotlight shone with hindsight on events separated from their busy surroundings and compressed in time. But although some of the criticisms were substantive, there would be nothing to justify the sacrificial resignation of the ministers under the spotlight, and I was soon convinced that all the serious charges levelled at them by our opponents and the media over several years were without substance.

It is worth putting in context the nub of these issues, for even now it is not widely understood on just how narrow a basis of fact was built such a balloon of fanciful indignation and abuse.

Britain has long been a world leader in the manufacture of defence equipment. It is an industry that at the time the Scott Report was published accounted for some 400,000 jobs in this country. We exported substantial amounts. Economic self-interest was allied to a strategic self-interest and to a respect for the right of other sovereign states to exercise their right to self-defence, a right explicitly recognised in Article 51 of the United Nations Charter. The right of our customer countries to maintain confidentiality on matters concerning their defence equipment is also one we respected. Clearly, however, a licensing system was necessary to ensure that weapons did not fall into hands that might use them either to threaten our own interests directly or to create instability or conflict in the world's danger zones.

The Near East was one such zone, and the leaders of Iran and Iraq were not regarded as safe pairs of hands. Hence the government decision in 1980, when their war began, to sell no lethal arms or ammunition to either side. Hence too the promulgation within the relevant government departments of guidelines in December 1984, concerned with the sale of non-lethal equipment. These guidelines were voluntary and self-imposed.

They did not have the force of law and were intended merely as an aid to officials in assessing whether or not to grant export licences. They were thus the operational arm of policy: they had an ethical base and were intended to allow for case-by-case consideration, embodying sufficient flexibility to allow officials to react to changing circumstances in order to maintain our neutrality between the combatants and to try to preserve an equilibrium in the region.

The Scott Inquiry therefore was not about selling bombs, bullets, missiles or rockets. They were banned altogether. That was in contrast to the policies of earlier Labour governments, who had sold two destroyers and eight Canberra bombers to Argentina in the 1960s and, in the 1970s, forty-two Sea Dart and 120 Blowpipe surface-to-air missiles and two Lynx helicopters. The Argentinian dictatorships had an appalling human rights record, and as a result of these sales British forces risked facing British weapons in the hands of the enemy during the Falklands War. In the Gulf War, by contrast, no such risk existed, and after that war no British lethal weapons were found in Iraqi hands. The Labour Government of the 1970s had also sold lethal equipment to Iran as part of total sales averaging £50 million per annum during the run-up to the Iran–Iraq war; and the value of such exports to Iraq rose in five years from £61 million to £427 million. Hypocrisy in foreign and defence matters had always been Labour's strong suit.

Such a record hardly gave the Opposition the right to embark on the campaign of vituperation that was later to form the basis of the Scott Inquiry. Moreover, the sales of these lethal weapons I have described were actually promoted and undertaken by the Labour government itself, whereas the Scott Inquiry was about the control by government of sales by private companies. The sales by such private companies, moreover, were not of bombers or missiles, but of such military equipment as spare parts for microprocessors or field telephones, or of machinery that could be used for making military equipment as well as for normal civil engineering purposes.

What a contrast with the behaviour of other countries in the Iran–Iraq war. Belgian ammunition, French Exocet missiles and Mirage fighters, Russian tanks, aircraft and missiles – all poured into the conflict. Britain, who contributed only 1 per cent of all Iraq's defence-related imports, agreed to the sale of hovercraft spares to Iran and defensive mobile radar equipment to Iraq, to deploy against surprise attack, but only after the ceasefire, whilst continuing to refuse licences for high-grade secure radios, metal detectors and phototypesetting spares. Against that background an outside observer might reasonably ask what on earth all the fuss was about.

The first and most direct charge against the Government – that of selling lethal weapons to Iraq – was demonstrably false, and in due course Scott was to confirm that that was so. You have to search for it in his Report, but when you find it, it is unequivocal:

> *The papers which I have seen clearly show that the Government was not prepared to countenance the supply of lethal equipment to either Iran or Iraq. When applications for such exports were made they were generally processed very quickly and were invariably rejected.**

The outlandish claims of Robin Cook, the ringleader in the charade who had talked of the 'political scandal of a government that privately, covertly, without public statement, arms a brutal psychopath who exposes British troops to fire from those arms'† were to look – to use one of his own favourite words – risible.

Sir Richard Scott was almost equally dismissive of the claim that, as Peter Mandelson MP chose to put it, 'Cabinet Ministers were willing to see innocent men go to jail rather than have their own shabby role in the

---

* Sir Richard Scott, *Report of the Inquiry into the Export of Defence Equipment and Dual-Use Goods to Iraq and Related Prosecutions* [*The Scott Report*], Volume II, page 784, para. D7.19.

† *Independent*, 23 November 1992.

Saddamgate scandal revealed.'* Although he held a minority view within the judiciary on the handling of public interest immunity, Scott concluded on the charge of 'seeking to deprive defendants in a criminal trial of the means by which to clear themselves' that: 'The charges to which I have referred are not, in my opinion, well founded.'†

To the extent that the Arms to Iraq issue had a core, it lay in the guidelines. These informal, self-imposed rules governed the granting of licences, and it was the alleged changing of the guidelines that led to charges of conspiracy and cover-up. They read as follows:

(i) *We should maintain our consistent refusal to supply any lethal equipment to either side;*

(ii) *Subject to that overriding consideration, we should attempt to fulfil existing contracts and obligations;*

(iii) *We should not, in future, approve orders for any defence equipment which, in our view, would significantly enhance the capability of either side to prolong or exacerbate the conflict;*

(iv) *In line with this policy, we should continue to scrutinise rigorously all applications for export licences for the supply of defence equipment to Iran and Iraq.*

Routine, unsensational, these guidelines were not the formal expression of government policy, but simply the internal benchmark by which the implementation of policy should be applied. Sir Geoffrey Howe, as Foreign Secretary, had had them drawn up in December 1984; and in October 1985, in the interests of open government, he

---

* *Sunday People*, 15 November 1992.
† *The Scott Report*, Volume III, page 1538, para G18, 106

decided to publish them although under no pressure from any quarter to do so.

Nor were these guidelines the exclusive determinant of the application of government policy. Other factors – humanitarian, strategic, terrorist, the terms of non-proliferation agreements – all came into play, but the guidelines were a useful tool for hard-pressed officials processing thousands of applications. They were intended to embody sufficient flexibility to be applied even-handedly and in changing circumstances. It was agreed by ministers that they could only be amended with the agreement of the relevant Secretaries of State and the Prime Minister. By definition, therefore, junior ministers could not change them in isolation and officials could not respond to any such attempt to change them.

As time went by the wording became obsolete. In 1988 the Iran–Iraq war finally ended, so Guideline (iii), which referred to prolongation or exacerbation of the conflict, lost some of its force. But the situation in Iran and Iraq remained tense. In 1989 Iran's *fatwah* against Salman Rushdie following the publication of his book *The Satanic Verses*, the arrest in Iraq of the nurse Daphne Parrish and of the alleged spy Farzad Bazoft, followed by the execution of the latter, caused our diplomatic relations with both countries to change. Then in the spring of 1990 the Supergun affair blew up and in August that year Iraq invaded Kuwait. It is a mark of the quality of their drafting that the guidelines, although obsolete, were able to accommodate such changing circumstances, being applied more restrictively to the situation in each country as events swung this way and that.

Quite rightly, ministers addressed from time to time the adequacy of the guidelines as these events took place. The ending of the war brought the prospect of substantial trading opportunities with both countries, not just in defence equipment. Finally in July 1990, after thorough appraisal by ministers and officials, the Foreign Secretary Douglas Hurd prepared to minute the Prime Minister to ask for changes to be made and announced. However, the invasion of Kuwait intervened and matters were left as they had always been.

Or were they? This was to be the vortex of the storm that was to rage around the issue for years: whether or not the wording of the self-imposed guidelines agreed by ministers in 1984 to guide officials in the granting of licences for non-lethal, defence-related equipment sales to two warring countries had in fact been changed at some point, even though no demonstrable consequence of any such change could be found. What was clear from official papers at this stage was that the many ministers and officials involved who met to discuss updating the guidelines all thought that the guidelines they wanted to amend in July 1990 were the same ones that had been put in place in December 1984. But that basic truth did not suit the convenience of the myth-makers.

As it became clear that Sir Richard Scott was slowly working his way towards a conclusion my preparations intensified. So did the pressure upon me. Media interest was reaching fever pitch and it became clear that when I came to present the Report to the House of Commons I would be the focus of intense interest. It was still impossible to say what form that attention would take, since we were still shadow-boxing and had no idea what Scott would conclude, but it seemed certain that I, and the Government, would come under concentrated attack. Too many people had invested too much of their credibility in the existence of a scandal. But while they could invent a new scare story whenever they pleased, I had to concentrate on the facts – and I was still trying to run the rest of my large department, at the same time as marshalling and absorbing as much material as I could on all the different strands of the Inquiry. It was hardly surprising that I lost almost a stone in weight over this period. It mattered not that, as the whole House knew, I had played no part in the alleged misdemeanours. I had to answer for the Government as a whole on the day; and I had to get it right.

As the days passed and publication approached there were endless wrangles both with the Opposition and media – one and the same on this, as on so many other issues – and with the staff of the Inquiry itself. Sir Richard had indicated in December 1995 that he might want to submit the Report on Ordtec separately from everything else, because he wanted to give extra time to a former defence counsel, now a judge, to respond to questions. We were not at all keen on the continuing uncertainty that this would engender, not to mention the apparent favouritism. Scott also dreamed up a scheme to present the Report not to the Government who had commissioned it but to a team of three senior backbenchers who would table it in Parliament on his behalf. At another stage he contemplated announcing his findings himself. He seemed not to realise that although he had been granted exceptional discretion on the way in which he conducted his inquiry this Report, having been commissioned by the Government, should be delivered to them, and, by precedent, published in part or in full by them within a reasonable period, in Parliament. At the same time the Government would normally be expected to respond with clear policy decisions, agreed in the light of their close study of such a Report. Many such reports were routinely held for several weeks before publication, to enable such close study and consequent policy decisions to take place.

On this occasion, long, complex and controversial though it would be, the Report would need to be published quickly and in full. Those who wanted fun and fireworks rather than facts demanded instant publication, to be followed by a free-for-all, with the Government to be called upon to respond instantly to a very long document that it had not seen. Sir Richard Scott even refused a modest request from my officials to see the proposed cover of the Report whilst printing was taking place, to ensure that it conformed to the established procedure for such parliamentary documents. This aroused their concern – misplaced, as it transpired – that he might be planning to give his report a 'soundbite' title.

Most of our problems with the Inquiry team, however, were over timing. When would it be published? How far in advance of that would the Government receive it? Who else would see it ahead of publication? And how far in advance? Although there were clear parliamentary conventions for the handling of such matters, there was now a mood to set aside all the precedents and procedures in order to feed the mob. The press and Opposition never understood or accepted it, but the reality was that whilst we like all governments wanted announcements to remain secret until they were made, on this occasion it was the Inquiry team, not the Government, who were behind all the fuss about confidentiality and security. It was they who were imposing the ferocious constraints upon how, when and to whom the Report would be issued.

Eventually on 31 January 1996 it was agreed that I would receive the Report on 7 February and would publish it and present it to Parliament on the 15th. Eight days was hopelessly inadequate for time to study its five volumes in order to prepare the statement I would make to the House of the Government's considered response and to answer questions upon it, but it would have to do. The Opposition, by contrast, could – and did – continue to say what they pleased regardless of the facts, as they had been doing for three years.

Further wrangling took place over which of the witnesses might receive the normal courtesies of seeing advance copies and when opposition spokesmen would receive their copies. The Government was criticised by the media for a lack of openness in circulating advance copies, but in fact our discretion was tightly constrained by the requirements of Sir Richard himself and his terrier-like but unsubtle Secretary to the Inquiry, Mr Christopher Muttukumaru.

I received a fearsome letter from Muttukumaru on the day the Report reached me, requiring me in formal legal terms to agree in writing to the most rigorous constraints on access by others to the document. It was even suggested, as my officials informed me, that the press should be shown advance copies on the day of publication – in confidence, of course.

Because of all this we had to put up with a lot of ill-founded adverse publicity. But there was nothing new in that and, given the fact that publication was to be on a much faster track than was normal for such a Report, and on far more rigorous terms of confidentiality, I was not inclined to distract myself with further wrangling with the Inquiry team.

It did seem to me to be right to let Robin Cook, the Opposition spokesman, see the Report earlier than the normal conventions for such matters allowed (of only an hour or so before publication) although we had to observe the Inquiry team's strictures. In the event though, when he came to DTI to collect his copy, he stood on the pavement outside for ten minutes talking to the press and repeating yet again his soon-to-be-discredited slurs upon ministers, instead of getting on with studying the document. I had also decided to let Tony Blair, as Leader of the Opposition, see an advance copy on Privy Council terms, but in the event, before I could so instruct my private secretary, it transpired he had already trenchantly rejected such a request from Blair's office, fearful as he was of the retribution of the Inquiry office and Mr Muttukumaru.

When I had received my five green-bound volumes of the Report, the first thing I did was to telephone Sir Richard Scott to thank him for discharging his task. I also expressed the hope that we might meet one day, in quieter times, to talk about it all. Then I and the nominated officials whom Scott had approved embarked on a rapid read-through. It was full of delphic, even self-contradictory, conclusions – often without supporting evidence, which made rapid analysis difficult – but it was soon clear that there was no smoking gun, no killer punch. Indeed, on the central charges against ministers, no sustainable case had been made. The contingent drafting I had already undertaken, both of my planned statement to the House and of my speech for the debate that was to follow, could now be firmed up, as we extracted the substance of the Report from its dilated 2,000 pages. But there was still a massive amount of work to be done. My special adviser Gregor Mackay was not on the list of officials allowed to see the Report, so I asked the Prime Minister to appoint David Willetts MP, the immensely able Cabinet Office Minister, to help in the preparation of briefing material, and this eased the pressure on me as the countdown to publication began. For Peter Fraser, who would repeat my statement in the House of Lords, the learning task was even more daunting.

My conviction, formed soon after I had started my preparations, that William Waldegrave, Nick Lyell and other ministers under attack had behaved throughout with complete propriety, was now reinforced by the Report. I was bolstered too, in preparing to defend them in Parliament, by a fierce sense of indignation that journalists and Labour politicians could have used such extreme language – Tony Blair spoke of a Government 'knee deep in dishonour' – without, as it now transpired, the evidence to support their claims. They had behaved despicably for party advantage and it was clear that if I was to turn the tide on the great flood of smear, innuendo and invention with which my colleagues had been defamed over a period of several years, I would have to go on to the offensive when I stood at the despatch box.

I chose to take a two-stage approach. This would not be the day for measured responses to the many sensible proposals and valid criticisms in the Report: that would need to wait for the debate later. Today was the day to concentrate on the main issues and to try to halt the flow of complacent vilification. So I decided to be robust in my statement. The press was to use the word 'chutzpah' the next day, and even the *Guardian* journalist Richard Norton-Taylor, one of the ringleaders of the press campaign on Arms to Iraq, was to describe it later, in a highly partial account of the saga that he wrote with two colleagues, as 'a pugnacious and crafty performance',* a compliment of sorts.

Despite every attempt by the media to breach the security so fiercely demanded by Sir Richard Scott's inquiry team, we managed to maintain the confidentiality of the Report until the appointed hour on Thursday 15 February. Even Cabinet colleagues had little knowledge of the Report's findings until I briefed them that morning, before slipping out of Cabinet early to continue briefing myself. Surprise suited the Government, as well as Scott. I knew from my experience the previous year with John Major's leadership campaign that whilst we held the initiative we must use it. First impressions mattered. The circumstances were different, of course. Here we were seeking to stop in its tracks a juggernaut that had been rolling for three years, in which the media as well as the Opposition had a strong vested interest. And we had to stop it within the next hour.

As I rose to speak in a packed and feverish House, members still had no idea whether it was to announce the acquittal of ministers or their damnation. We had kept the tactical advantage of surprise, but to say that I was nervous at this point would be an understatement worthy of the Duke of Wellington. I held the fate of two ministerial colleagues in my hands; and some in the press had been writing of a government on the brink of meltdown. Almost numb with tension, I wondered whether the mass of briefing I had absorbed over recent weeks would emerge in proper order or whether, with so many different issues intertwined in the Report, I would blow a cerebral fuse and be unable to respond to the barrage I would soon face from the benches opposite. But I was buoyed by a sense of the justice of my case.

Such was the noise and excitability of the House, however, that no sooner had I got to my feet than the Speaker felt obliged to take the

---

* Richard Norton-Taylor, Mark Lloyd and Stephen Cook, *Knee Deep in Dishonour: The Scott Report and its Aftermath* (Victor Gollancz, 1996).

unusual step of suspending the sitting for ten minutes whilst MPs rushed out of the Chamber and clamoured for copies of the Report at the Vote Office, at the instant of its official publication. Given the bulk of the Report and the smallness of the Vote Office, the logistics of the distribution process were not easy.

If anything, the hiatus heightened rather than diminished the tension as, once more, I gripped the worn brass corners of the despatch box, took a deep breath and began in the time-honoured way: 'Madam Speaker, with permission, I should like to make a statement about the Report published today ...'.

I made it clear at once that the Report had concluded that no lethal weapons had been sold to Iraq. We had not 'armed Saddam Hussein'. I then went on to spell out the Report's findings that there had been no conspiracy and no cover-up, a point which Sir Richard Scott, asked later by a journalist, confirmed: 'I think that is a fair summary.' But I was also careful to make it clear that the Report contained a number of criticisms, mainly of an administrative nature, and many of which we accepted.

For example, the legislation to control imports and exports was still based on an emergency wartime act of 1939. Scott was right – it was long overdue for updating and replacing with something more relevant. There was legitimate criticism of the way in which sensitive intelligence reports were distributed within government: ministers signing PII certificates were sometimes not shown relevant intelligence material. The Inquiry Report was also critical of the ministerial guidelines and on the nature of ministerial accountability. It recommended changes to the law relating to prosecution practices by HM Customs & Excise and on the approach to public interest immunity. I had something to say on all these issues and I address most of them again in this narrative.

One of the most bizarre elements in the whole saga was the Supergun affair, or Project Babylon, as it was known. This James Bond-like tale involved spying, murder and an international plot to build for Saddam

Hussein the world's biggest gun, alleged to be capable of carrying nuclear shells from Iraq as far as Israel. Mossad and MI6 were involved; so was the unfortunate Dr Gerald Bull, a Canadian ballistics expert, and his Belgian company Space Research Centre. So too, were various Midlands engineering companies – and, inevitably, a government minister, Alan Clark.

Scott takes 151 pages to cover this 'almost unbelievable concept'* as he described it, which I will not try to summarise. Suffice it to say that the most dramatic British involvement was over the manufacture of four high-quality steel tubes, the longest being 39 feet, ostensibly for an oil pipeline, or a petrol plant, or as pressure vessels, or for the nuclear industry, or as gun barrels . . . The story was a confused one, involving muddle, delay, poor communications, the issue and withdrawal of licences, the making and dropping of charges. The pipes were eventually seized at the last minute by HM Customs & Excise at Teesport, just before they were to be loaded on to a ship.

Scott's main conclusion was that there was inadequate investigation by MI6, despite being alerted by various of the manufacturers involved. He also identified a serious omission in failing to pass on the information they did gather to the committee monitoring arms exports, which included Customs, intelligence agencies and Whitehall departments. In consequence, senior officials in those departments were unable adequately to brief ministers. It is not a conclusion with which one can argue.

The charge that had given William Waldegrave most difficulty was that he had deliberately misled Parliament by sending to MPs letters, drafted in his department, which referred to the guidelines as originally published. In an inquiry, unlike a trial, the accused is guilty until proved innocent; and William's case had not been helped by a serious leak, some

---

* *The Scott Report*, Volume III, page 945, para. F1.1.

months before, to the effect that William would indeed be found guilty of this charge. The other two ministers who had been involved in discussions on these matters, Alan Clark and Lord Trefgarne, had long since left the Government, so it was on William that all the vicious attention of the Opposition and media focused. He had the invidious task of having to prove a negative; and in the meantime he had undergone what Lord Howe of Aberavon was to describe in the House of Lords later in February 1996 as 'three and a half years of pre-emptive recrimination'.

When the final Report appeared, the earlier leaked verdict appeared to have been modified, though only to the extent that he had misled Parliament, but had not done so deliberately. In a letter in March 1989 describing the guidelines, he had had, said Scott, 'no duplicitous intention'.* This, as Scott should have realised, was even worse than a 'not proven' verdict. It left William stigmatised and in limbo, yet technically on the right side of the terms of official guidance on ministerial behaviour. But the charge and verdict were only sustainable if the guidelines had been changed. Margaret Thatcher's typically trenchant view on that was expressed in the later debate in the House of Lords: 'If there was no change in the guidelines – and there was not – then the question of deliberately misleading the House does not arise.' After all, she had agreed the original guidelines and it was self-evident that any change to them could not take place unless it, too, came to her for agreement.

The alleged changing of the guidelines was anyway irrelevant to the Matrix Churchill trial that had caused the Scott Inquiry to be set up, because Scott concedes in his Report† that William would have turned down the export of their lathes on any version of the guidelines, had he received the relevant military intelligence, which he had not.

However, in making my statement to the House I kept my main fire-

---

* *The Scott Report*, Volume I, D3-124.
† *The Scott Report*, Volume I, D6-169

power for Robin Cook. Uncharacteristically, I did not pull my punches. He had fomented the poisonous row over this matter for three years, feeding the House, the press and the public, as I said in my statement, 'a sour stream of invective, innuendo and invention', ruthlessly smearing my colleagues and seeking to tar the whole Government with what I described as 'one of the most odious campaigns of manipulation and black propaganda that the House will be able to recall.' I called on him now to withdraw his disgraceful allegations, and when he failed to do so I said that he 'has blighted the rest of his career in this place. He will never be trusted in the House again.' Strong words, but no stronger than some of the things Opposition MPs had been saying for years about Government ministers. Emotions were running high.

After the initial exchanges, questions rumbled on in the House for about the time it takes to play a rugger match at Murrayfield, including injury time. Fierce charge and counter-charge flew across the Chamber. But my thorough preparation paid off, and about ninety minutes after I had got to my feet Madam Speaker brought the proceedings to a close. Bruised but still in one piece, I left the Chamber with the Prime Minister, to take stock in his room with him and Michael Heseltine. They were kinder in their comments than I deserved, but I was able to embark on an intensive round of media interviews feeling that, although there was still a full Debate to come, we had already begun to achieve our objective. We had lanced the boil.

During the many media interviews that filled the next few hours it became clear that my concentration on the central points – that there had been no conspiracy and no cover-up – was making the running, and the news reports were positive. The next day's papers could hardly be so helpful, after years of peddling the libels fed to them by Opposition MPs. In fact, though, their headlines were largely neutral. The *Financial Times* summed up the general tone with: 'LANG AND COOK BATTLE TO A COMMONS SCORE DRAW'.

The sketch writers had more fun, on a personal note. To Boris Johnson in the *Daily Telegraph* I had mounted a 'one-man blizzard of propaganda, a snow-job of Himalayan proportions'. To the *Daily Express*, 'in confident naval officer style, Mr Lang belched out a good old-fashioned smoke-screen'. Matthew Parris in *The Times* said: 'This cool and understated character has never been seen in such storming form.' But, he also got the point: if I 'had stumbled during the first critical quarter-hour … things would be different. They are now set and no broadcasting studio will change them.' That was absolutely right, and it was why I took the stance I did. Facts do not always speak for themselves, especially when unproven, so I knew that the spin-doctors had to be beaten at their own game.

Some testing media interviews followed over the next few days. *Breakfast with Frost* the following Sunday was straightforward, even though Robin Cook was also participating. I think it was on this occasion that while waiting to go on I tapped the shoulder of the studio floor manager, who was standing in front of me watching the start of the programme, and asked him for a glass of water. 'Yes, of course, sir.' He bustled off, and it was only when he reappeared with the water that I recognised Rory Bremner, as ever the great impersonator. Then it was on to Jonathan Dimbleby and a live studio audience. He came at me hard, but that interview was later to be held up as a classic example of how robustly adversarial interview techniques can actually help the unfortunate interviewee to win his case. As a justification for media bias, I am not sure that I wholly agree with that, but it was becoming clear that as a 'scandal', the 'Arms to Iraq' issue was losing its force. As the *Sunday Telegraph* put it on 18 February: 'The moment of maximum danger for the Government has passed.'

During the lull before the big debate, both sides regrouped and took stock. Doubtless they also wrestled with the impenetrable morass of Sir

Richard Scott's Report. I knew now that we had won the argument and that the press knew it, even if the Opposition would not admit it. I knew too, however, that the debate would still be difficult, not least because Opposition members would try to revive a sense of scandal by lifting sentences and phrases, and even single words, out of their contexts. Whilst they would continue to say whatever they liked, wrapped in inventive rhetoric, I would have to measure my every word. Also, there were several serious issues on which Scott had made legitimate criticisms and I would need to respond to as many of these as possible. There was not much time to thrash out agreed policy decisions across government.

I had already been able to reassure the House in my statement that the inadequacies in the distribution of intelligence material within and between government departments, identified by Scott, had been quickly rectified. I had also committed the Government to produce a consultation paper with a view to improving export controls and licensing procedures.

An aside to the issue of export controls was the strange case of the Labour Party's reaction in 1990 to the legislation proposed in order to make permanent the Emergency Act of 1939. On the advice of officials, the Government consulted with the relevant shadow ministers, Gordon Brown MP and Joyce Quin MP, and offered to include in the new Bill a negative resolution which would have enabled the legislation, once enacted, to be reconsidered each year, should the Opposition request it. DTI officials' notes recording various meetings and exchanges involving Government ministers Peter Lilley and Tim Sainsbury with their Labour counterparts record that Gordon Brown and Joyce Quin preferred not to include a negative resolution in the Bill. One can only speculate that this was because they were concerned about how their left wing might exploit such a debating opportunity in a future Labour government. In the event therefore, ministers, who had planned to include it even if Labour had not requested it, decided not to do so. It was important to get the new legislation passed smoothly as the 1939 Act, as it stood, was now considered vulnerable to legal challenge.

In her evidence to Scott on this issue four years later, Joyce Quin's recollection rejected the proposition that she had asked that the negative resolution be excluded. Peter Lilley, Tim Sainsbury and their officials claimed that they had and submitted the contemporaneous written evidence contained in departmental records. Scott, in his Report, stated that he had not had time to resolve the factual issues, but chose to ignore the history of negotiations and the detailed and rational statements of the ministers, as well as the unambiguous written evidence of departmental officials that supported them. He made excuses for Mr Brown and Ms Quin, pointing out that they had not had the advantage of the submissions from officials that ministers had had and blamed the Government, who were responsible for putting forward the Bill.* I find this very puzzling.

When it came to replacing the 1939 Act after they had come to power in 1997 the new Labour Government seemed to lose the sense of urgency and outrage of a year earlier. They did not introduce the new legislation that Scott had called for, and they had promised, until their second Parliament, in 2001. Even that leaves in place parts of the 1939 Emergency Act to which Sir Richard had taken such exception.

Returning to my preparations for the debate, now that the temperature had dropped over the substance of the Scott Report I was keen to take a more moderate tone and to deal with the remainder of the issues that I had flagged up in my statement ten days earlier. The crisis had not gone away, because the arithmetic of the Chamber had not changed. On this, as on so many issues in those difficult times, we had one or two potential rebels on our own side and, for reasons unrelated to the issue under debate, the exigencies of Ulster politics were threat-

---

* *The Scott Report*, Volume I, para C1.111.

ening to drive the nine Ulster Unionist MPs into the Opposition lobby. A defeat in the division lobbies looked highly likely; and a defeat is a defeat. Regardless of the reason for it, it would still cause William Waldegrave and Nick Lyell to have to resign. In Nick's case, as a Law Officer, his head was only on the block because Sir Richard Scott happened to hold a different – and minority – view about Public Interest Immunity law. In addition, as it was I who had recommended to Cabinet the position we had taken over the Report and I had invested so much personal capital in it, I had by now decided that if we lost the vote I would feel obliged, at the very least, to offer my own resignation to the Prime Minister. So, again, we had to take great care in the presentation of the Government's case.

David Willetts and Gregor Mackay (now free from the constraints of Scott's embargo) did sterling work in preparing and disseminating briefing on a range of issues. My Cabinet colleague Roger Freeman undertook the challenge of preparing himself for the sensitive task of winding up the debate on behalf of the Government, which he was to do with masterly skill. In my own case, in preparing my opening speech, it was largely a question of updating my already extensive briefing and of analysing the reaction to my statement and the media coverage of the Report's many facets. At the same time, though, I was still fulfilling many routine DTI engagements and running my Department.

I was summoned before a packed meeting of the 1922 Committee where I had a strongly supportive reception, but we were now beginning to identify one or two potential rebels in the forthcoming vote. One of these was Quentin Davies MP. I had a meeting with him on the Friday before the debate in my room at the House, and found him impervious to argument or explanation. Quentin took the straightforward view – frustrating to those of us immersed in the detail of the Report and the answers to its criticisms – that Scott had found against Waldegrave and Lyell and so they should resign. Another potential rebel, Rupert Allason, had concerns about PII certificates and wanted a presumption of disclosure of documents, rather than suppression, in their future use. Following a discussion between Michael Heseltine and myself in which we agreed a form of words on this issue that Roger Freeman might deploy in his wind-up speech, Rupert was to come back onside when the vote came, but Quentin was not to be persuaded.

In my speech opening the debate I set off at what the *Independent* was to describe as 'a steady drone' – at this stage I was not averse to boring the House. I addressed two related issues causing concern: openness in government and accountability to Parliament. I pointed to our record, which included the establishment of the Select Committee system in 1979, the first White Paper on Open Government of 1993 and the Intelligence Services Act of 1994, the Citizen's Charter initiative, the publication of Questions of Procedure for Ministers, and the publication of lists of exports licensed for Iraq. I indicated that we were willing to consider what further steps we could take in this area.

I addressed the convention to which successive governments had adhered of declining to answer questions on defence-related exports, and invited proposals, across parties, as to how this might now be modified. I proposed that the Public Service Select Committee be invited to consider whether change was desirable in this and in other areas of ministerial accountability. Sir Richard Scott had himself recognised in his Report the sensitivities involved in such an issue. I accepted Sir Richard's concern about the behaviour of HM Customs & Excise as an independent prosecuting authority, and undertook to place it in future under the supervision of the Attorney General's office.

But the House – and the Press Gallery – were less and less interested in the detail of the Report. All hinged on the outcome of the division at ten o'clock. It could not have been closer. But for the Ulster Unionists, we would have been comfortable. With them and Quentin Davies in Labour's lobby, our majority was reduced to one. But one was enough.

The real crisis had passed. The bogus scandal evaporated. The discredited rhetoric would resurface, with diminishing force, only in the litany of spurious grievances with which Labour politicians are such seasoned propagandists. Of course, as they knew all along, mud sticks.

Delphic utterances lose their delphism when quoted only in part. This was the tactic to which Mr Cook and his colleagues had switched after publication of the Scott Report. They had moved from invention to selection. Judgements which Sir Richard Scott had felt unable to make without equivocation, and for which the evidence adduced was often hard to find, were awarded cast-iron certainty when the balancing qualification was ignored. The absence of a concise summary of conclusions added to the opaque nature of the Report. So, too, did the use by Scott of certain words, clearly selected with care, that carried an emotive imputation beyond their literal meaning. To express an opinion – it was no more than that – that a failure to inform Parliament on the current state of Government policy was 'deliberate', or that the public were 'designedly' led to believe that policy was stricter than it really was (and there were many other examples), served neither truth nor understanding.

On one level, it would have been naïve not to have known that these comments would be quoted selectively; on another, Scott appeared to attribute guilt, only to back off for lack of evidence, leaving an unworthy stain, unsupported by facts. Could he have set out expecting to find that William was guilty of misleading MPs, only to be confronted with evidence to the contrary at a late stage in the Inquiry, when he showed his preliminary conclusions to William? Did he have to amend his draft accordingly, causing the narrative, the whole cast of which implies an expectation of guilt, to lapse into an unsatisfactory muddle that at times becomes almost meaningless? Scott thought he had established that in

February three ministers – Clark, Trefgarne and Waldegrave – had agreed that the guidelines should be changed if they all agreed on the nature of a change. This led Scott to conclude in his draft report that the guidelines had been changed.

The evidence that William managed to produce at that late stage, after a Herculean scouring of back papers, was a contemporary handwritten note by Lord Trefgarne on his copy of an interdepartmental minute which stated that the three ministers did not, in the event, agree. Consequently no change could have taken place. The *fatwah* against Salman Rushdie also announced in February 1989 was particularly in their minds at the time. It was indeed fortunate for William that he was able to find the evidence that cleared him and his colleagues, but the chilling conclusion is that the case that seems to have been built up against him was unfounded, and if William had happened not to have found the evidence that vindicated him and the others, a serious injustice would have been done.

In the fetid political climate of February 1996 and under daunting pressure, in a short period of time, to absorb, rationalise and try to consider a response to the substance of what the Scott Report said, I did not have time to appraise the quality or strength of its arguments. There were no runs to be made then by saying Scott was wrong, even though I sensed from the outset that he had not made his case. When a judge pronounces, one's natural instinct is to assume he is right, and in the climate of the times I would have made little headway with the public in trying to demonstrate otherwise. It was strange how a searching inquiry for the truth seemed to have taken on the hue of an adversarial polemic, coloured by emotive language and unsupported assertions.

More leisured scrutiny in calmer times confirms that what the Report lacks in pellucid appraisal of the facts it more than makes up for in the wilful promotion of various theories. If the guidelines were changed, I asked myself, where, when, how, why, by whom, on what evidence, with what proof and with what consequences did that happen? It seems a reasonable set of questions, but where are the answers? I have read and re-read the relevant parts of the Report and cannot find them.

There are sections of factual narrative which are as uncontroversial as they are incontrovertible; but they are punctuated with *obiter dicta* and reprises suggesting just where events are claimed to have reached at supposedly key points of time in the unfolding story. These seem to me to constitute not so much proof as benchmarks on the chosen route down which the Report seeks to take the reader. Contrary points of view or of fact that do not fit the formula are dismissed as 'sophistry' or as 'untenable'. I do not believe that Sir Richard 'designedly' misleads the reader, but I do believe that on occasion he fails to make his own case. Indeed, the ambiguities of several of his conclusions and the lack of a summary of his findings suggest that in the end Scott failed even to convince himself. 'A summary would risk distortion' was his explanation at his press conference on the day of publication, pleading also 'writing fatigue'.* However, if he had proof, dispersed within his complex ruminations, was it not capable of being laid out in a summary? Summing up is something judges do. If his proof was incapable of summary, was it because there was no proof?

Consider some examples. One of the central planks of his argument is that the revised Guideline (iii), a change to the wording of which was contemplated by ministers at one stage simply to reflect the fact that Iran and Iraq, at war when the guideline was drafted, were now at peace, represented a real change of policy. Scott argues that because a category of goods, namely those which would directly enhance defence capability, would be permitted under the proposed new guideline but were not allowed by the old one, it was not credible to regard the new guideline as an updating of the old. He does not seriously address the argument,

---

* *Daily Telegraph*, 16 February 1996.

widely used at the time (and clearly more relevant than engaging in over-literal semantics), that in a time of peace a strengthening of defensive capability was consistent with a policy of avoiding steps which might contribute to new conflict.

Again, Scott seizes on the casual drafting of one letter by an official in William Waldegrave's office which refers to a 'more liberal policy' as evidence that ministers and officials really did think they were changing policy. With clear hyperbole, he says that the contemporary documentation shows that it is 'impossible to quarrel' with the expression. Yet against that one phrase are also to be found in contemporary documents such alternative comments as: 'The revision is more in the spirit of implementation of the guidelines rather than a dramatic change of policy'; 'The fact that the modulation is so fine ...'; '[Lord Trefgarne] would now be content to agree to the use of the form of words to provide interpretation of the guidelines in respect of Iraq'; 'the amendments were mainly cosmetic'. These four contemporaneous comments* seem to me to carry rather more weight as to what was in the minds of ministers and officials at the time than the one loose phrase on which Scott perches his claim.

In another key paragraph in Scott's case† he claims, without proof, that the fear of adverse publicity prompted ministers' reluctance to announce a guideline change. But he ignores other more plausible factors. For example, it seems clear from paragraph D3.40 that US concerns over Iran rather than popular concerns about Iraq were what motivated ministers. Also relevant were British government concerns over the attitude of the new administration in Washington; fears for the British hostages; threats to British shipping and concerns about our relationship with Saudi Arabia. A more rounded consideration of such factors could not have led to so simplistic a conclusion.

---

* *The Scott Report*, Volume I, Paras. D3.43, D3.41, D3.45 and D3.64.
† *The Scott Report*, Volume I, Para. D3.97.
‡ *The Scott Report*, Volume I. Para. D3.61.

In another paragraph‡ Scott suggests that the reformulation of the guidelines considerably extended the scope of Guideline (ii) in respect of attempts by British companies to fulfil existing contracts. But if, as Scott claims, the guidelines were being changed in a more liberal direction, how could agreement to fulfil existing contracts possibly extend their scope when those contracts had been entered into at a time when the earlier and supposedly more restrictive contracts were in place?

Where anyway, is the proof of his contention that the guidelines had been changed? There is not a shred of evidence that British defence exports to Iran or Iraq either grew by any palpable amount or changed their nature to any discernible degree as a result of the alleged, but invisible and unproven, guideline changes. As Tom King MP was to point out when as Secretary of State for Defence he visited the battlefields after the Iraqi invasion of Kuwait had been repulsed, he saw evidence of arms and armaments from almost every country with a major defence industry, but all he found from the British defence industry was one Land Rover.

The contemptuous dismissal as not even remotely tenable of arguments that, in the documentation of the time and with the benefit of hindsight, seemed to be both entirely reasonable and corroborated by cross-references, is something I still find disconcerting. Literalism, semantics, assertion and the use of words deliberately (designedly) imbued with emotive undertones – these are not the features one expects to find permeating a report by a senior judge into a complex series of events of international importance and political sensitivity. By contrast, the acquittals of ministers of the lurid charges of conspiracy and cover-up are to be found tucked away in the dense undergrowth of the Report, couched in such bland terms as 'not, in my opinion, well-founded'.*

Another puzzle is Sir Richard's handling of Alan Clark's role in the affair. He knows – and recounts – that Alan was the driving force in seeking to

---

* *The Scott Report*, Volume III, page 1538, para G18-106.

change the guidelines and thus allow our trade to increase, both with Iran and with Iraq. Alan never made any secret of this. As first a trade minister and then Minister of Defence Procurement, he consistently pursued his aims with patriotic fervour and through the proper channels. Yet more than anyone's it was his initiatives in this area that led to all the textual wranglings in the minutes of ministerial meetings, on which Scott expends so much energy and sheds so little light.* And it was his action in giving encouragement to Matrix Churchill over their export licence applications which, however well intended, had breached government policy and led to the prosecution of the company's senior executives.

If Alan had not, at the last minute, recanted and changed his evidence, the trial would not have collapsed. That would have led to a terrible miscarriage of justice. In his Report, however, Sir Richard finds almost no fault with Alan Clark's behaviour, either then or, indeed, during the whole saga.

Public Interest Immunity Certificates – PIIs – pervaded the whole complex Arms to Iraq affair. By signing such 'gagging orders', as the Opposition now described them, ministers were alleged to have risked sending innocent businessmen to prison by depriving defendants, in their trials for illegal exports, of the means to defend themselves. 'None of these businessmen would have been convicted in the first place', Robin Cook had claimed,† 'if ministers had not abused their power by placing gagging orders before the Courts.' But Sir Richard concludes that all the ministers who had signed PIIs had done so without any impropriety. The judge in the trial was, after all, the arbiter on whether or not evidence subject to such orders should be disclosed.

---

* See, for example, *The Scott Report*, Volume I, D3.143.
† *Daily Telegraph*, 8 November 1995.

The PII issue took on an edge, however, because Sir Richard Scott himself had views about the use of PII certificates that were controversial among the legal profession. The underlying principle of the certificates was to ensure that when a minister considered that the public disclosure of certain information in a trial might be against the national interest, the signing of a PII certificate would ensure that the matter was brought before the judge in the trial. He would be best able to weigh the claimed public interest against the interests of justice, and he would decide whether or not they should be disclosed to the defendant's lawyers and thus used as evidence. The procedure was well established and had been used in both civil and criminal trials. It is designed to ensure, not that ministers reach a view on the merits of the case, but that they act consistently and according to the right legal principles. If so advised by the Law Officers, ministers had a duty to sign certificates. In the Matrix Churchill trial the judge saw all the documents, acknowledged that PII claims had been properly made and decided that most of the information subject to PII certificates should, in fact, be disclosed; and it was. All but one of the defence counsel in that trial have stated publicly that in their view the PII claims were properly made.

In fact, the documents did not show the defendants to be innocent – if they had, the prosecution brought independently by HM Customs & Excise could not have been brought – and the trial proceeded normally until four weeks later Alan Clark changed his story under cross-examination. Then the whole case collapsed.

Sir Richard Scott's view was that the use of PII certificates in criminal trials should be reconsidered, that they should not be used 'on a class basis' and that ministers should not have a duty to sign them if they felt that the documents in question should be disclosed. This was a perfectly reasonable point of view, even though a minority one. It differed from the view of the Court of Appeal, presided over by Lord Justice Bingham (later Lord Chief Justice), and also from the views of such distinguished

Law Lords as Lords Lloyd, Wilberforce, Simon of Glaisdale, Slynn and Ackner. But it was a view of what the law on PII certificates should be in future, not of what it was at the time in 1992; and what it was was court-made, not Parliament-made. Indeed, the courts have subsequently modified the procedures. Whatever the merits or demerits of the argument at the time, it never formed any basis for criticising the Attorney General, Sir Nicholas Lyell, who behaved throughout with propriety and in accordance with precedent.

When Sir Richard gave evidence himself to the House of Commons Public Service Committee just three months after his Report had been published, he largely destroyed his own case when he said: 'As to the legal conclusions, they may be right, they may be wrong. I think it was Lord Wilberforce in the House of Lords [in fact, it was Lord Lloyd] ... who said he thought that I had failed to distinguish between the law as it was and the law as it ought to be and maybe there is an element of truth in that.'*

Should ministers have resigned anyway, either at the outset or when the Report was published? In a clear-cut case, it would be right and honourable to step aside at once, perhaps in the hope of reinstatement once vindicated. But this was not a clear-cut case. At the outset, there were a dozen or so ministers in the spray of Labour's muckspreader. It was obvious that the allegations against them were wild and preposterous, so why should innocent ministers step down just because their political opponents were libelling them? Some of them, such as Lord Trefgarne and Alan Clark, had left the Government several years before, which concentrated the focus unfairly on those who remained.

Certainly, the long drawn out nature of Scott's Inquiry, the leaks that took place and the rumour machine all spread a stain across the

---

* House of Commons Public Service Select Committee, Wednesday 8 May 1996, Minutes of Evidence.

Government that could never be fully expunged. It was part of a bigger picture that our opponents were seeking to paint. But in the climate of the times resignations in this case would have fed the flames. By the time the targets had been narrowed down to William Waldegrave and Nick Lyell, the Report was almost complete and there was no reason for them to resign before publication. They both believed passionately in their innocence and they retained the confidence of their colleagues. That remained the case after publication and to have gone then would have been unjustified by Scott's ruminations, but would have been taken as an admission of guilt from which their reputations could not have recovered.

So the Opposition, who clearly subscribed to no code of good behaviour, made it impossible for either of them to do what in other circumstances they might readily have done, confident that their reputations would in due course be restored. Had the vote been lost, however, at the end of the Commons debate, they would both have had to go; and they knew and accepted that. It would have been unfair but unavoidable.

Perhaps the form of Sir Richard Scott's Inquiry lay at the root of its problems and led on to the inadequacy of its long and ill-defined Report. It was not, for example, established under the disciplines of the Tribunals of Inquiry Act 1921, nor under any other recognised form. So anxious had been John Major to be seen to place no constraints upon Sir Richard that he had left the form and nature of his work entirely to him to decide. After all, Sir Richard was a distinguished and experienced judge, who could presumably be relied upon to know how best to serve the interests of justice.

The consequence, however, was a form of *ad hoc* Inquiry that was to be described by one distinguished commentator as 'procedurally extraordinary, from start to finish and unprecedentedly controversial.'* Whatever

---

* Anthony Barker, 'The Inquiry's Procedure', *Parliamentary Affairs*, 1991.

benefits Sir Richard might thereby have hoped to achieve – whether in terms of justice, brevity, speed, clarity or even intelligibility – were manifestly absent from the finished product. The Report that appeared after more than three years was very long, obscure, often ambivalent to the point of meaninglessness and lacked an executive summary of its findings. I believe The Plain Language Commission awarded it its Silver Rhubarb award for 1996.

Partly this was the result of the judge's decision to sit alone, without the benefit of lay assessors or expert assistants. He did have the assistance in questioning witnesses of Ms Presiley Baxendale, a lively and very able QC, but the adversarial nature of their twin-pronged attacks on witnesses, whose own counsel were allowed to be present but not to participate in the proceedings, spread a deep sense of unease over whether or not the interests of justice were being served.

Lord Howe of Aberavon has observed, to general support, that it was like facing a double-barrelled inquisition. As he put it in an article published in *Public Law* after the Inquiry had reported: 'There was no cross-examination of any witness save by the Inquiry itself, no closing speeches, no face-to-face dialogue between the Inquiry and any representative of the outside world ... Defence lawyers may be seen but not heard.'*

Witnesses, who thought they were helping the Inquiry to establish the truth, were perplexed by their treatment by a hostile QC and an aggressive judge, who allowed no balancing defence involvement. It did not help that this hostile cross-examination was held in public, whilst their right of reply was confined to the privilege of putting their case later in writing to the tribunal in private.

Procedure for the conduct of inquiries of this kind had been well established by the distinguished Salmon Royal Commission of 1966, whose findings have been generally respected since. Scott cheerfully discarded

---

* 'Procedure at the Scott Inquiry', *Public Law*, Autumn 1996.

these when he felt so inclined, describing some of them, strangely, as 'alien'. After dismissing most of Salmon's six principles of justice during a lecture to the Chancery Bar Association nine months before his own Inquiry ended, he concluded with the sweeping assertion that: 'The overall problem [is that] they are too heavily based on procedural require-ments of fairness in an adversarial system.' Hmmm. His own procedures have not found favour, however, with his fellow judges in subsequent inquiries, which have reasserted the Salmon principles as the best way of ensuring fairness, clarity and justice.

From the very outset Sir Richard was determined to ensure that he, and only he, should have access to the whole picture of his Inquiry. Not only did he insist on sitting alone, with no oral argument by defence counsel and no expert assistance concerning the operation of ministerial policy and departmental guidelines, but he also insisted on an undertaking from the Cabinet Secretary Sir Robin Butler to the effect that 'no attempt will be made to coordinate the written or oral evidence of witnesses'.

At one level one can of course understand why a judge should not want witnesses to cross-check and harmonise their evidence before going before him. This was not a criminal trial, however, but an inquiry after truth; and to deny witnesses the broader perspective of his concerns, that might have enabled them to enlighten him or even save him from various fruitless digressions down highways and byways, hardly seemed to serve justice.

More seriously, it revealed a streak of ingenuousness about the nature of governmental decision-making and administration that underlay the whole Inquiry. 'In an inquiry of this complexity, the judge will have the best overall perspective of the matters under investigation', pronounced the Inquiry Secretary, Christopher Muttukumaru, in 1995. Tony Benn MP spoke for many more, on all sides, when he said in Parliament a year

---

* Hansard, 26 February, 1996, Col. 620, quoted by Geoffrey Howe in 'The Management of Public Inquiries'.

later that it was 'entirely wrong that such political matters should be handed to a judge who knew nothing about administration.'*

'*Juge unique, juge inique*', say the French. That was not, of course, the case with this inquiry, but to be labelled 'a media darling',* as Scott was, should have made him feel uneasy. Certainly he seems to have proceeded from a number of fundamentally false assumptions. As I said in Parliament on the day I published the Report on 15 February 1996, in answer to a question from the Liberal Democrat MP, Menzies Campbell:

> *As far as the question of sophistry is concerned, the Hon. and Learned Gentleman is asking the House to believe that my Rt Hon. Friend the Chief Secretary [William Waldegrave] with two other Ministers, single-handedly changed Government policy, without telling their Secretaries of State, against the advice of many of their officials, and sustained that change for several years with nobody knowing. That is palpably incredible.**†

And so it was, as Sir Richard ultimately, grudgingly and making smoke, admitted. With adequate outside advice he might have learned that lesson very early on and realised that the central thrust of the whole 'Arms to Iraq' issue was an unscrupulous Opposition scam that could quickly have been disposed of as such. Ministers act collectively; their decisions are based on written advice from officials; their meetings with ministers in other departments are minuted by officials and their decisions are disseminated, often widely, within departments and across departments and implemented by officials in those departments and beyond. Ministers come and go, sometimes with excessive regularity, and so do their officials, but the governmental machine rolls on and so does its record of

---

* *Financial Times*, 16 February 1996.
† Hansard, 15 February, 1996, Col. 1149.

what is government policy. If it is not in that machine, it is not government policy.

It is strange that Sir Richard Scott allowed himself to be swept up in the storm that swirled around the guidelines, elevating them, if not to Holy Writ, at least to the status of law. If they had been intended to have the force of law they would have been the subject of legislation. In fact, they were intended to guide officials in applying the Government's policy and, if necessary, in advising ministers. They should have been kept in perspective by the Inquiry, instead of being subjected to endless and ultimately meaningless analysis, of the angels-on-the-head-of-a-pin variety.

'The underlying purpose of the Guide is to provide a framework,' says the introduction to another set of guidelines. 'The directions and guidelines prescribed in the Guide are intended to be used as tools to achieve the desired purpose. They must not be allowed, by an over-rigid application that fails to take into account the circumstances of each case, to become a constraint on effective and sensible case management ...' That puts the case very well. It was written during April 1995, whilst the Scott Inquiry was in full swing and appeared in the HMSO booklet *Chancery Guide*. The author was Sir Richard Scott.

THIRTEEN

Game Over

O ne day in the summer of 1994 I was sitting in the smoking room in the House of Commons enjoying a reflective drink when the familiar form of Ted Heath drifted into view, like some great whale moving calmly through a quiet ocean. 'I hear you've been saying some sensible things', he intoned. I shifted uneasily. 'Thank you, Ted. Have a drink?' 'No.' He made to move off. 'You must keep on saying them.' Then he swam slowly off, lost in the fathomless depths of his own thoughts.

He was referring to the 1994 Swinton Lecture that I had delivered the previous week in York. In it, under the title 'Doing the Right Thing', I had warned my party not to allow itself to be driven off the centre ground of politics, just because Tony Blair's Labour Party was advancing on to it. To resist Blair, I urged a common sense and instinctive approach to the development of new policies, founded in our party's philosophy instead of falling back on ideological templates:

> *I think it would be wrong, as you may guess, to settle on the adoption of*
> *an ideological approach as the solution to our problems. An ideology is*

often the rationalising patina that is overlaid, in hindsight, across a range
of decisions and events that at the time were much less certain in their
outcome and much more pragmatic in their development.

Ideology can be a substitute for thought, and an ideologically driven
party ultimately becomes a pastiche of itself, entirely in the grip of ideo-
logues applying, uncritically, yesterday's answers to today's problems.

What I was trying to say was that whilst our party's time-honoured ideals
and principles could be applied in a pragmatic way to changing circumstances, in order to refresh policy development, to fall back instead on
the hardened arteries of ideology would sterilise new thinking. The rigid
authoritarianism of some colleagues was not only making us extremely
unattractive to the electorate, it was also offering a false analysis of what
was needed; and it was dragging us off the battlefield where the next
election could be won, leaving it clear for New Labour.

I thought we should be seeking to connect with a new electorate, in
new circumstances, and to persuade them – not instruct them – that our
priorities were also theirs. 'We need the defining phrase, the striking
perspective of an applied philosophy that once more gives all our activity
coherence and freshness.'

I identified two specific challenges we needed to face. We had to get
right in our approach, first, the balance between community and the individual and, second, the balance between rights and responsibilities. I
pointed out that scale was a distinguishing feature of Conservatism and
that in developing policies that related to the scale of people's everyday
lives, we had to relate them to the reality of those lives, not to an idealised
version of how we thought they should be. It seemed to me that we
needed a new social awareness if we were to develop relevant policies, not
the slogans of the past. I pointed out that the social changes flowing from
the 1960s had not all been bad. 'Divorced people; young people; women;
homosexuals; ethnic groups – these are just some of the groups whose lot

has improved. And though we rightly honour the importance of the family in our social thinking, it has not suffered at the hands of improved individual rights.' The speech was widely reported and well received by the press. The party, however, was too tightly in the grip of the ideologues. Had we changed our tone then, instead of after the rout of 1997 as some belatedly did, we would surely have fared much better.

I believed in smaller government and in reducing the proportion of Gross National Product to be taken by the state and I never once failed to support the Chancellor in Cabinet when he called for tighter controls on public spending. But I did not find it difficult in government to reconcile sound monetary and fiscal policies with compassionate and well-directed social welfare programmes. After all, the latter can only flow successfully in the long run from the former. It was a formula that Margaret Thatcher had pursued, though not one she spoke about. Talking tough but acting soft had never seemed to me to be the right approach. It might have been better the other way round. I suppose Margaret Thatcher felt she had to overcompensate for being a woman in what was still largely a man's world, in order to establish her authority. John Major by contrast had to overcompensate to show that his tone was different from hers. They both paid a price, but in fact their achievements were complementary and their policies quite similar, though presented quite differently.

Where Margaret Thatcher established a new political paradigm, John Major consolidated it. But for his years in power, much of what she had achieved might have been undone. Yet it was by taming the trade unions that she made New Labour possible; and it was his period of consolidation that gave Labour the time to become credible – a credibility founded on our policies, better presented than we could do but with presentation replacing principle.

Some of John Major's policy initiatives flowed directly from the Thatcher years. The Citizen's Charter for example, derided as boring by the fundamentalists in the party, and milk and water compared with the red meat of privatisation, flowed directly from the privatisation programme. There were still in our later years many further candidates for privatisation. I myself identified in a speech in December 1996 such examples as Companies House, the Meteorological Office, the Valuation Office and several more, chosen not to comply with dogma but because it seemed sensible. These, though, were hardly the commanding heights of the economy. The Citizen's Charter filled the void. Peter Riddell wrote in *The Times* that 'most government initiatives are taken more seriously than they deserve. The Citizen's Charter has suffered the reverse fate.'

He was right. What the Charter did was to recognise that in those major public services where privatisation was impossible or inappropriate, what mattered was to recognise the continuing need to assert the rights of the individual in his relationship with such state monoliths and to codify that relationship in a way that drove up quality and service. As such it was a natural successor to the philosophy of privatisation and it has transformed attitudes in such services as health and education, both among the providers and the recipients.

Similar sabotage by indifference greeted John Major's 'Back to Basics' initiative, which was deliberately misconstrued by some in the media and by some in his own Cabinet as moralistic preaching. It was no such thing. Rather it was, at a time when the Party was getting bogged down in debates about Europe, a call for a return to first principles. Like the Citizen's Charter, it was an approach intended to improve the quality of public services for the benefit of the user, and to cut a path through the thicket of policy initiatives and programmes that filled every department, with a clear statement of the underlying principles and objectives of policy. New policies could only be developed if we restated our fundamental aims and ideals.

So it was not the morality of single mothers or gay couples or drug abusers that was being addressed. 'Back to Basics' was readdressing what

Conservatism stood for and how its ideals should translate into better education; a more effective assault on crime; a new approach to what John Major called 'housing on a human scale'. Certainly it meant, too, sustaining the old instinctive values of personal responsibility, not just to family, but to neighbours and the community, but that was not preaching. It was simply acknowledging the better qualities of human nature and seeking to develop policies that respected them. This approach could have fulfilled the Prime Minister's objective of showing his party's human face again but, whether deliberately or by sheer insensitivity, one or two Cabinet colleagues completely ruined the initiative with crude, intemperate, moralising speeches that made Conservatism look authoritarian and outmoded. The press set off on a sexual witch-hunt and soon found enough quarries amongst Conservative MPs to kill the distorted initiative stone dead.

I tried, in my own contributions to the debate, to restore the balance. I addressed the dramatic changes that were taking place in society: the liberation of women into working careers and the changes in family life that were happening in Britain as elsewhere. 'Family loyalty,' I said in a speech to the Scottish Conservative Women's Conference that same autumn of 1993, 'affection and respect are just as possible in the dispersed families we see more of today as they are in the traditional nuclear family. And in going back to basics, we should not pretend that the only family worthy of the name is to be found in the traditional nuclear family.' Of course, my own ideal was just such a nuclear family and I said: 'We must not be afraid of stating that it is better if at all possible for children to be brought up by both parents.' It remains my firm view that that is so and that a happy family life, if it can be achieved, is the strongest building block in a stable and law-abiding society. Conservatives should always support that, but I also pointed out that nobody married to get divorced, no couple started to build a family unit with the intention of knocking it down. Our policies had to address the reality as well as the ideal.

I well remember John Major saying, in an impromptu speech at a Downing Street victory party after he became Prime Minister: 'Let's see what we can do with this Conservative Party of ours.' It was one of the first indications I had heard from him that he had a political agenda of his own. It had not emerged during five years in the Whips' Office, which did not encourage such creativity. I knew that, like Margaret Thatcher (and myself), he revered the memory of Iain Macleod, that hard-headed romantic with a voice like a rifle shot who was rigorous on economic and fiscal matters but driven too by a sense of social obligation and compassion: a One Nation Tory. John Major's career in office shows a similar attitude. Of course, Enoch Powell was also a One Nation Tory, but as Iain Macleod said of him: 'I go along the same rails as Enoch, but I get off at the station. He goes on until he hits the buffers.' Like Macleod, John Major understood the difference between freedom and licence. He knew that the civilising moderation of common sense should always override dogma.

The Conservative Party is now coming back into balance after the burn-out of its ideological digression. Had it stayed in balance in the first place the almost terminal traumas of 1997 and 2002 need not have happened. But John Major's problems were not confined to the policy front. Europe was a more visceral issue than one of mere policy. Any chance he had of managing it – which for a while he did skilfully – was ruined by the retrospective codification of Thatcherism that denied its own record in office and split the party to its core. Added to that, where he needed more team players he had too many egotists, high on their own rhetoric and unpersuaded of the value of unity and loyalty. The party that chose him because he wasn't like Margaret Thatcher refused to support him for the same reason.

His circumstances also differed from those of his predecessor in two crucial ways. First, his remarkable 1992 election victory, when more people voted Conservative than ever before, did not bring him a manageable majority in Parliament. Secondly, the large new intake of MPs that year was markedly different both in political outlook and in personal behaviour from the older stalwarts they replaced; and among the residue there were many who, having failed to prosper under Margaret Thatcher, had hoped to do so under the new leader. Rejected again, they became bitter.

When she had come into office, Mrs Thatcher had the support of a demoralised country, an agenda that wrote itself, a discredited opposition and a largely united party. That is not to detract from her great achievements, which probably only someone with her tremendous force of character could have encompassed. But John Major inherited a demoralised party, which lacked both momentum and an agenda. In 1990 he had to take up the hand she had dealt him. It was a hand that included the European split, the poll tax riots and an economy that had run amok and into a world recession and was only beginning to respond to his restorative actions as Chancellor.

Also as Chancellor of course he took us into the European Exchange Rate Mechanism, a policy then universally supported across the political spectrum, now universally derided. But it was the policy he inherited, of the government she led. My own puzzled scepticism, I confess, had gone unvoiced except in private. I was alongside him in Glasgow when in September 1992 he strenuously defended sterling and our continued membership of the ERM to a large CBI audience, before heading off to Balmoral for the weekend. Happily for me, I was in Los Angeles on 'Black Wednesday' the following week, when it all fell apart. I was surprised to find Norman Lamont still in office when I got back, and to see the ashen faces of all my colleagues. Although leaving the ERM was traumatic and shattered our reputation for sound economic management, it is ironic both that joining it had helped to stem inflation and turn interest rates downwards, and that leaving it had continued the process and set us on a strong path to economic recovery. The overall verdict on the economic performance of the Major government deserves to be much more positive than it has been so far. Its strength took the country to new heights and continued to sustain the incoming Labour government throughout its first parliament. In time the credit will surely be paid where it is due.

At John Major's farewell dinner in the House of Commons just before he ceased to be an MP, Lord Mayhew, himself a brave and distinguished former Secretary of State for Northern Ireland, told the gathering that John had 'shown more moral courage than anyone I have known in politics.' That is surely true. The usually mild and courteous exterior concealed a steely grit. It is a quality that all Prime Ministers need, to meet the myriad challenges they all face. The Gulf War tested this early on and so did repeated European Union negotiations. Something that demonstrates it well was his commitment towards achieving a durable peace in Northern Ireland.

He once asked me – we were standing in the Locarno Room in the Foreign Office, just after the Remembrance Day ceremony at the Cenotaph in Whitehall – if I thought he should respond to feelers received from the IRA, hinting at a change in their position. It was well understood that there could be no negotiations with them unless they first renounced violence. The Prime Minister was considering adding to that the proposition that if violence were to be renounced then talks would be possible. It was new ground, which he did announce at the Lord Mayor's Banquet a few days later. My advice was simply to be sure to get something concrete in return. In due course the peace process got under way and by the time we left office in 1997 a successful conclusion seemed attainable, without conceding any fundamental principle. Sadly, since then much has been conceded for almost no return.

The biggest test of his moral courage, however, came in the repeated cupped-hand betrayals from within his own party and government. The corrosive impact on the Government's standing of these cowardly attacks was considerable. The running rebellions of some backbenchers were also reprehensible, but at least they stood up to be counted. His ultimate reaction, in suspending the party whip from eight backbenchers, I thought mistaken, given the parliamentary arithmetic. They might have been better tackled earlier in the parliament, individually. However, in placing his leadership at the disposal of the party in the summer of 1995 he made a brave attempt to confront and dispose of the issue once and for all. Perhaps the most contemptible of the critics he faced, though, was the coterie of senior, high Tory editors and columnists who so demeaned themselves with the personal abuse they unfairly heaped upon him because he did not conform to the purity of the ideology in which they luxuriated. He could not have done so, for party management reasons, even if he had wanted to. Despite the damage they did to him and to the Conservative cause, he retained his integrity and his rapport with many of those people in the country, who had accorded to him the record 14 million votes in 1992 that was more than any other Conservative leader had ever achieved – and which Tony Blair could not match, either in 1997 or 2001.

'Thatcherism' was a programme for its time, not a philosophy for all time. There was no 'Majorism', because John Major was a mainstream Conservative. The party is only now beginning to limp back on to the ground he tried to hold for it. I think John Major subscribed to the Michael Oakeshott view of Conservatism, as 'the name, not of a creed or doctrine, but a disposition'. It has always been the mainstream view, a view of a reactive party that had become uncharacteristically proactive, of a common sense party that had fallen under a spell. I am no Oakeshott, but I tried to say something similar in a speech entitled the 'The Fulfilled Society' in early 1993:

> *Intuitive, not doctrinal, Conservatism imbues politics with respect for the law, for freedom under it, for individual rights balanced by responsibilities. It honours self-reliance and excellence and, whilst asserting no over-*

riding ideology, seeks to set the scene in which the individual, the family,
the community, society, the nation can flourish. These concentric circles
are the arena of Conservatism and it is their concentricity that gives it
such confidence and stability.

Political memoirs are doomed, I know, when they lapse into quoting endlessly from old speeches, so I will quote no more, but this extract still seems to me to have relevance today – though in truth I should admit it made little impact at the time. As the 1992 Parliament advanced it became increasingly difficult to make oneself heard unless one was being extreme on Europe or disloyal to colleagues.

As we headed towards the 1997 general election the whole cauldron of philosophical dispute, party divisions and personal sleaze came to the boil. Just when we should have been presenting a united front and a tone of enlightened altruism we were caught up in doctrinal battles dominated by high-handed authoritarianism. After eighteen years of power, the physical wear and tear and the creative exhaustion were beginning to show. We had won so many battles that there was no longer an identifiable enemy to beat. Our opponents were using our language. So with nothing to react against, we started talking to ourselves instead of to the electorate.

Europe was an issue of genuine and visceral disagreement, as it had been for thirty years. But John Major offered a sound policy around which all strands of the party could rally. 'Wait and see' or 'negotiate and then decide' may not have a great ring to it, but for a split party it offered a way forward, from a standpoint of deep suspicion of the integrationist forces at work in the European Union. At one stage in the election campaign he was to say: 'I will not lead Britain into a single currency. Only the British people can do that.' But by then the split was too deep. It was not our stance on Europe that lost us the election; it was our public divisions on it. A little more maturity in some quarters, a little more team spirit and a little more loyalty would certainly have made our defeat less dramatic than it was to be. Those candidates – some of them government ministers – who broke ranks during the campaign to repudiate their own leadership, bear a great burden of responsibility for what followed.

I had returned from India in January with some kind of 'flu virus that was to recur, in stronger bouts, over the next few weeks. Several times I had to take to my bed and I was feeling distinctly jaded as I eyed the prospect of the long election campaign. Several times I was summoned from my sickbed to the House of Commons to vote in some important division or other, or to fulfil some vital engagement in the party's run-in programme ahead of the official campaign, or to do a round of media interviews culminating with the usual Paxman sneer and barrage on *Newsnight*. I even undertook the last of sixty House of Commons dinner engagements in eighteen months, in aid of the visiting constituency association of parliamentary collegues. In the middle of March I managed to fly to Berlin to take part in the Königswinter Conference; and before that I delivered a thirty-minute speech in Düsseldorf – in German – on the horrors of the European social model. So unused to speaking that language was I that by the end my face was numb with the effort.

The following week the phoney war ended and we were off. There was a brief respite as the media stopped its one-sided battering and started to pay lip-service to its statutory obligations of impartiality. All the operational plans provisionally laid months ago began to drop into place both nationally and in my constituency.

In the early stages of the campaign I had a few successes in skirmishes with a very nervous Labour Party on the trade unions and industrial relations, but whenever we tried to keep the issue running we were ambushed by some new sleaze scandal. Mainly these had involved English MPs – and I suppose they had been stored up to be used now to our maximum disadvantage – but two red hot Scottish scandals soon dragged the Scottish party into the arena as well and by Easter, with a full month to go, our prospects were looking bleaker than ever.

The rest of the campaign sticks in my memory as a kaleidoscope of Smith Square press conferences, television studios and frantic dashes by jet or helicopter to destinations all over the country, interspersed with the country towns and villages of Galloway, where the air was cold but the sun lit the green fields almost every day. Bad national news was balanced by buoyant determination in my bucolic fastness. I thought we would probably lose the election nationally but that somehow I would hold on to my small majority.

There were a few bright spots in the pervading national gloom. I was whisked by Dassault Falcon jet from Prestwick to Birmingham to launch with the Prime Minister our Small Business Manifesto, with its new Rates Allowance Scheme and a promised move towards a lower small business corporation tax. That went quite well. Malcolm Rifkind, Michael Forsyth and I held a joint press conference in our Scottish headquarters in Leith, five years to the day after Russell Sanderson and I had held one there to mark our 1992 victory. It fizzed and crackled; the press were in good humour and the event was well reported. But I think ours was gallows humour and the press were in good cheer because they knew they would soon be rid of us.

Nevertheless, by mid-April it was Labour who despite their huge lead in the opinion polls were tight-lipped and edgy; we were jaunty and relaxed and the mood of many we met seemed friendly – they, too, knew it would not be long. This was as true in Reigate and Cambridge as it was in Berwick and Aberdeen. I was scoring a few runs on the social chapter, the working time directive and trade union immunities, but it was still Europe and our divisions that dominated the news. Just a week before polling day a rogue opinion poll from ICM published in the *Guardian* showed us just 5 per cent behind Labour – who immediately retaliated with a brazen lie that we had plans to dismantle the old-age pension, a complete fabrication but one that had a marked effect on the electorate.

Over the final weekend one could discern a decisive firming up of voting intentions. I sensed that there was a massive shift against us; and so, of course, it transpired. Privately, I felt burned out and not a little bitter at the indisciplined party colleagues who had brought us to this. But I could see now, despite all the smiles, waves and nods of the past weeks, that I, too, would probably join the rout. My horizon narrowed to the next few hours as, late on polling day, I arrived in Dumfries for the count. I was comforted to have with me for the first time my whole family, and also Greg Clark and Alan Young.

At first we seemed to hold our own as the rows of counted votes snaked along the table. At one stage we were even a thousand votes ahead, but that did not last and soon we started to echo the dire news that had begun to come over the television set in our bleak little cell at the back of the hall. Gloom descended, intensified by the cheers we heard from neighbouring cells as each result was announced. Soon it was all over. I was out by over 5,000 votes. It seemed a terrible result until I heard how much worse others had fared in the south. Before I could try to comfort my loyal supporters I was cocooned by the press and whisked from one camera and microphone to another. By the time I was free of them the hall was already almost deserted.

I have never believed that all political careers end in failure. It depends on why you go into politics in the first place. I look back on my own political career now as a rewarding, fulfilling experience. The fulfilment came from promoting the ideals in which I believe and seeing them make a real difference to people's lives, from opposing the socialism I so despised and from serving the cause of parliamentary democracy. And, of course, as a career, with all its uncertainties, it is an exciting rollercoaster ride. For those rewards one was willing to endure the deprivations – the long hours, the pressures on one's family, the loss of privacy and the financial sacrifice.

One does it knowing that one day it will all end. The pendulum swings; events intervene. I was particularly fortunate in that I entered Parliament at the start of a long and uninterrupted period of Conservative government, during which I had the good luck to rise to two of the best jobs in politics. So I was ready for it when the end came so unambiguously, in May 1997. 'It's the cause that matters,' as Margaret Thatcher had said, 'and that goes on.' I had done the state some service, but I had run my course. I was worn out, physically and mentally. I needed a complete break and I would now do something different. The moment my result was announced, I decided I would retire from politics.

The Conservative Party needed a break. It, too, was worn out. After so seismic a period of political life over the previous quarter century, there was a need to regenerate both people and ideas. First, though, it would need to make peace with itself and recognise the calamitous consequences of disunity. And it would need to search its soul and discover again where its true identity lay. I fear it is still searching.

Of course it was disappointing to lose and I felt a sense of having let down my constituency supporters. More than that, though, I felt a kind of unsurprised resentment at the sheer force of the rejection of our party, which had achieved so much, by an uncomprehending electorate. They would in time discover the destructive triviality of Mr Blair's rootless modernism. For days, weeks, months my brain had churned with all the facts and statistics of our past successes: the record growth in jobs and prosperity; the record exports; the record productivity gains; the low inflation; the advances in the health service; the strides in education; the falling crime figures – on and on it went. But nobody wanted to know, because that was not what the election had been about. It had been about connecting with a public mood and we had not connected. Labour had. The golden legacy would fall into other hands and over time they would dissipate it, but there was nothing at all to be done. It was time to let go. The long day's task was done.

Most of all, that night, as I walked away finally from the viscera of the political battle and we climbed into our car to drive home, I had a sense of relief. A heavy burden had been lifted. I felt suffused with an elegiac calm. Then through the exhaustion there began to seep a sense of liberation. I was my own man again. As we sped up the empty road, I wound down the window to smell the freshness of the spring countryside and my spirits began to lift. To the east I could discern in the sky the first pale grains of light that would lead in a new day. Deep down inside me, my heart began to sing.

INDEX